C000101493

FROM MICROLITHS TO MICROWAVES

THE EVOLUTION OF BRITISH AGRICULTURE, FOOD AND COOKING

Colin Spencer is an author, playwright, painter, journalist and lecturer. His first writing was published in *The London Magazine* at the age of 21. He has had six plays produced, nine novels published and from 1980, eighteen books on food and cookery published. For thirteen years, until 1993, he wrote the food column for *The Guardian*. He was President of the Guild of Food Writers from 1994-99. Recently he has written histories of vegetarianism, homosexuality and the award-winning, *British Food An Extraordinary Thousand Years of History*, also published by Grub Street.

By the same author

NOVELS
Poppy, Mandragora and The New Sex
Asylum
Panic
How the Greeks Kidnapped Mrs Nixon

NOVEL SEQUENCE CALLED GENERATION
Anarchists in Love
The Tyranny of Love
Lovers in War
The Victims of Love

NON-FICTION
British Food An Extraordinary Thousand Years of History
Cordon Vert
Colin Spencer's Vegetable Book
Green Gastronomy
Homosexuality A History
Vegetarianism A History
Which of Us Two?
Vegetable Pleasures

FROM MICROLITHS TO MICROWAVES

THE EVOLUTION OF BRITISH AGRICULTURE, FOOD AND COOKING

COLIN SPENCER

GRUB STREET • LONDON

LIBRARIES NI	
C700711492	
RONDO	22/07/2011
641.5941	£ 20.00
OMAOMA	

First published in 2011 by
Grub Street
4 Rainham Close
London SW11 6SS
Email: food@grubstreet.co.uk
Web: www.grubstreet.co.uk

Copyright © Colin Spencer 2011
Jacket design: Lizzie Ballantyne
Design and formatting: roy.eclipse@btopenworld.com

The moral right of the author has been asserted
A CIP record for this title is available from the British Library

ISBN 978-1-908117-00-7

All rights reserved. No part of this book may be reproduced or transmitted in any form
or by any means, electronic or mechanical, including photocopying, recording or any
information storage and retrieval system, without permission in writing from the publisher.

Printed and bound in Great Britain by MPG Books Ltd, Bodmin, Cornwall
Grub Street books are printed on FSC (Forest Stewardship Council) paper

Contents

Preface

It is more than ten years since I wrote *British Food: An Extraordinary Thousand Years of History*. In that work I charted the influences and changes on the cooking and dining habits of the British Isles from the Norman Conquest through the Black Death, the Enclosures, Reformation and Industrial Revolution to the start of the new millennium. But the subject is vast and complex, there is always more to search out and unravel, not least, the history of our food before the Norman Conquest, and most particularly, how much the land that would become Britain must have forged the integral nature of our national cuisine.

When the last Ice Age retreated what was the land beneath, the land which appeared to the first settlers? It is perhaps an unpromising premise, for the land was bleak and forbidding as the glaciers shrank. Yet it is here that our food must have had its origin, its basis must originally have come from indigenous flora and fauna, as these are the roots from whence all else grows. Our ancestors selected what was agreeable, what gave them pleasure and ignored other ingredients. From these beginnings a diet is moulded by travellers, traders and invaders that bring new seeds, plants and animals and the ideas that transform them back home. Hence I felt the urge to begin a new history of our food by examining the landscape of the land that was left above the rising seas and which had so recently been colonised when the glaciers retreated.

It was a time which had echoes of our own; a climate gradually becoming warmer, a familiar landscape changing, altering so subtly, but noticeable to the attentive food gatherer and hunter. The evidence we have from these times shows foods that indeed became ensconced within our national diet, some still loved passionately – cod and shellfish, onion and beetroot – and at least one which we feel ambivalent about because for hundreds of years it was over cooked – cabbage.

I do believe that our feelings about food are influenced by a genetic inheritance. I also think that all food histories are notes towards a study in semiotics. The food we grow and prepare communicates messages, information about us and about what we want to tell others.

We largely accept that in the study of the past there will be lessons to learn for the present, if only we can interpret them correctly. We read the past subjectively through the prism of the age we live in, each succeeding age finds different interpretations from the one before. Let me say now that there is a tendency to disparage the past, our ancestors and their achievements, to belittle the people, as being less clever, less civilized. This is a great error. The more we examine the past, the more we must respect and honour our ancestors and this becomes clear when we study their food and nutrition. A striking example of this was to find in the evidence of the habitation of the first colonisers to this land in 8700 BC great carpentry skills from felling trees, cutting planks and jointing them together and contriving walkways across marshes. So unlike our vague ideas of the life of hunter-gatherers, but then reality is always sharply different from pre-conceived notions.

But then our idea of hunter-gatherers has been thrown into complete confusion with the recent find of a house, which can be dated around 8500 BC in North Yorkshire. This indicates that the people were not nomadic hunter-gatherers but settlers and that also generally means farmers and I explore this fascinating question in the first two chapters.

I also find it tiresome when hearing speakers relate 'that Jesus lived in a time of turmoil and strife'. When has there ever been a time that was not filled with turmoil and strife? The answer is that if such a time existed it needed two factors for it to exist at all, one, that the population had to be small and, two, the territory had to be large. As far as the evidence goes, one of the peaceful ages could have been the first few thousand years this land was re-colonised. For the cause of war, of fighting and slaughter, is always about dispute over territory which means the ability to grow food and this is still the major factor though those at war sometimes maintain it is about religion.

No doubt a casual reader might think what possible gastronomy could occur in 8000 BC among a group of hunter-gatherers who are skilful carpenters, have domesticated the dog, but don't even have a cooking pot? Gastronomy is defined as 'the art of cooking' and in any group there is always one individual who excels in the arts, who cares more than the others, about the selection of food, the fusion of flavours, the amount of time it is cooked. I am certain gastronomy is as old as cooking, and such people like the innovators above are the nameless ones in history, but their ideas are taken up and pursued by others that come after them.

In western society today we live in an age that is crucially aware, at times it would seem almost to a hysterical degree, of the food we consume. It examines it with forensic attention, endlessly theorises and speculates as to its specific role, condemns or approves of methods of cultivation and production, is hypersensitive to threats, imagined or real, of pollution, worries endlessly over nutritional values and bodily health. In the past the main anxiety was lack of food and the ills of malnutrition. In the present within the rich western industrialised world there has been an excess of food and we have been noted for its waste. In the immediate future we face huge problems. We know that we cannot feed the world population now or in the future under the threat of both climate change and dwindling oil supplies, without more radical changes in cultivation and production. But it is doubtful that these alone can feed the world. People themselves will have to alter their diet to one that sustains the planet rather than devastates it. There is in this concern over our food a new realisation of the value of wild foods, as they disappear we realise their significance. It is then of particular interest to me to discover the richness of the food resources in this land when it was first becoming isolated from the continent. Tragically, we will never see its like again.

Colin Spencer
East Sussex 2011

Prologue

Food is the key to explaining so much that is mysterious and puzzling in our evolution, its history is full of mesmerising lacuna where we can only speculate. For example, why is only one third of humanity lactose tolerant? What dietary changes encouraged the growth of the brain and nervous system? What was the spur towards language? How did food also become art? Here, I am tentatively suggesting new theories which occur in our early pre-history, far beyond the time scale of my other book which deals in the relatively brief last ten thousand years of British food history.

When does sound communication between species become a language? Cats when they wail communicate as much as their prey, birds, do in their dawn chorus and that is language for them. But our language is defined as having syntax and grammar and being formed in sentences. It is a highly evolved system which depends on organs, mouth, tongue and parts of the brain that have evolved beyond other primates. As bipedal hominids our range of sounds in which we communicated must have been greater than other species of primates because these organs had begun to evolve. There was a real need to create a great range of sounds; communal activities stimulated them, new words to show how new flint tools were made, laying and starting fires and then after millennia eventually to have made drawings that could be recognised as symbols of them. Writing down sounds is recent, the earliest are what seems to be jar labels from Harappa in Pakistan and Sumerian cuneiform script on clay tablets, both dated around 3500 BC. Some of the earliest words were: hand, bread, barley, water, flax, ox and head. They were accounts of food production, what was traded, what was stored, what was sold. While around fifteen thousand years earlier there were those amazing cave drawings their aesthetic beauty sings to us across time, what was the impetus behind drawings that encapsulate the essence of an animal in so few lines? A form of prayer perhaps, a ritual towards the success of a hunt, as if in capturing the essence of a beast halted its flight from the hunter.

Or, imagine the encyclopaedic knowledge of any food gatherer and the necessity in a brief life to pass on such knowledge to the children. How important language was to describe the nature of a plant, where it might be found, how it might be used, what afflictions it could cure and how it might be cooked. Example, of course, was deeply illustrative, but as hazards always exist and nothing is uniform, the unexpected occurs and explanations are needed – language is a vital tool in controlling our living context. And especially and essentially on the necessary daily search in finding food; so I am sure, though it can never be proved, that the quest for food, a constant pursuit, must have been a vital part of enriching and refining, if not instigating languages.

We tend to forget that the first requirement of the early hominid was a source of fresh water and it is water that is the habitat of one of the most easily gathered of all foods, which also happen to be highly nutritious – clams, in their many and different forms. One of the signs of early habitation and settlements are piles of clam, mussel and oyster shells – importantly the soft flesh inside can be easily digested raw and if necessary swallowed on the move. For brain encephalisation and the growth and strengthening of the whole nervous system you need a one to one ratio of omega 6 and omega 3. All forms of shellfish are rich in the latter while meat has omega 6. Carnivores, like the big cats, have no omega 3 in their diet, which is why their brains are small compared to their body weight. Our ancestors were fortunate in that for millennia they must have relied on shellfish as a significant part of their daily diet before they added meat and continued to eat shellfish afterwards, so that precious one to one ratio between meat and fish was achieved. I make this point because Richard Wrangham in his fascinating book, *Catching Fire* (Profile Books, 2010) omits the vital significance of shellfish in his theory about cooked meat and brain expansion.

How early in time did we take to drinking animal milk? I believe that lactose tolerance which only a third of humanity have came as a response to a cold and icy environment. It may be a dietary change that only occurred sixty thousand years ago when we migrated out of Africa and again colonised parts of Europe that became colder and the usual foods grew scarce. It could have been discovered after killing a female that had just calved, or else domestication of one or two animals occurred much earlier. But milk for the lactose tolerant could only have become a staple part of the diet after domestication of the herds, so is as recent in these islands as six thousand years ago. As, of course, is cheese and butter, we forget too easily how recent such staples are.

Food and sex are the two great driving forces in life, the desire for both is the stimulus to act, to travel, to explore, to colonise. Yet both for our earliest ancestors were cloaked in mystery, how soon was it that there was made the connection between orgasmic coupling and the birth of a baby? How soon could it have been that the connection was made between assuaging hunger and vigorous health, how soon the connection between a particular plant and banishing an illness? We must have felt that we were the playthings of gods, the mysterious, invisible forces which surrounded us and must be pacified and made benign by the same gifts that gave us health and well being – food. How very recent this driving instinct within us is. For in my view religion led to flour. The desire for physical survival then was very early entwined with mystical faith and ritual. 'Give us our daily bread…' The Lord's Prayer was a late expression historically of this connection.

Yet, how did we go from an ear of wheat to flour? Indeed, how on earth did flour become bread? And how or why did it become the first staple food so early in time? Why a staple, instead of a variety of foods? I pose the question because we are only too happy, it strikes me, to take a Panglossian view of the past and consider that our decisions were 'the best possible ones'. I am not at all sure that this was so. For example, I am against having one staple food and consider historically that this was a major error.

Then why is it that food is not just grub, fuel for human energy, why does it have to be on special occasions, art as well? Why throughout history do we care about good food? I don't mean the food that is fuel for our survival, of course we care about that, because otherwise we grow ill and die. No, I mean why should we still care, when we often do not even have the time and the money to expend on it; why do we still make a great effort to create good food? Though let me add that the concept of what it is, is a deeply subjective one. Nevertheless, it is part of the culture, far back in pre-history; the food for ritual meals would have been prepared, cooked and arranged in a different manner than day to day grub. Again, this can only be speculation but I know that this need is deep within us, to make the food we consume special, distinctive, remarkable, even though it is transitory.

The gastronomic urge is a real driving force within us. But why? Our bodies need the nutrition which food has, not an art form on a plate. Yet this is what we contrive, a psychologist might answer, because if the look of the food is enticing with its fusion of aromas, then your appetite is stimulated and you will digest the food more efficiently. No doubt true, but it doesn't quite answer my query. Admittedly, our response to gastronomy is not uniform in the human race; yet no society, no civilisation is without this profound need to elevate food, its cooking and presentation as an art form. An art form which is so transitory it vanishes within a few hours of being created, this I find even more mysterious, the creation, then the consumption, the destruction and final complete disappearance. What can be the motivation behind such a continual and energetic display?

CHAPTER ONE

Becoming an Island

The British Isles are a recent occurrence, having been isolated by the sea only in the last seven thousand years. We know little about human habitation in that period of four thousand years after the glaciers began to retreat, because so much of the human remains, the evidence of living and dying, lie now beneath the sea. For the ice which had once extended as far south as northern England had begun to melt and so began to drown huge expanses of dry land which had joined us to the continent. Yet much of what we do know is due to excavations done over the last forty years at a site in Yorkshire at Star Carr that astonish us in their revelations.

But let us set the scene. For hundreds of thousands of years over the northern hemisphere the ice sheets had advanced and receded, (there is evidence of human existence on the East Anglian coast as early as 780,000 years ago); the furthest south they came was to reach that part which is now north London diverting the Thames from East Anglia into its present valley. Human populations moved south as the ice advanced, then north again as it grew warmer. The area that was to become the British Isles was reoccupied around 10,600 BC (500 years later than nearby parts of the continent); it was a period of astonishing climatic changes, which radically altered the landscape and what grew in it.

Eighteen thousand years ago the sea level was one hundred and thirty metres lower than it is now, for so much water was locked up in ice sheets covering the northern hemisphere. When the glaciers began to melt, shrink and then retreat some few thousand years before this land became an island, it left a treeless, watery landscape of bogs, marshes, great shallow lakes and rushing rivers – a wild but virgin land with enormous food resources in the

rock pools of the coast, marshes and intertidal zones, the deltas and estuaries
of vast rivers. First of all coniferous forests colonised the new areas. Within a
few hundred years these lands were one great pine forest, trees which smother
the earth below in darkness, allowing only the tiniest filtered sunlight and
hardly any rain to enter, not an environment for food plants to thrive or the
mammals to live off them. But after one thousand years the pine forests moved
northwards as deciduous trees invaded the land, and it is then that we find
some initial semblance of the British landscape beginning to form. Heath lands
were invaded by birch and pine, then deciduous woodlands of oak, elm and
lime, while the large mammals, elk and reindeer moved north.

Now, the land was newly colonised by a few groups of hardy people, who
were to become the nucleus of the British nation. For DNA taken from burial
sites at Goughs cave in Cheddar from this time (10,000 BC) are recognisably the
same as several present day residents in the area. This land was growing
warmer through many generations (a time span from roughly 10,000 to 7000
BC) so why should people travel at all? The answer was simple enough; they
were following prey, mammals of many different species and sizes. While the
mammals themselves were following a food supply which was flourishing and
abundant. How fascinating it is that though this land newly uncovered by the
ice sheets must at first sight have seemed barren, the seeds already locked up
within the earth touched now by the warmth of the sun would have sprouted
and grown. Yet even the first peoples living near the retreating ice would have
made use of the ferns, mosses, lichens and liverworts which clung to the rocks
and seashore in that freezing climate.

In the coastal waters, there were enormous shoals of fish: sardine, herring,
tuna, mackerel, cod, hake, all the flatfish that like to bury themselves in sand
and on the rocks themselves many forms of crustacean. The warm Gulf
Stream mingles with the icy Arctic waters which then flow from Iceland to
Portugal, encouraging the growth of plankton which the fish thrive on, while
their seasonal migrations to spawn can be learnt and followed. Another great
advantage of the coastal region was the endless supply of salt, a source of iodine
and a preservative for the hard winter months, as well as being a commercial
commodity to be traded to the peoples of the landlocked inner regions. The salt
pedlar was a character who appeared very early in history in the central parts
of these islands.

Becoming an island was to take three thousand years. As the sea levels rose
the water slowly covered the huge land bridge – now called Doggerland that
joined us to what would become Europe. One could walk from Yorkshire to

Jutland, from Hull to Holland and on to Denmark; there is evidence that this land bridge was occupied until 5800 BC, used for migration and also for living. Trawlers now dredge up spears and other artefacts from the depths of the North Sea, which date from this time.(Time Team has done a programme for Channel 4, which mistakenly identifies tiny barbs of flint as arrow heads which could easily also be saw or grater teeth used for food preparation.)

A Varied Diet

Once the temperature had become pleasantly warm, it could be argued that the nutritional value of our food supply in the British Isles, was never greater than in those few thousand years after re-colonisation and before farming. That is those five thousand years from roughly 8500 to 3500 BC, from when the last glaciers receded, the land was finally separated from the continent and in the south east the first primitive ploughs scratched the earth's surface. These ancestors of ours were largely gatherers with a substantial vegetable diet; it is possibly difficult to appreciate for us in the degraded ecology of modern Europe to envisage the abundance of the food that could be gathered. The European Temperate forest of 8000-4000 BC was an area of very high edible productivity, as rich in wild foods as any areas in the world at that latitude. The dentition of its peoples reflects the consumption of leaves, shoots, roots, fruit, seeds, flowers, buds, nuts, supplemented by insects and wild mammals, a great range of other creatures more easily trapped, snared and gathered than the big game of elk and caribou. The mammals were much smaller than they are now, even in the winter there would be red deer, wild ox and boar, small game like stoat and water birds, while in the summer there were beaver, wild cat, badger, fox, wild cattle, ducks and geese, while huge heaps of shells show that they were a favourite meal along the coast. Worldwide, there were 3000 species of plants that could be consumed, in those parts of Northern Europe that would be colonised after the glaciers had melted, that number would have been much smaller, but growing all the time, as it grew warmer, every year. Do not forget though, that even in the coldest lands there are various lichens that are highly nutritious as well as algae which flourish in the warm summer months; reindeer and caribou also manage very well.

The food value of what we have eaten ever since has declined steadily to reach the present nadir of our contemporary diet. The other striking difference in the food we ate in those first five thousand years is that then there existed no staple; no daily gruel, no porridge, no flour, no bread, no daily consumption of processed carbohydrate, though, of course carbohydrate existed in the diet. A gruel made from mixed grains would have been the first staple (inspired possibly because its composition and consumption was linked with fermented drinks) but this meal would have been the prelude to settled farming and one of the stimuli towards it. I would guess that grass seeds were first used as a basis for fermentation which must have been discovered by accident, the resulting drink enjoyed and used in rituals and much later it became a gruel, then later still the grains ground and baked as a dry biscuit, before they ever became flour.

In my view a staple food is a huge dietary error because it creates a monoculture and a large working class, allowing a small governing class to use such a food as a tool to manipulate and control society. A staple is also addictive and narrows the range of a diet. If a diet is diverse and arbitrary, it cannot be taxed, stored, traded and generally controlled for the benefit of the few and the detriment of the many. Food commodities which large parts of the population believe are a daily necessity, like a secure salt supply, becomes a means of governing and a source of exploitation. Choosing a staple is the initial step towards tyranny.

But why no staple food existed then and why one came into existence later is one of the stories behind these first two chapters. The short answer is that there was no need for a staple, as the range of nature's larder was so varied, so high in quality, so easy to gather and slaughter, so much in fact to choose from that any food which needed stages of preparation, which producing a flour from roots, tubers, seeds or bulbs did, was not even considered. There are, of course, no artefacts that have ever been found concerned with milling and flour production until agriculture begins, which is a strong indication that flour was never made. One only has to imagine the detailed preparation from gathering the ripening seed heads, then threshing, roasting or grinding them, while getting rid of the husks, then turning what was left into a paste and cooking it. The whole rigmarole would have to be taught, and then the end product found to be amazingly satisfying and enticing to ever catch on. When their surroundings were rich in easily gathered, trapped or hunted foods it is very unlikely that a food which needed such preparation would become popular.

Re-colonisation

Many of our ideas about the life of hunter-gatherers have been based upon ethnographic observation today and this has been profoundly misleading in conjuring up a picture of our own immediate past. The tribal groups of people that had reached the north where the ice sheets had melted were not nomadic but settlers and the only reason for settling was the existence of rich and inexhaustible food sources. Our natural curiosity to experiment with strange and new edible forms has given us a dietary flexibility, which is one of the unspecialised characteristics that have led to our pre-eminence upon the planet. In this virgin land as well as the animals mentioned above, there were significantly aurochs (the ancestor of modern cattle) while the dog had been domesticated ready to herd them, and small mammals were legion: wild boar, sheep and goats, shrews, moles, hedgehogs and red squirrels. It was thought until recently that the homesteads were seasonal (saplings tied together then covered in skins) and that the appearance of food dictated where they were sited, whether it was a particular shellfish or plant, and there there are indications that people travelled south in the autumn to another area, or west to a particular coast. These temporary buildings surely existed, giving shelter when needed, but what has now been discovered are permanent houses which were used over a period of several hundred years.

The astonishing record of human existence at Star Carr tells us that it was occupied for 250-300 years by around 30 people in the winter and spring and it goes as far back as 8700 BC. The house was round, about three and a half metres wide held up by a circle of wooden posts.[1] The archaeologists who discovered it think there are bound to be others and that such houses completely change our idea of the first settlers to move back into Britain. Found at the site were boat paddles, arrowheads and antler headdresses. Because the groups of people were no longer nomadic the size of the group shrank and as they stayed in a particular environment they grew to possess a detailed familiarity with it. This in turn must have expanded certain characteristics of scrutiny and memory and changed the purpose of the artefacts away from big game hunting into smaller tools created for more precise work. We know by studying hunter-gatherers today that even in environments where there is a paucity of food, as in the Kalahari, they need only spend thirty hours per week collecting what they need. This leaves time for building, for exploring, for tasting herbs and their effect on possible healing, for specific planting, craft and art work.

What amazed the specialist archaeologists at Star Carr was the level of expertise in carpentry; a wooden track way was dug out of the peat made from poplar and aspen which would have been built only by using flint axes and antler wedges. (The remains of another track way have recently been found on the seabed off the Isle of Wight.) Flint creativity was then superlative. Microliths – tiny flakes of razor sharp flint inserted in wood and bone handles – were made in a range of designs. When flakes got blunt they were easily replaced. Scythes, saws, knives and graters (the only ethnographic evidence that remain for these in Britain as the tiny cutting edges were set in wood which vanishes) in various designs take the breath away with their dexterity, sharpness and efficiency. (Flint blades are still used today – because of their extreme sharpness, brain and eye surgeons use them for the most delicate eye and brain operations.) For many thousands of years we had used the same technology. A butcher today using a flint axe found at Boxgrove near Chichester, a site that goes back to an inter-glacial half a million years ago, found its sharpness and dexterity as efficient as any modern knife if not more so. Flint is widely distributed in the British Isles, much of the early flints used for tools were found on the surface or prised from stream beds. The even harder flints used for the best tools were found by mining.[2] Flint dates from the Cretaceous period around 100 million years ago.

I cannot stress the efficiency and range of these flint tools too highly, for the whole of their quality of life stemmed from it, while the preparation and cooking of food was at the centre of it. Flakes of flint glued with birch bark resin into antler bone or into a triangular chunk of wood could be used as graters for root vegetables which could be fermented with the addition of water, honey and herbs. Toxins could be leached out of other grated roots, nuts and fruits by placing them into hair bags and suspending the bag in a running stream. Coiled baskets made from close woven rush will hold water, but all human habitation had to be near a source of fresh water, a fact that is a worldwide truth before the advent of a piped water supply.

Lakes, rivers and seas were easily fished, by using flint and wood spears or tridents, waters were dammed and we know that sea-going craft were constructed which could go some miles from the coast, for the remains of deep sea fish species have been found at settlements. Herds of red deer, roe deer, wild sheep, goats and boar, were hunted with the help of dogs. The evidence for the dog in Britain being domesticated was found at Star Carr. The dogs were buried near the human remains and their bones showed no marks of the flesh being consumed. Dogs are descended from wolves and wolves take their live prey back to the communal lair where it is killed by the leader wolf who takes a few bites, then offers it first to his current bitch; afterwards, it is thrown to the rest of the wolves. Dogs, in the belief that their master-trainer is the top dog, follow the same pattern and round up the kill taking it back to the hunter.[3] Herds of wild animals are at their most vulnerable when they have young to guard, it is then that they flock easily and can form tight clumps when a dog or dogs approaches them. The use of dogs in this manner must have been enormously appreciated by early hunters, for it made their main task so much simpler.

These hunter-gatherers cooked the meat by boiling it in skins with the addition of hot stones, as well as roasting, cooking buried in embers, cooking on hot stones or between hot stones and slow cooking in flint-lined pits. One can cook with no utensils at all over an open fire by wrapping food in damp leaves then burying it in the embers, or pierced by a stout, long stick and grilled. It is likely that wild grains, roasted, then pulverised in animal fats, flavoured and made into discs were eaten as biscuits as travelling food with wind-dried meat and strips of smoked fish. Birch bark containers carried sustaining food for a long journey. Both fish and meat, cut into thin strips, could be wind-dried, salted or smoked.

I believe that the art of cooking, as we think of it now, that is the addition of flavours from a selection of ingredients to enhance a piece of meat or perhaps fish, did not come about in an arbitrary fashion and certainly existed then. Such compound flavours would have derived from medicinal concerns, the art of gathering for healing purposes must have occurred at the dawn of humankind's evolution. Fermented drinks were also an earlier discovery and would have been made from grated roots, berries and honey. Many of these flavours found to be agreeable would have been added to cooking broths, besides they would also have had their own significance and when days of celebration occurred, special meals would have been cooked and eaten. At Star Carr there is evidence of headdresses made from the skulls of deer with their antlers attached; one can imagine rituals, meals and much booze drunk to celebrate spring or other seasons.

Unlimited Food

But what were they eating? We find Mesolithic sites near coastal waters, fresh water marshes (British Fens) and the deltas, estuaries and lagoons of the major rivers; these have greater edible production than any other zone, partly because of the frost-repelling winter warmth of the sea. Whole plant communities from shore marginals and floating flora, are directly edible by humankind, while supporting a wealth of molluscs, crustaceans, fish, mammals and wildfowl, all benefiting from the nutrients washed down from land drainage.

The northward spread from the Mediterranean basin of hazelnut, apple, pear and other food species in the oak and hazel forests would have been encouraged by extensive and deliberate fire clearance and even planting. At Star Carr we know that in late spring they burnt the reed beds around the lake, this might have been to encourage wild animals to eat the new shoots and thus be an easy target, or simply to help them harvest new shoots and tubers –

probably both. The nut-bearing beech trees and some edible-root species seem to have made a similarly preliminary advance into north-western Europe. There is evidence of forest fire-setting which open up the forest canopy allowing grazing and browsing resources for wild deer, cattle and boar; it also allows the growth of edible bracken root. Also, where the edible roots, grasses, seeds, foliage, nuts and fruits grew in season, there too would be the wild pig, sheep, goats, cattle and deer. A diet composed of plant foods, bird eggs, fungi, molluscs, crustacea, fish and herbivores best approaches high subsistence efficiency.[4] They would have discovered and used numerous plants which flourished at the water's edge that were nutritious and easily gathered: *Glyceri fluitans*, a wild rice-like plant, or club rush (*Scirpus lacustris*), a type of water chestnut with large tubers, lower stems and seeds which has a productivity higher than maize (*Zea mays*); water lilies, reeds, water plantain, water gladiolus, water parsnip, water speedwell, marshmallow, marsh samphire, marsh marigold, marsh cress, bog moss, swamp potato; also the tubers of the waterlily (*Nuphar*), arrowhead (*sagittaria*), and the bulrush (*Schoenoplectus*) were all dried, stored and eaten. Growing upon the coast were the edible root ancestors of our beets, kales, turnips, cabbages and parsnips, *Brassicas Beta*, *Crambe* and *Echinophora*. Also in the shallows were the edible seaweeds: *Zostera, Atriplex, Lathyrus maritimus, Scirpus maritimus*.

Star Carr was on the edge of a post-glacial lake where we find a range of mammalian meats, birds, eggs, fish, seeds from a huge range of plants as well as middens of oyster shells and other shellfish which are found up and down the coast of these islands. A later Mesolithic site at Morton Tayport in Fife (4382-4115 BC) shows that there were over forty different species of molluscs eaten, the most common being the cockle (*Cerastoderma edule*); crab claws were also common among the shells. Of the fish eaten large cod far outnumbered any other (maybe our love of this fish is a genetic inheritance), more proof that they fished from boats that could go some miles out to sea. Other fish were haddock, turbot, salmon and sturgeon; the last two were probably caught in shallow water on their way to or from the river mouth. Remains of sea birds were also found, the most common being the guillemot (*Urua aalge*).

The consumption of shellfish which is particularly rich in minerals that are washed down from the uplands and mountains is vital to the growth of our nervous system. So such a diet is significant in brain expansion, the health of our nervous system and our general mental capacities. For shellfish is rich in omega 3 and if equal in our diet with meat rich in omega 6 we achieve that 1 to 1 ratio of both which is the vital nutritional component (See Preface). Isotope analysis of bones excavated near Llandudno shows that about a quarter of the protein came from fish, shellfish and marine mammals like seals.[5]

Half of the bones analysed from Star Carr came from wild cattle, followed by elk and red deer, then roe deer and wild pig. The bones of smaller mammals were also found, red fox, pine marten and beaver, but these might have been hunted or trapped for their pelts rather than their meat. A word on the quality of the meat – samples from wild herbivores show, without exception, the meat is rich in the essential polyunsaturated fatty acids with minimal saturated fat.

But what might they have gathered? It was the women and the children who used woven reed panniers and baskets to collect the roots, bulbs, shoots, seeds, leaves and tubers. Imagine the knowledge that such women would pass on to their infant daughters such as where to find a certain tuber and at what time of year, they would also teach them which part of the plant was edible, which part had to be soaked so that the toxins were leached out, which part of the forest it grew in, what side of the hill it flourished on, whether the seeds could be eaten, or whether they required roasting or grinding. Fungi would be strung and dried. Nuts were a great provider, evergreen oaks with edible acorns, once they had been soaked in running water and the toxins leached out from them, could be roasted and dried, there were high yielding hazelnut trees, which were extremely popular, large amounts of their shells have been found at various sites. Other foods for the winter were roasted seeds, dried meats, fish, fungi, while gathering always included digging for roots, which were roasted or dried for storage. As already stated it is now known that a diet composed of plant foods, bird eggs, fungi, molluscs, crustacea, fish and mammalian herbivores best approaches a high subsistence efficiency; so our ancestors were vigorous and healthy, able to adapt to sudden changes of both climate and habitat.

In Britain as we became an island it was a little warmer than it is today and the range of edible plants had become high and the population was small. It has been estimated that in about 5000 BC there were between 2750 to 5500 people only upon this island. Incredibly small, they would have been broken up into small groups or tribes of 30 or so. Hunter-gatherers have in-built birth control, but also remain as a small group as there tends to be four-year gaps between pregnancies; this is due to constant breast feeding of the children who were not weaned until they were around four years old. Breast feeding produces the hormone prolactin which stimulates the secretion of progesterone and stops conception. Foods suitable for weaning and infancy would have been troublesome to contrive, necessitating stones to grind the raw and fibrous, in the summer months made easier by soft, pulpy fruits which must have been the first foods accompanying the mother's milk for the growing child.

In the temperate regions, as we know, there are distinct seasons, plants store up their energy to tide them over the winter months, once growth is possible again, and the plants mobilise these reserves into growing tissues. In early spring the bulbs of the wild onion (*Allium*) and the rhizomes of Solomon's Seal (*Polygonatum*) appear. The bulbs lie conveniently near the surface; such areas where they are seen to be growing would have been marked and remembered, as would those covering the rhizomes of a bracken (*Pteridium aquilinum*). Apart from wild asparagus and sea kale, there are bulbs and rhizomes where the new shoots are at their most nutritious. Also fern and nettle shoots when very young and tender are edible, while both become toxic or unpleasant when more mature. It is then that people benefit from using the storage or growing tissue, or by intercepting the food as it passes from one stage to another, hence all types of growing shoots become a delicacy, both tasty and enormously nutritious. Also, the young, staminate cones of pines and buds of trees such as lime are a rich source of protein and were all used as food.

Sea Levels

Sea levels were still rising until Britain finally became an island around 5500 BC, the process probably took about fifteen hundred years, but the rate that the seas rose and the land disappeared altered, sometimes slowly, sometimes very quickly. Every year the sea rose imperceptibly about 30 millimetres, for in 9500 BC there was a huge land expanse covering what is now the North Sea joining the East Coast to Denmark, but the glacier continued to melt slowly covering what we have now named Doggerland. By around 6900 BC we were still joined to the continent with a bridge of land going from what would be Hull and Norfolk to the Netherlands, but by 6400 BC the North Sea broke through creating a thin gash, soon to be a ravine, in a great torrent pouring into what would become the English Channel. This must have contributed to folk memories of the flood to be eventually described in the Bible and elsewhere in worldwide legends. All in all the sea rose 130 metres in two and a half thousand years and submerged countless Mesolithic sites, which has limited our knowledge and understanding of our enterprising forefathers.

But sometimes their ghosts emerge, passing us briefly and hauntingly as in footprints which for much of the time are submerged beneath the sea, but are revealed at very low tide. Hundreds of footprints of people, children and animals in layers one on top of the other which dried out in the hot sun baking the mud of the salt marshes, can be seen at Goldcliff when the Bristol Channel tides are low. They date from around 6000 BC; here also are remnants of food, bones of wild boar and cattle, eel bones and burnt raspberry and elderberry seeds.[6] Charcoal and burnt wood show us that they were clearing the reed beds, harvesting both reed and wood for panniers and building. There may have been few of these ancestors of ours but they were industrious.

However sudden the climatic changes appear to us now, to the people living at the time, the most sudden would have occurred over the length of a lifetime – about thirty years. But what were these changes? The horizon changing from land to sea, the realisation that a salt water marsh was deepening to that of a wide estuary, less rainfall, trees, shrubs, plants and lichens never seen before given now the chance for their properties to be explored, fresh water lakes filling up with pike, new mammals both large and small, a large island appearing off the south coast and huge estuaries forming that were sheltered and would become useful as harbours for trading and shallow fishing. To the people living through these changes, though they must have been aware that their land was shrinking – the coast line changing radically on the east and south – they must also have been aware that the food available was becoming more interesting, that new creatures and new plants and fruits brought new flavours, and what is more these flourished in a warmer climate and were thus more accessible. Also, the memories of long, cold winters, which necessitated stored foods of nuts, dried vegetables and fruit were fast fading.

I cannot envisage a better diet than the one they had; it is high in every conceivable mineral, it is seasonal and fresh, and it covers a huge range of natural foods. There was spring water to drink, though potions made from fermented roots or seeds with honey would also have been drunk, but it is likely that such a beverage would have been kept for ritual celebrations. Meats would have been slowly baked in closed pits, or simmered with vegetable roots in animal skins, or roasted on spits. Much of the vegetable food would have been eaten raw with a high consumption of leaves and roots. All of the alliums would have been eaten, as well as the brassicas, campanulas, chicories, sorrel, dandelion and nettles; others could have been the salt bush (*Atriplex halimus*), Turkish rocket (*Bunias orientalis*) and garlic cress (*Peltaria alliacea*). Women and children – the gatherers – ate as they progressed, keeping some in their basket for later and to offer to the hunters. The there must have been other foraging days when the whole group set out to the seashore perhaps – shellfish, like mussels and clams were eaten almost in situ. One imagines these visits to the rocky shores armed with sharp stiletto-like flints with bone or wooden handles, which would pierce between the shells and prise them open, with the sea birds circling above watching for a chance to snatch a portion. Then perhaps some of the men would gather gull eggs from high up on the cliffs, throwing down great bunches of rock samphire.

I should add that my view that the abundance of food meant a diverse, healthy diet is not shared by some, who believe that we must not confuse diversity with abundance. 'If deer, boar, and roe deer had been truly abundant, would Mesolithic man have added rabbit, birds, and snails to his diet? If a few plant species had supplied all of his energy needs, would he have scoured the area around his campsite for fruits, vegetables and nuts?' Apart from the fact that humankind is reduced to one gender and inhabited dwellings reduced to a 'campsite', the argument is specious and utterly ignores the rich complexity of human nature. We are an intensely curious animal given to experimentation of all kinds. Long, long before the Mesolithic we would have tasted everything that grew, every shape and colour of egg, clam and fish; some of the experiments would have made us ill, some were so toxic they killed, but I imagine they took safeguards over that and experimented first on something small. How did they know to leach acorns in fresh running water? These were clever people, adept in all the forest skills, fisher folk and hunters. What clinches my supposition is that the people were taller and healthier than the farming folk who would succeed them, so much so, as we shall see, for the farmers took the hunter-gatherers as mates. They recognized good breeding stock when they found it.

The People
They were resourceful and intelligent, with senses acutely tuned towards their environment, certainly their hearing, smell and eyesight must have been of far greater power than we can ever imagine, a power long lost to us in our contemporary world which has little use for it. There must have been other senses too that we can only suspect existed, but senses of instinct which gave a depth of knowledge we now lack. They were skilful at all manner of crafts, from making hair sieves and reed baskets, to felling trees and preparing animal skins. What we forget in our industrial and technological world full of gizmos and gadgets is the sense of attunement such people had with their living context, so that when they interacted with it, as in felling a tree, stripping the bark and cutting planks from its length, they took the time to explore and discover the rhythm of the inner, hidden laws of nature, but also gave praise to the hidden gods that blessed their success.

Their gods were extensive, we know they had religious rituals augmented no doubt with fermented drinks, where they wore antlered masks and headdresses, which have been excavated at Star Carr. These would have been in honour of the horned god of the hunt, but also an earth goddess would have been praised, for from the earth came their life and sustenance. But there would have been gods of the sun and the moon, of fire, of water, of springs and stones and great forest trees. The range of dense forest itself, so limitless then, containing the secret lairs of beasts that could kill, the tusked wild boar, the great bear and wolf, this place too inspired fear and awe. We also know, as in the cave paintings we have since discovered in the interglacial fifteen thousand years earlier, that humankind could describe in linear form the fluidity and precision of animals and their movement with a skill which has never been surpassed. There is bound to be far more of these paintings still hopefully to be discovered, but many could be lost to us beneath the channel and the North Sea.

Trade existed between different parts of Britain and certainly while Doggerland was still dry humankind could have travelled from the Middle East to the highlands of Scotland, without having to cross a sea. I believe that where it is possible to travel we do so, and have always done so, and that with trade goods ideas are also shared. But becoming an island meant another change of climate; our land became wetter and windier. While the sea meant we had a natural defence against invasion (though that was to happen countless times in the next six thousand years), there was still not the complete freedom to colonise that came on the northern European land mass which had no natural barriers. What influences we allowed were selected, chosen for the most part, rather than being forced upon us. There was also on our western coasts what has been called the Atlantic mindset.[8] There was a huge food resource which gave people an assured level of productivity, (there is ample evidence of deep-sea fishing in the later Mesolithic, of bottom feeding fish, cod, haddock, ling and hake). People settled in defensive positions between land and sea, their fleet of boats made them highly mobile and in pursuit of fish they travelled, sometimes great distances, but often on voyages of discovery.

In an age of hunters and gatherers how did the cohesion of individuals into groups begin? How did leaders appear, become an elite and what part did religion and ritual play in this drama? In a hunter-gatherer society could food be used to manipulate and control its members as would happen in the future? Is everyone equal in this society? Does everyone get the same amount of food? The women and children eat the vegetables and fruits as they go. Do the men eat more meat than the women? Does any one person lead these societies? Or are they led by groups of elders ruled by democratic assent? Society, as we think of it, a group of disparate people living and sharing the advantages and disadvantages of life and obeying rules of conduct began here, as the tribes grew in number.

One aspect of this group is also obscure, which is did the family exist then, a pairing off between a single man and woman who would stay together while their children grew up? Pictorial representations always depict a small nuclear family. But though no one can say, I suspect that this is a myth that we have projected onto the past. I think the nuclear family began to be born with ownership or the working of plots of land. At this time before agriculture women were shared, children were reared by the group as a whole, for this arrangement makes sense. The women gave birth in four-year intervals, but it was important for a group's strength to have as many children as possible. Also, there was no concept of property and ownership in shelters, chattels or people, except that things belonged to the group or that particular tribe. The group was the family and their loyalties were to each other within that group. However, one must balance such a conjecture with the knowledge that interbreeding could have been a problem which early groups would have had to acknowledge, so that close incest between brother and sister or father and daughter, might well have been an early taboo and become enshrined in religious observance.

These are all basic questions, which we puzzle over when society is so small and still being formed. But alas, there are no firm answers, as the fragmented evidence that we find never includes written hieroglyphs, the picture is always partial and afterwards there is only conjecture. But there are some details so strongly suggested that we feel we know them. For example, these early hunter-gatherers absorbed every detail of the natural world and being totally attuned to it used every observation to build up a pattern by which they led their lives. The tides, so noticeable compared to the inland sea of the Mediterranean, violent in their speed, mood and range yet comforting in their regularity and seasonal pattern must have given coastal communities a vivid sense of time passing, while the sea's relationship with the moon and the night sky bequeathed a sense of design, which the stone circles so common along the many coastlines have attempted to capture as well as to mollify the mystery of the Gods. A close scrutiny of the night sky was essential to early navigation and these stone circles and Megalithic monuments register such knowledge. The direction of the flight of migrating birds, the time and season of their gathering, the movement of the sun, moon and stars, the direction and power of the winds, as well as particular high tides and formation of clouds, rocks and soil were all vital sources of information. It is not surprising that the peoples of these regions on long fishing voyages traded in polished stone axes, pottery, seed grain and domesticated animals creating a common language by the first millennium BC. This was a branch of Indo-European which we now know as Celtic.

Living and learning to survive on the edge of the Atlantic Ocean over countless millennia instigated a toughness in its people, no doubt mirrored in the plants that grew upon these windswept shores, the beets and kale, as well as the birds that nested on the high cliffs which all shared the same tenacity, a will to survive. But the people also had a strong streak of independence and competitiveness. I would also add that their character is enlivened by a singular sense of humour, for the more bleak the life, the more mordant the wit, but the ocean also bequeath a sense of security and power against aggressors as well as a seamanship which is breathtaking in its dexterity and daring. These qualities are entwined into the character of the British peoples who returned again and again to these shores as the ice receded once more then at last as it finally retreated they stayed and built their first houses.

CHAPTER TWO

God, Flour and Family

During the two thousand years from Britain becoming an island, to when ploughed land began to exist in the southern regions – around 3000 BC – three radical changes occurred which still dominate us. They were organised religion, the family group and a food staple that meant flour production. They are all closely related, almost united, even though they happened slowly, as bit by bit they sprang out of each other and are still today part of the structure in our society. But why should organized religion appear at the same time as farming, and what causes the birth of the family all at the same time? Property is the short answer, but how could ownership of land, shelter and things within it, create a religion and the first existence of milling stones? But before we can answer these questions we have to look more closely at what went before, for in the inherent disadvantages of the hunter-gatherer system is buried the energy to begin something quite different.

There lies a paradox at the centre of the hunter-gatherer existence; wild foods can only feed a limited number of people. As a population grows it needs more and more food and wild plants can easily be exhausted – a wise person sensing and observing this would gather the seeds and save them, possibly strewing them later nearer where the settlements were. But was there any need for this hypothetical person, for are not people naturally untidy and careless, dropping some of their gatherings as they return home? Edible and favourite plants springing up around their living spaces must have been somewhat of a miracle once itinerant peoples settled. How early was it when they realized that spitting out the seeds generated more plants, or that the soil around defecation pits were also places which seemed to harbour favourite plants? One could conclude that once there were settlements there were also food plants growing around them, that the natural garden was an inevitable result of the growth of the homestead. Therefore the paradox that exists is if hunter-gatherer tribes are to flourish and to grow they inevitably turn into farmers.

How did it Start?

When nomadic tribes of hunter-gatherers discovered a group of regions rich in plants and small mammals, they built settlements and inevitably there were new food plants that grew around them. Thus agriculture must have begun with tended plots around the habitat, plots that would have been kept for favourite foods, or plants found further away which they wanted near. These were likely to have been the grasses and the flavourings – sage, thyme and the allium family. So the staple and the herbs to make it palatable were there, near at hand, trampled over day in, day out as recognizable as their own hand axes. Also, the food gatherer with her or his acute observation and powers of memory must have realized early on that where animals defecated plants grew more lush and green, tall and fuller leaved. This basic knowledge, though not the reason for it, must have been familiar lore, as familiar as an earlier observation, that thriving vegetation needed water and sunlight, for they must have been long aware that nothing green grew inside the darkness of a cave.

It is now becoming clear that there is an evolutionary stage between the hunter-gatherer and the farmer, which is the settler who has chosen a particularly rich and fertile habitat, who still hunts and gathers from the home site, but who also has a plot outside the settlement that grows favourite plants. Though this is a transition stage it is far from being a brief one. If we take the Star Carr site as an example the settlement began from around 8700 BC and farming did not reach there for another five thousand years, for a stage to last as long as this it must have been a successful and thriving way of life. So why change it at all? What was so great about agriculture anyway?

Agriculture began in the Middle Eastern regions around 11,000 BC, when people grew the cereals wheat and barley, which they harvested with flint sickles, though there were many weeds among the grasses, including rocket, one of the earliest in the original regions. But then so many of our favourite foods began as weeds insidiously worming themselves into the main crop where we took an instant liking to them. For, as agriculture spread northwards, but incredibly slowly, both oats and barley began as weeds and then became secondary crop plants. Agriculture reached Europe around 5500 BC and began to flourish in the Balkans and the Danube basin. Rivers were vital to agriculture's existence because the annual flooding fertilized the soil. It was a time of increased rainfall with warmer winters. The Danube itself was one of the main thoroughfares across Europe linking the Black Sea via rivers in northern Europe to the Channel. Yet farming took another two thousand years to reach the south of Britain. As an idea it hardly moved like wildfire. In fact, this extreme slowness indicates some resistance or, at the very least, indifference. I suspect the latter though when it is ingrained it is reinforced by the former.

In fact, as I have already indicated, there seems to me looking back from our crowded noisy, technological age, aspects of sylvan beatitude in the life of these last hunter-gatherers who were also settlers. There was no violence (if there were signs they would have shown up on human remains), they were strong, healthy people, which indicates happiness, so I can well understand them clinging onto this way of life. Apart from the inevitable drift towards it, there must have been some pressure placed upon their society, or some trigger which hastened the process, for them to become seduced; for they could well observe the toil of early farming. What was it about these farmers then that made their life seem attractive? But surely the first question to pose is how did farming, as a way of life, first manifest itself to them? For they didn't one day walk out of the forest and onto a farm.

Communities hear things from travellers, for travellers love to tell stories, to be the centre of attention, to command an audience and very likely these stories got embroidered, but the core of them would have been based on fact, yet to the audience, I daresay, would still sound incredible. Travellers are also and always traders, and goods were exchanged across all the lands free of ice where people existed. Goods came from the Mediterranean to northern Europe, there was in the summer months a constant flow using the great river system from the Black to the North seas to a Britain rich in minerals. Though among any group there are always individuals eager for travel, expert at trading, communities tend in their nature to be fixed in their ways, it is their security, their nature to reject change and when the food supply is more than satisfactory, there is no impetus towards it. Weird and wonderful stories remain fables, are listened to with pleasure but are rarely acted upon. The mining communities in the south west would have been the first to hear such stories and the fishermen along the south coast. Such fables would, I am sure, have accounts of great walled settlements built upon the banks of rivers with gardens of plants, of land which was cleared of brambles and scrub, then ploughed, dragged with a flint tool and planted with grass seed. How these listeners must have laughed at some of the stories, thinking the people to be such fools when they could have gone into the forests and gathered whatever they wanted for a few days. But the traveller would continue, talking about food which was wrapped not in bark, but in something edible made from this ground grass seed, or from ground bulbs or tubers sometimes, of a drink made from soured milk and many descriptions of trees and vines hung with huge and colourful fruits. This picture golden in the rays of a hot sun was such a far cry from the dense, damp greens of Britain. There would be stories too of herds of cattle pasturing in the highlands content to be led by the farmer (a new word and new concept to the listeners) and being slaughtered whenever the need arose. Imagine, no need to stalk patiently and silently, failing to kill instantly and continuing to trek after the wounded creature.

Generation after generation must have listened to these tales, tales heard and loved and becoming part of folklore, and they never imagined it was a way of life for them. They knew that they had settled near to their food source, whether a river estuary or a lake in the midst of forest glades, that they already managed their environment, they burned the scrub and made clearings in the woods, they plucked the brown wool from the sheep, they already encouraged the wild pigs to eat their scraps. Their children were adept at taming ewes and drinking milk from their teats. We must have always been aware of the advantages that grasses possessed – they seed early in the year, the seeds do not drop from the plant for a week, so are able to be picked. It has been estimated that one person can cut six pounds (almost 3 kg) of wild wheat in an hour, so why bother to plant great fields with the seed? They knew that many seeds could be dried or roasted and last throughout the winter. (Forty different kinds of seed have been identified in the diet at this time.) It is easy to cultivate two crops in one summer. They appear to give energy from very little; they must have been appreciated as a form of travelling food.

A theory is that agriculture instead of being a slow conversion by the people already living in Britain was brought by newcomers, invaders or immigrants, who arrived piecemeal, a slow immigration across the channel. Small farming families in skin boats, no bigger than the currachs still used along the west coast of Ireland, one loaded with seed corn, another with a small pig secured in the bottom of the boat while the family paddled across the channel. This happened sometime after 5000 BC. Certainly boats existed, there are classical allusions to osier boats covered and stitched with skin, and 'they marvellously fit out boats with joined skins and often run through the vast salt water on leather'[9] and immigration of this nature may well have occurred. One might ask why would they have embarked on a difficult sea crossing in such frail crafts? The immediate answer that springs to mind is the acquisition of land. But the population of mainland Europe was small, there was plenty of land ready to be cleared and tilled at this time. So why should they journey into the unknown at all? Some historians have said they could easily have been refugees from one disaster or another, a theory that has slowly lost validity. But why not accept both theories? Surely, this great, radical change happened very slowly, piecemeal and over a very long time, it was the gradual bowing down to the inevitable. Like the slow rise of the North Sea, so gradual it seemed imperceptible unless you marked it and returned year after year, so agriculture crept across Europe, the putative farmers floating up the wide rivers and scanning the landscape for the virgin lands.

For centuries the movement towards farming occurred without the main event. There were signs of forest clearance from Star Carr onwards, men cut down trees to make walkways and log boats, build dams, construct dead hedges and protective barriers against wind and predators. It must have seemed such a small step also to erect fences and dry stone walls to keep in animals. Indeed, there must have been many experiments along the lines of domestication early on. So we were taking charge of our environment from almost the first years of settling in these islands, taking charge of it in a moderate manner which suited our needs at the time. But there is some evidence from bone analysis that a sharp change in our diet occurred towards cultivated foods and away from the wild (particularly shellfish) soon after we became an island. But this has to be placed against the evidence from the Black Patch settlement later (see page 49) where both cultivated and wild are represented equally. While, of course, at this earlier time there is no evidence whatsoever of large scale cultivation as we were to see two thousand years later.

So in my view for that first thousand years after we became an island people were aware of agriculture in far distant lands, but only used cultivation spasmodically, almost in an arbitrary way around their settlements just for a few flavouring plants or brassicas, while the domestication of wild sheep could easily have been begun by children looking after a sick lamb and this too would be fairly arbitrary.

But there is more precise evidence which points strongly to a mixed way of living from around 4000 BC. Because pots were unglazed, not fired in a kiln, the fats inside were absorbed into their walls and these can now be analysed. The pots contained milk and butter and archaeologists think that the skills to make these must have been brought to Britain from the continent. But not necessarily, both butter and cheese can be created by accident, by the movement of the container of milk on the side of ponies or the backs of people.

However these first farming families were not well nourished, they had bad backs and rotten teeth; their labour was so arduous in clearing soil, tilling and harvesting and though cow milk allowed the women to wean their children at an earlier age, the farmers tended to take their wives from the hunter–gatherer clans as they were far healthier and stronger. So the first farmers, made up of families and the hunters shared this land amicably together, intermarried and must have also exchanged ideas, about gathering and cooking, about spirits, fermentation, as well as the mysterious forces behind the living world. Each could see the attractions and disadvantages of the other way of life and there must also have been much bartering between them.

How does a change in social construction occur, where several people become obsessed by the same idea and diverge from the main group, their example finds favour and is followed? Perhaps some uncommon, charismatic leader who saw the future and desired it, led some of them towards the new ideas? We have this concept of a 'natural leader', what we mean by it is that it is someone who is dominating and whom we allow to dominate because we are in rough agreement with their policy. In these times such a person was likely to have been the most astute, skilful and successful hunter. For meat would still have been the most highly prized of foods, because its presence within a small community signified the greatest effort and skill, also the whole carcass enriched every part and person in that community. The leader or the one that makes the decisions, the one the group trusts, is also given privileges by the group and these range from sexual to food and habitat, here the tribe is the family and it is the disintegration of this social unit which the onset of farming began.

No longer was the tribe or clan the central grouping within daily life, where all women were mother to all children. But now when pieces of land were shared out and sometimes, choice fertile stretches bitterly fought over, that territory became a prize for a leader who would have gathered a family that would continue to own it in perpetuity. But first the land itself has to be selected, ringed initially by natural barriers, generally the sea shore, rivers or streams, but sometimes woods, hills or mountains. So the decision to farm the land throws up leaders and families and if a community is to live in peace some form of council develops, so that decisions are made and adhered to and if that council is to have any real power in its control of people and land it has to have religious jurisdiction so that people fear it.

We know that farmers took their mates from out of the hunting tribes. It seems to me that one of the great attractions for the desired young girl in that new farming family, that must have made her decide to leave her tribe would have been the idea of nurturing your own children, of living closely with them, of bringing them up until they were strong, sturdy young adults. The idea of not sharing your four-year-old infant after it had at last left your breast with the other women of the tribe, that ownership, of blood and kin must have been a strong instinct to urge the young female huntress into the arms of the farmers, who were so eager for her health and strength.

Evidence of this change has recently been discovered in a burial where the arrangement of the bodies, children were buried facing their parents, has been found and DNA extracted from their bones and teeth prove their kinship. These have been dated to 4600 BC and come from Eulau in Saxony-Anhalt about 120 miles south west of Berlin.[10] The family burial was among group burials and all showed signs of a violent death, for the land where they were buried is particularly fertile (one of the richest in Europe) and the evidence points to a battle over ownership of it. Another interesting find through analysis of the bones was to discover that the males came from a nearby area while the females came from far further away, which indicates that the men were choosing their mates elsewhere to stop inbreeding and to build allegiances with neighbours.[11]

Religion and Ritual

After 4000 BC what is most striking about this period are the communal field monuments, the great burial mounds, barrows and standing stones, all of which demanded a large community to work upon them and to erect them, for their scale is awe inspiring, exactly the emotion that they were intended to inspire. There can be no doubt that religion with its ministers or shamans (it is difficult to decide what title to give these priest-like figures) held power and dominated society. This was a social structure, a system of thought based upon the night sky and planetary movements that involved the whole community. For it must have been observed that the heavens, whether by night or day, ruled the growth and well-being of their food plants, whether by sun, moonlight or rainfall, or other mysterious happenings.

The monuments also include the causeway enclosures which contain artefacts including querns, the precursor of milling stones, often deliberately broken or set on edge or placed upside down to show that their function had ceased. The querns were of the type called saddle quern, having a deep U shape, which meant it had been in use for some years. It got this characteristic shape because the person grinding the corn was astride the stone holding a smaller stone to grind the corn, powdering the seeds with such force it caused over time the U shape. The existence of querns points to the first indication of a staple food – bread. Or does it? It certainly points to the manufacture of flour, but it would be wrong to leap to such a conclusion, because broken quern stones are found in many of the religious sites. The querns were broken obviously to stop them being used again, but making flour surely was a daily necessity and quern stones have to be found and adapted for use. Not an easy task. So destroying one is a deliberate act of vandalism, a public act, like breaking a glass after a toast, but the quern stone was of far greater value.

The indication surely is that the flour that was ground was of special significance, that whatever it was made into had great metaphysical meaning; which points to the making of cakes, offerings for the gods, as in the classical ancient world. Foods fit for the gods were only suitable if they were foods that needed labour and time spent on preparing, processing and creating them. Wheat seeds have to be cut when they are ripe, then beaten to break the spikes into spikelets, then winnowed, tossing the spikelets to let the wind blow away unwanted bits of straw, then pounded to free the grain from the protective husks before they are either boiled to make gruel, or ground into flour. But for the religious ceremony that flour would have to be the finest, so it would be repeatedly ground and sieved several times through an ever finer hair mesh. The cakes would have been always flavoured with sacred herbs and hallucinogens among a host of other variations and the priests would have eaten them while drinking mead. The hallucinogens could have been the most common weed that grew around settlements, black henbane (*hyoscyamus niger*) or the opium poppy (*papaver somniferum*), also hemp (*Cannabis sativa*) cultivated at this time, thorn apple (*Datura*), sweet flag (*Acorus calamus*), deadly nightshade (*Atropa belladonna*) or mandrake (*Mandragora officinarium*) while fly agarics or ergot could also have been used.[12] Ritual use of such plant hallucinogenic drugs for the ministers, elders and the elite would help to explain the immense passion and piety which suddenly erupted in this formerly pastoral, hunter-gatherer society which had now begun to turn towards farming and which bound them all together in a cohesive whole.

Emerging slowly out of the forests seems to have been a time of heightened consciousness, of the dawning realization of the immensity of the world, the fragility of life, the brevity of existence (under thirty years), and the possibilities of new beginnings. Our living context shapes our vision of the world obviously, so imagine if most of your life you existed beneath a canopy of tree branches, or at the edge of tree and water, the sky is hidden or masked, night and day, by giant interlaced forms that dominate your existence. No wonder tree spirits are worshipped, as is the earth they rise from and the great stones and rock faces that block track ways. The forest disguised your existence, it hid you away in its darkest recesses like another animal, and once humanity emerged from its embrace a new dawn arrived. Then when forest clearance begins and agriculture encroaches upon the canopy of trees, the whole majesty of the sky is revealed. This was a time when the first writing appeared in the Middle East and where the megalithic monuments were raised from the islands of Malta to those of Shetland. We know later in the classical period of Greece (500 BC) that sacrificial cakes were made in various shapes, flavours and colours and they had the sanctity of tradition. I think this ritual would have travelled from the Mediterranean slowly northwards, taking on the indigenous flavours of those lands. In Britain as well as the hallucinogenic additions, they would have been made from the finest wheat flour with honey, butter or soft cheese and ale, flavoured with berries or raspberry, coloured with cowslip. There must have been numberless variations, the best of which would have been revered.

Causeway enclosures appeared around 3500 BC and lasted for about a thousand years; they are great earthworks, communal monuments, sometimes as large as 200-300 metres in diameter marked by ditches and several entrances. They are known all over north-western and central Europe, they are positioned sometimes in valleys and on plains, at other times they are on hills and have commanding positions and panoramic views. In Britain they are found in the south and the Lincolnshire and Yorkshire Wolds, they are prominent in Wessex (that area of south-western England that was to become an Anglo-Saxon kingdom, its fertility always to be farmed) where they are no more than 30km apart and sometimes as near as 10km, so that they are easily walked to and fro on foot. All have a defensive ditch dug around them, which is constantly broken in intervals and which suggests that different families had their own sections and entrances and exits. The causeways puzzled prehistorians for some time, but now it is thought that their size denotes a need for large collections of cattle or sheep as well as the whole community, so were tribal meeting places for trading goods, stock tending, initiation rituals, exchange of stock and seed corn, for rites and ceremonies involving flocks and herds. A meeting place for the whole of society, which combined religion and commerce, public ritual and private bonding, where the sons and daughters of the most affluent and powerful of families could meet and start new scions.

How do social groups begin, we might ask, but looking back at this time it is not difficult to understand that two or more families which have begun to farm in a verdant landscape of valleys around a river would have a friendly relationship exchanging and bartering seeds, goods and stock, that their children would pair off (there was a high mortality rate among small children) and start their own families, then travel a little further away to farm themselves. Such a loosely related society would have a powerful tie in kinship and would want to meet for the important days in their life to celebrate; these were bound to coincide with the long and the shortest days of the year. In such a society, as we have said, the night sky and what they could learn from it would dictate much of their life; for there, far outside of them, was a great sense of structure that ruled the year and the minutiae of their lives, but which mysteriously cloaked itself in invisibility all day, but though operating from afar seemed to recognize their needs.

Such meeting places included funeral rites which are why so many fine and beautiful artefacts have been discovered, polished stone axes and pottery. Remains of food eaten have been mutton bones, pork ribs and hazelnuts. This then was a society of tribes and group alliances, loosely led, one feels, by benevolent rulers or ministers of their religion for it is an age where the long barrows are also found. I use the word benevolent because again there seems to be little violence in this society, it is, one feels, an agricultural community that has a small population over large expanses of land. It is a community that believes strongly in the afterlife that was a continuation of the present one. Such a last ritual would have been celebrated with food and drink and hallucinogens taken by ministers and mourners alike. These foods which are seen as elixirs, keys to the mysteries of the next world, allow those that mourn glimpses into the future, but also have a practical aspect. They are prepared by women who have to be skilled cooks, skilled because these are foods of superlative value that have to look perfect and taste divine. Once these skills are learnt and practiced, they are used in a more moderate way for other occasions, at a feast for honoured guests or tribal leaders. The skills are not forgotten. On the contrary they are polished and honed, especially when they involve the hardest labour. In this case it would mean the finest grain of flour. So we are nearing the birth of our staple. But first we have to produce the product itself – grain. Cereals need space and tilled soil.

Gods and Crops

Britain can be divided agriculturally into the north-western Highland Zone, rocky uplands and heath, useful for grazing, but too exposed for crops and the south-eastern Lowland Zone, fertile and alluvial, watered by many wide rivers. A diagonal line from the river Exe that bisects Devon to the river Tees across the

Yorkshire moors roughly marks these two different geographical areas. So this great Lowland Zone was ripe for cultivation and it would be the first area to begin having dedicated forest clearance. This started in the period from 3500 to 2500 BC and the main cereals that were sown were emmer wheat (*Triticum dicoccum*) and barley, in particular the naked variety (*Hordeum tetrasticum*). These were the main crops, which must have been brought in from the continent as they were tried and tested and relied on there. Emmer wheat grew wild in the Middle East, it is hulled wheat like einkorn or spelt, which means it has strong husks that enclose the grains; they very easily propagate themselves, as when the temperature changes at night the husks expel the seeds and when they hit the soil they drill into it. Emmer wheat is still grown in Switzerland and Italy and made into bread, in Italy called *pane de faro*. Naked barley is so called because it has an easily removed husk and high sugar content, so was to be found useful for all fermented drinks, much enjoyed still today. Both are morphologically wild with small grains and a brittle rachis that is easily harvested, but unpredictable in growth and difficult to process compared with later varieties.

We know that wheat (*Triticum diococcum*) comprised over 90 per cent of the crops grown, with a little einkorn (*Triticum monococcum*) and always barley which remained the most popular cereal for thousands of years. This proves I believe that it remained the staple grain for fermentation. The querns show that the wheat, of whatever kind, was ground into flour; both a saddle quern and a rotary quern or hand mill were used. (A quern with a central spindle fixed into the centre of the lower stone.) Stone pestle and mortars were also used. The grains would have been coarsely ground and much of the attendant weed seeds with it and a thick porridge or gruel made by the addition of a little water so that it was a stodge that could be either boiled and eaten as a porridge or rolled, flattened and then baked on a hot stone.

Flax (*Linum usutatissimum*) was grown for its oil, also made into a cloth or just the seeds, eaten after light roasting. Orache (*Atriplex*) was eaten as well as watercress (*Nasturtium officinale*), chives (*Allium schoenoprasum*), wild thyme (*Thymus*), mint (*Mentha*) and edible fungi. Vast quantities of hazelnuts (*Corylus*) were consumed. Acorns were hung in close woven baskets in running water so that their toxins were leached out, then dried and pounded into meal, being rich in both starch and fat. Wild crab apples (*Pyrus malus*) were split and dried and hung on threads for storage. Other popular fruits were raspberry (*Rubus idaeus*), blackberry (*Rubus fructicosus*), rose hips (*Rosa sp.*), sloe and wild cherry (*Prunus spinosus arium*) and cranberry (*Oxycoccus palustris*).

As the population increased and farming became the necessary daily labour the demand for tools and axes of flint and stone grew also, when before the flints had simply been found and gathered from the earth, or on beaches, river beds and high moors. Now the tasks of building and fencing and necessary forest clearance demanded a steady supply of high grade flint, and this had to be quarried. The remains of these mines still exist and are impressive; they follow the flint deposits which sweep from Wessex and the South Downs up towards and over East Anglia. At Cissbury in Sussex, shafts were excavated through the chalk to a depth of 15 metres. Miners went deep to find the best flint which is the last layer; once that was reached tunnels were excavated horizontally, the walls are holed with antler picks and on the roof there still remain the sooty remains from the miner's lamps.

It is interesting to note that the first farmers built the tombs for their dead on top of the hills that overlooked the land they cultivated. Also these houses for the dead were much larger, took far greater energy to build, than the houses for the living. The tumuli across Britain are countless and are in various designs: round cairns or barrows, long cairns and barrows, passage graves and wedge tombs among others. In the period between 4000 BC until 2500 BC one feels that the ancestors ruled over the living as their graves became greater, constructed with huge stones (the capstone of a tomb at Tinkerswood, south Glamorgan weighs 50 tons) with burial chambers roofed and sometimes vaulted. At the beginning of this time these tombs were group burials, with people added as they died, many with their personal belongings. But by 3000 BC the tombs were built for one person, denoting a group mourning a leader, his tomb taking a central position over a ring of smaller tombs. Many of the tombs have been blocked and stone circles erected instead, as if a living leader now wishes to command the messages from beyond. Sometimes, there is an uneasy mixture where a tomb is set in the midst of a stone circle as at Callanish on the isle of Lewis.

The power of the leaders continued to grow throughout the building of the great henges and circles which covered the British Isles through the two thousand years from 3000 BC. 'We can only speculate about the social structure...certainly to talk of kings at this period is an anachronism, though some prehistorians have argued for the existence of chieftains capable of controlling and directing their communities.'[13]

From the awesome setting of Castlerigg, Cumbria in the midst of the highest mountains in England to Land's End and Ireland they proliferate, but the only area where they are rare is in the south east; they all remain mysterious and impressive, however. Wherever the wedge-shaped tombs and tumuli were situated they are carefully aligned with the heavens. Here, we imagine, lay the power which the leaders could invoke, the full moon and the setting sun must have appeared in a divine guise; as they died and were reborn, they ruled the heavens as the summer sun ripened the harvest. The moon vacated the night sky but reappeared as a thin crescent, only the correct rituals within the circle made by the priest or chief could ensure that the heavenly order continued.

The skill in carpentry noted some thousands of years earlier at Star Carr continued; it involved chopping, splitting, planing, whittling, cutting, grinding and smoothing. Also, different timbers were now selected for different purposes: hazel for pegs and posts, oak, ash and lime split for planks, while wooden objects found alongside the track ways, (across the marsh at the Somerset levels around Glastonbury) – a pouring funnel, a dish, spoons, a wooden spurtle, a porridge or gruels stirrer – show a precision in methods of cooking. While a spear, bows, arrow shafts, mattock, paddles, awls, pins, toggles and fishing floats tell us that hunting was still as important as cultivating. The yew bow could shoot an arrow over a hundred metres and was the same length as the classic English longbow used in medieval warfare. These objects, which were always newly wrought and finished to a high degree of craftsmanship (the bow was decorated with criss-cross leather bindings) are thought to be votive offerings and their presence shows us that the task of cultivation and hunting, preparation and cooking, were considered as sacred, needing the blessings of the gods and the mysterious powers that controlled existence.

If these artefacts and architectural remains tell us anything it is that the relationship between the objects that bring the food to the table and a fervent mystical belief (which must always have been there) now appear to be celebrated and strengthened. The megaliths and stone circles still exert an awesome power. Graeme Barker points out that 'the emergence of elites was the key factor which simulated agricultural production.' (*Prehistoric Farming in Europe*) But elites only came into power through the growth and then the manipulation of religious belief; it was that structure which kept a growing population in control. Their existence was and is solely due to agricultural surplus, for the elite do not toil in the fields, they and their necessary underlings, the bureaucracy that manages the social structure, are fed by the labour of the workers. So here we have the beginnings of a staple food, allied with religious belief and the beginnings of a fixed social structure. Fixed in the sense that the top echelons comprised the rulers, ministers of religion inevitably fused with secular administration, while beneath them were the workers, builders and farmers and a new skill appearing in the latter, stockmen. Farmers would now have to combine the best qualities of their animals as they would their plants.

Mediterranean farming used hand tools or light ards (a tool for scratching the surface of the soil, the most primitive form of plough, in fact) which merely scuffled the top soil, trapped moisture in the soil and allowed seeds to germinate more easily. But these tools were useless for the heavier clay soils in northern Europe, so a new technology had to be invented and that took time. The great expanse of temperate forest, a perfect environment for so many edible species, remained inviolate from man's labours at cultivation until 3500 BC and another thousand years passed when only arbitrary and spasmodic, experimental attempts at cultivation and domestication occurred. By then oxen were used to pull the ard or plough with a man behind guiding the furrow and urging the oxen forward. But agriculture certainly began in those last few hundred years before 3000 BC even in far parts of Britain and Ireland in the lowlands where the soil was good. This transformed the natural world into land division, communal labour and social control, and population levels immediately began to rise.

Immigration
Around 2100 BC the rich copper and tin deposits in the south west of Britain attracted new people with new skills from what is now Switzerland, and they brought with them bronze weaponry and also very likely, beautifully fired terracotta pots. The pottery needed baking in a kiln at a high temperature, for a potter's kiln is closely allied to the type of smelting furnace needed for extracting copper from the parent ore. Bronze is made from adding 10 per cent tin or arsenic to the copper; fortunately most of the copper ore in Britain already contained arsenic as an impurity. These immigrants were later named the Bell Beaker people because of the shape and design of their pottery. There seems to have been no struggle for supremacy between the migrants and the farmers, in fact on the existing Stonehenge monuments there are signs that the migrants began to work on them and continued at Avebury and Silbury Hill, so the cultures merged. No doubt the original farming community was only too happy to welcome such fresh advances in the quality of their living, in fact the migrants may well have been invited to live in Britain, having met through trade and recognized that such a move was beneficial to both communities.

Thus the Bronze Age began and lasted until 650 BC, and almost immediately we find that the grave goods buried with the dead are made from bronze, weaponry of exquisite workmanship and beauty, while there is jewellery for men and women of gold and amber. Gold cups have been found similar in design to those found in Mycenae indicating trade between Greece and Britain. Textiles also began to be made, woollen skirts, tunics and cloaks.

The earliest copper mines were in County Cork, then in North Wales near Cardigan Bay, they were extensive, the one in North Wales at Great Orme was excavated from 1900-900 BC. Though they used just bone, antler, bronze and stone tools they could sink their shafts and galleries to seventy metres, and this mine has five kilometres of passages and two huge caverns, one of which was where three seams of ore came together; indeed it is estimated that thousands of tons of ore must have been removed to have created the space.[14] The chief or group which could corner this production acquired extensive powers, which led inevitably to power struggles between households, the desire to accumulate personal wealth by marital alliances, and exchange and force of arms became an integral part of life. The earliest artefacts were axes, daggers and spearheads, and sadly with greater weaponry that was more efficient came greater violence. One must conclude that once land and property began to be owned bloodshed then ensued – that inevitable tale of human greed and vanity.

Our understanding of the Bronze Age has been enlarged by finds of hoards of bronze artefacts which had been immersed or thrown into rivers or lakes. At Flag Fen in East Anglia archaeologists have discovered three thousand bronze swords, spears and tools. A find at Runnymede included a range of bronze tools, implements and ornaments, as well as bone and antler tools, clay spindle whorls, loom weights and imports like armlets and amber beads. This was most apparent in the Eastern Zone of Britain and seemingly had ritual and religious significance, as many of the finds were newly made and of particularly fine workmanship. But it also has an economic and social relevance and such practices have been titled as prestige goods economy, deriving from the necessity of removing surplus bronze from circulation so that the metal retained its high value within society. Thus, the rulers keep control of the economy and retain their prestige. We should also bear in mind that the rulers were given their dues by the people in food: ale, dough or bread, meat and honey, furs and pelts, cheese and butter.[15]

Because of these watery graves, added to the fact that the old ritual sites geared towards astronomy were now abandoned, it is surmised that the belief system had radically changed. Can this shift be connected with the climate change? Another shift in weather conditions after 1000 BC meant lower temperatures and increased rainfall, cold and stormy periods became frequent. This led to greater swamp areas in the north and meant another change in farming – the uplands, too cold and wet, had to be vacated. So it was in the greater settlements of the south-east where cultural and technical developments took place. These factors, greater rainfall and lower temperatures, meant that the upland farmers had to move down to the valleys, more lakes and tributaries would have appeared, so were they trying to appease the gods by their golden offerings in the rivers and lakes?

There are now new mining projects and techniques, while stronger boats are being made so sea voyages become commonplace and deeper sea fishing possible. There is evidence of foods being smoked and wind dried. While the new pottery now refined preparation and cooking techniques, storage jars for example could be made airtight, while slow cooking of a mixture of dried beans, peas, vegetables, with or without meat simmering in large terracotta pots in the embers of a fire would become the standard dish of the day to return to.

Then early in the first millennium BC the migrants changed the crops. Naked barley was replaced by the hulled variety (*Hordeum texasticum*) and emmer wheat gave way to spelt (*Triticum spelta*). The farmers were reacting to new weather conditions, emmer being vulnerable to frost it can't survive throughout cold winters. Spelt delivers a higher yield than emmer but prefers a heavy soil, barley grows almost anywhere in Britain. The growth in cultivation of spelt meant that heavier soils were being cultivated than just the chalky, limestone uplands of the south east and farmsteads were moving onto heavy clay soils. Spelt and barley were often grown together in the autumn known as maslin (or beremancorn in the medieval period), but barley was also sown in spring. In the late iron age crops of oats and Celtic beans were also grown (there may have been a decline in the fertility of free draining light soils which had by this time been under cultivation for 2000 years).

Evidence from settlements and barrows show that cattle, pigs, sheep and goats were now herded and the two latter were kept on the drier uplands while the rest were in the river valleys. Grain production formed the basis of the economy at this time; it was used to make flour but also sprouted and fermented to make ale and mead. We must remember also that wild honey was relied on to sweeten food and drinks.

All foods were divided into those to be eaten straightaway and those to be treated for storage. Storage foods did not only mean those foods to be eaten throughout the long winter months, but those foods also that could be used when travelling long distances. These were all dried, thus smaller and lighter to carry, foods that had to be chewed slowly, sometimes reconstituted with water. Fresh meat was cut thin, then wind dried or smoked, fish could be split, boned, skinned (bones used for needles and skin for waterproofing) then dried and smoked.

The population was steadily rising, by 2000 BC it had become a quarter of a million, in the next one thousand years it would double, which showed that farming, plus the family and a settled agrarian community were factors that increased the birth rate, leading to food surpluses, a bureaucracy and an elite. There is evidence that the scale of prehistoric sheep farming rivalled that of the post-medieval period. These early sheep shed their fleeces in early summer so had to be herded in order to be plucked instead of shorn, as they are now; the easiest method was to pen them in a small paddock and then collect the wool from the fences and bushes that the sheep rub against. The country had a field system and was traversed by myriad tracks and paths. Horse harness fittings are to be found from this point, so we know that riding existed and from the width of wheel tracks people as well as goods were carried in light carts. But the track ways were also used by herds of sheep and cattle, which were routinely driven from one community to another for purposes of breeding. The moist warm climate was particularly suitable for the growing of lush grass. Around some Bronze Age farms there are remains of flax retting pits, the first stage in the production of linen, which in the summer must have been worn instead of wool.

Though there were hill forts most people lived in farms dispersed over the lowlands, houses were rectangular, made from timber supports filled in with wattle which supported a thatched roof; a style of rural architecture that would continue for the next five thousand years until the nineteenth century. The buildings were roughly 7.5-5m and had a central hearth; they would have housed a family group of anything from six to twelve people. Much the most well preserved dwellings have been found in the Orkney Islands at Skara Brae and elsewhere.

The Food

In the period from 1400-900 BC there was an extension of arable agriculture in the south and over the chalk uplands; the order, regularity and pattern of the fields show a coercive authority behind the planning. Leadership, of whatever nature, directs and affects the quality and character of the people's diet. In order for a leader to ensure his or her continual power funds are necessary in a ceaseless flow to trade, barter and sell. They are necessary to impress visitors, traders and society as a whole with the grandeur of the leader, their power in all things, funds are necessary to pay underlings in goods to continue to serve and obey, funds are there to bribe and flatter. The funds must come from the workers and the workers have to be told what to mine, what to cultivate, harvest, forge and spin. A labourer is no longer free to grow anything he might fancy in the fields he tills, once agriculture is controlled the range of the diet shrinks. Oh, he or she is free to pick and gather still from the wild in the few hours they might have free, still able to grow a few plants for his own use, favourite herbs and vegetables in the narrow plots next to the dwelling, but none of this is central to the diet. Women too spent long hours in the fields, sewing, hoeing, gathering while the men toiled with the harder, heavier jobs, forest clearance, moving the megaliths and the earth. It has been estimated that each of the earth causeways that are straddled across the hills of Wessex would have taken one hundred thousand hours of labour. But a leader who speaks with the authority of the gods is obeyed without question.

The diet that could fuel such heavy unremitting labour must have been high in calorific value – over five thousand calories per day. Bread and meat would have served, while the ubiquitous hazelnut, a supply of which was easily carried around, would have given more protein, easily digested if meat was scarce. If the women worked in the fields as they did, a large terracotta pot could be left in the embers filled with cabbage, carrot, onion, lentils or beans with animal bones left over for flavouring. Such soup would be the mainstay of the labourer for the next five thousand years. The first terracotta pot (the first ones were introduced into Britain around 4000 BC) made stews possible, an improvement on boiling in skins. And as the tools grew in practical design the food within the utensils undoubtedly became tastier and slightly more complex. It could not help but be noticed that long, slow cooking of meat, vegetables and herbs in a pot which is half buried in the embers or suspended over a modest fire, was pleasanter because of the herbs than without. Herbs had already become known as antidotes to aches, fevers and illnesses, either made into a poultice then wrapped around the infected limb or taken orally. Terracotta pots, created a radical difference in cooking techniques, because they were valuable as storage jars as well as cooking containers. Milk could be soured or drunk fresh, while butter and cheese were made. Ponies were used for pulling ploughs and carts. The animals were necessary to manure the fields, as well as for their hides, wool, horns and meat. A careful balance was achieved between growing cereals and the rearing of stock, a field of stubble was turned over first to the cattle, then to sheep and finally to the pigs. It was appreciated how fecund the last creature was, valued for its ability to consume waste, bracken, brambles, grubbed-up roots, still births and carcass scraps.

It is interesting to examine at a site at Black Patch in Sussex (inhabited from

1400-900 BC high on the downs, a village which covered over a kilometre) what was cultivated and what was wild in the diet. The growing crops were barley, beans, cabbage, emmer, and spelt; from the wild they ate chickweed, earth or pig nuts, goosegrass, orache, sloe, wild cherry, blackberry, raspberry, rose hips and hazelnut, from the nearby sea coast they gathered cockle, limpet, mussel and periwinkle. They ate meat from their own domesticated cattle, sheep and pigs (but two cattle to one sheep), they hunted birds and red deer. They stored their food in pits and in pottery jars, they had quern stones for making flour and hammer stones for crushing food, they used flint scrapers for treating hides and pelts and flint flakes for cutting and grating, awls (a fluted hand tool for making holes in leather and wood) and needles of bone. They had iron pyrite nodules for fire making – this is a yellow mineral, a source of sulphur, also named fool's gold or firestone that can be struck for sparks to ignite a fire – and they used charcoal. The Sussex Weald has been a source of charcoal making as long as it has been inhabited. Settlements of this type were self-contained, but produced a small surplus among the local centres of exchange.

Celts and Iron

The accounts of food consumption in Britain that have come down to us from classical authors such as Tacitus, Strabo and Julius Caesar have entered popular mythology and all are derogatory; too keen to prove that we were barbarians with no finesse or manners. They deal with the Celts, who may or may not be the people of these islands, in the past it was assumed they were, and that they were part of a whole nation which straddled Western Europe. As in fact these people never wrote anything down it is impossible to say with any precision what they were, but in terms of language, religious beliefs, their art and decoration and technology the peoples of Western Europe have many similarities. They have left remnants of their language in place names all over these islands. Albion is a Celtic word, while the Cornish word for river 'avon' has been used seven times in Britain and there are several others in Ireland. It was thought that there were a series of invasions by the Celts from 700 BC; certainly there are many hundreds of hill forts built over a triangular area in the south east. While the daggers, swords and shields that were sacrificed into the river Thames show an extraordinary artistic skill. The swords were often long ones for slashing used only by horsemen – mounted warriors had the advantage as many rural communities had already discovered.

According to the classical writers the Celts were great feast givers, their favourite meat being pork, and the strongest warrior chief had the right to carve the pig and keep back the choice cuts for himself. This was enough in itself to provoke fighting among them and it would appear more than just animals could be slaughtered. Such incidents were sung in ballad form to celebrate the greatest of one chief or another and were perfect fodder for one society to demean another, for the classical Mediterranean world (which imported most of its tin from Cornwall) looked down upon the Celts as barbarians. Strabo the Greek historian, geographer and philosopher 64 BC–AD 24 comments that the whole nation 'is war mad, both high-spirited and ready for battle, but otherwise simple and not uncultured'. He also tells us that large quantities of milk, fresh and salted pork could be consumed at a single meal.

Warfare and agriculture were given a further boost when iron weapons and tools appeared, around 650 BC. It has been estimated that local smiths served several communities within a 15-20 km radius, working on small and large tools as well as weapons and personal ornaments like the necessary clasps for the heavy cloaks that kept both wind and rain out and were exported elsewhere in Europe. Smiths now made cauldrons, shields and buckets as well as knives, razors and horse fittings. Horse harnesses appear around 1000 BC for the first time; the domestication of the horse transformed life in an astonishing way. Farms could be larger in area; hence there would be territorial expansion and the inevitable fighting or small tribe warfare which would ensue. People could travel further and faster and take luggage with them. Moreover the horse rider had a sense of strength over mere walkers and once armed tended to be invincible. Horse riders were also helped by the introduction of the trouser which travelled from the Orient across northern Europe (bypassing the Mediterranean for a millennium) which made riding a horse more comfortable and pragmatic.

Though the method of roasting and smelting within the smithy did not change overmuch with the advent of iron, iron agricultural tools were much more widely available, so such objects became commonplace. The population is now expanding, around two thirds of a million, there are vast numbers of Iron Age settlements across Britain, and in fact some believe our islands to be as densely populated then as they were at the time of the Domesday Book.[16] But as that was two and a half million it seems unlikely. Whatever the actual figure there was a sense of affluence and expansion in these years. We see the emergence of many specialist trades, jeweller and furniture maker, carriage builder and wheelwright, armourer and potter. Both hill forts and hundreds of farmsteads possess underground grain silos. Once emptied of grain the farmers cleaned the pits by setting fire to them, so now archaeologists can tell what food was stored there – wheat, spelt and barley.

Strabo listed Britain's most valuable exports as metals, hides, corn, hunting dogs and slaves. Perhaps it was the last that drew Caesar and his army to the French coast in 47 BC. When the Romans finally colonised Britain over a hundred years later they brought with them so many new food plants that it might be worth remembering what was here before they came. Plums, wild pears, strawberries, sloes and possibly the chestnut were here. There were also Alexanders which still grow lush on the south coast, a useful plant, for the stalk, leaf and black seeds were all used in cooking, the broad bean, celery, carrots, kale and asparagus, several of the vetches, coriander, beet, hemp used for rope and canvas as well as a drug and the opium poppy. People kept bees in wickerwork hives, set traps for fish and exported both grain and tin to the rest of the world. Caesar saw no gardens at all, either for pleasure or for produce. But as he was here for only a brief time he possibly never noticed them. For every homestead had a small plot protected from animals by a hazel hedge which grew the vegetables, fruits and herbs needed for daily cooking. What of course Caesar possibly meant was that there were no gardens, designed, planted and arranged simply for pleasure, to walk and recline in. Caesar also commented on the absence of the chicken. This has always struck me as odd, chicken flesh and chicken eggs surely would have travelled here, but chicken bones are not among the food debris in any excavations of the period before Roman occupation. I wonder whether there was not some religious objection to the use of the chicken as food, for Caesar mentions that we had cock fighting.

Cake before Bread

The food of the Gods – small, round delicately spiced cakes – coming before bread for the people, might seem an odd assertion. But quern stones have been discovered at the religious sites that are earlier in date than any domestic ones. Between 3800–3500 BC, so a mere three hundred years. As mentioned earlier, the stones have been either buried upside down, or deliberately broken at the site, or buried on their side. Whatever the position it was symbolic of burying the dead, so that its practical use was over; to deliberately destroy the central artefact of family life seems illogical and unlikely, but to destroy the means by which the sacred food was made after the ceremony is perhaps an act of piety.

Like any radical change in society, several factors are always involved: population was rising, numbers which wild foods could not hope to feed, except for meat; much of the domestic herds had to be killed by the end of October because there was no cattle feed after the pasture had gone, but there was plenty of game, so meat was no problem. But people also needed carbohydrate. For many thousands of years some of them may have gathered grass seeds and cereals which grew wild, then cooked them up into a gruel or porridge. This was true certainly of the far north where the use of grass seeds as protein and carbohydrate was necessary.

The people of Britain had known of bread and cakes before they began farming, from traveller's tales and many a sailor had also eaten them; they must have known too, that cakes were the food of the gods that in the countries far south and to the east of the Inner Sea, they were placed on the altar and burnt as they thought that the smoke full of aromas would entice the gods. That some form of the same ceremony was imported back to Britain seems reasonable. And a small acreage would be given over to wheat especially for the purpose of making such votive offerings. It was cake making then that was the stimulus and driving force behind bread, it was religion that gave structure and meaning to their lives. We still have the remnants of such a practice in the wafer and communion bread, both in the service and in the Lord's Prayer. I imagine that on the ritual site, for some days before, the grains would have been milled into the finest possible flour, but only a small amount, for the ceremony; then a larger coarser amount of flour was made for the people themselves and made into flat breads which would be cooked and eaten after the cakes had also been cooked, blessed, then consumed by the shamans. Lastly the mill stones would have been broken.

But why should organized religion come with farming? Because farming needed organization, rules had to be set down and observed as to which part of the land and how much of it went to whom. Though one can well imagine that in the first few hundred years people took what they wanted when they wanted it, this in time would only have led to fighting and slaughter and you cannot have savagery cheek by jowl with farming, the former will destroy the latter; hence a higher authority has to lay down laws which are guiding principles for the farming. Farming then to exist needed religion, not just secular legislation (which is a modern concept in itself), for that would not have had the power to constrain the people, nor the law needed to coerce the gods.

How far did the religious beliefs and rituals circumscribe the people themselves? These were the first farmers who were attentive to the changing night sky so it is likely that this is what ruled their life anyway, sowing and planting when the moon is full or waxing, and believing their gods must have ruled the earth, the rain, the sun. This argument stems from the artefacts which so far have been discovered, as nothing was ever written down, no set of beliefs or ethics, this is the only evidence we have. But we have plenty of evidence that the role of kingship was held in great reverence. I believe that in these few thousand years before the Roman occupation a change came over the structure of society, whereby the sacred gods also consumed the role of king, priest and leader, so that the divine food made for the gods was also made for the living gods. The grave goods buried with the kings were of the most exquisite workmanship, in urns and jars there was also food, long since vanished, but it would have been food of the highest quality and refinement. The great driving force behind this early gastronomy then is to praise the divine, to sacrifice to the gods to adore and revere him with cakes, and whether it is god or king hardly matters. This theme continues after Christianity where even one medieval king is likened to Jesus.

CHAPTER THREE

Rome

The power of good food played a vital part in the Roman conquest of Britain, nor should we underestimate its insinuating and growing presence in the century before Britain's colonisation. There's nothing quite like new flavours upon the palate which are markedly delicious so that they entice and stimulate, entreat, flatter and beguile, weakening the resolve, undermining what we might have thought of as high principles or general decisiveness. Whatever quite happened we can only imagine but the Celtic soul and its new Belgic settlers felt enthusiastic over Roman goods and quite the most important was Italian wine.

Trade and Slaves
The main trading port on Britain's south coast was at Hengistbury and Poole harbour; these were linked to the Channel Islands and to ports on the north coast of Brittany, the commodities then passed to the mouths of the Loire and Gironde. From there they reached the Mediterranean coast of Gaul. Strabo tells us that the curious Romans ordered a war galley to follow a Phoenician ship to discover their trading secret, which was how Poole harbour was discovered. One would have thought that among seafarers it was well known, as trade from and to the Mediterranean coasts had been continuing for some centuries. But Poole is hidden by the Isle of Wight, certainly, even more curiously Julius Caesar appeared ignorant of its existence as he landed in 53 BC on the Kent coast without natural shelter and many of his ships were destroyed in a storm.

Roman interest in our wheat, cloth and tin had first began around 120 BC and their desire for them led to a reciprocal need in Britain for Italian wine, luxury goods, yellow and purple glass and figs which gave enormous prestige to those that could afford them. Trade with Rome permeated through Britain, grains travelled from the south east, hides and furs came from the north, metals from the west coast, and all were transported to Dorset ports: lead and silver from the Mendips, copper and silver from Dartmoor and the inevitable tin from Cornwall. Hengistbury was a hive of activity, spilling over with life and wealth. Four tribes ruled southern Britain; the Dumnonii in the west controlled the tin trade, then the Durotriges, the Atrebates and the Cantiaci in the east where Caesar was to land. We can imagine that for any chief of these tribes to possess a marble figure of Venus, or a wife sporting an emerald and gold brooch, they would be puffed with pride, bathing in reflected glory from their tokens of worldly prestige for the rest of their life.

Slaves were another matter. Slavery of some kind must have always existed – where there is war and fighting there were trophies and human slavery, to be used as servile labour by the most important within society, was the most precious trophy of all. But a continuing demand for slaves from the most powerful trading nation and empire was not only a great economic asset, but changed radically the structure of society. The slaves themselves now had to be searched out and found, one imagines that small collections of armed horsemen would have been sent out to the poorer parts of these islands to find young men and women and most valuable of all, their children too. Once found they were told lies, given food and drink, spun stories and coerced into accompanying them. Only when they travelled nearer to the south coast would they on that last night be taken by surprise, then chained and brought to Hengistbury and the waiting ships, suddenly realising that they were leaving their land and homes forever. The captives, having cost nothing would now be sold (neck-irons and chains have been found from this time, a set of four in Anglesey); though the capturers were paid off, the slave administrator pocketed a handsome profit.

However, slavery was rather more complicated than it appears to us now, with our awareness of the tragic and horrific saga of the African slave trade and its connection with the sugar plantations of the West Indies. It is true that within the Roman mines and the arena slaves led short lives of hard labour ending in deaths of brutality. But slavery in the ancient world was a universal state where all but the very elite were plunged, many had important jobs in the household and administration, many were educated, talented, teachers, singers, musicians and scribes. Philosophers rationalised the state by saying that no one was free so slavery was a matter of degree, however what could not be denied was that slaves were property, had a cash value and were bought and sold like kitchen pots and pans. It is difficult to discover how much they did cost – the pretty young women were the most expensive, as they would end up as concubines – but the slave trade boomed in Britain because of the new found British love of Italian wine. A slave cost a single amphora of wine. One young woman cost 600 denarii, which was the equivalent of a year and a half wages for a legionary. The British wine lovers were paying over the odds for their wine.

The effect of this new affluence in the south was that the old hill forts were now abandoned and urban centres grew up at strategic trading places. The other result was that this new trade attracted the migration of a Continental Belgic community, which settled around the Solent. There is little doubt too that when such changes happen new foods and ingredients also permeate a society, apart from wine and figs, we can guess that other dried fruits, peaches, apricots and currants also made their appearance, not for the first time, but would now be common occurrence. Northern Europe had its dried and salted fish, but would the dried, salted and pressed fish roes, botargo, be something new? Fish roes were long extracted from a variety of fish, then salted, pressed, smoked and became a favourite delicacy (and still are) in all the eastern Mediterranean countries. Then surely too, the array of pickled vegetables that the Romans used as condiments with their food, would also find favour among the British.

We must remember that Roman cuisine had embodied not only classical Greece but also that of Persia, for each powerful empire fed from the culture before it and Persian cuisine was highly aromatic with its use of sweet and sour combinations, decorated with flowers and colour. As Rome's empire grew, so did its curiosity and acquisition of new products and ingredients produced from these new lands. The range of wines and foods it brought to this northern island lying off the edge of the continent must have been astonishing. Not all would have been new to the British, for trade with the Mediterranean had been active for centuries, but now the foods would have been presented in a different manner. One can imagine a sea captain explaining how to eat a slice of botargo with pepper, oil and a little citron, or adding some drops of garum to a fish stew, or watching a ship's cook make and dry pasta. It is not that the British elite might like these new foods, they probably spat some of them out, or that they would immediately introduce them – both their heat and their cooking utensils were too crude to cope with such cooking, lacking steamers and charcoal burners – it was that now they had a notion of how this great nation hovering at the other side of the channel lived and ate and it would have been disconcerting. One of the strangest aspects of Roman dining would undoubtedly have been the way they reclined on couches, while slaves stood and served them. 'In the ancient world, to lie down to eat and drink while others stood to serve you was a sign of power, privilege, of prestige.'[17] The affluent Britons now took to using Roman pots, tableware, combs and mirrors, drinking vessels and silverware for their ablutions, they used Roman gaming sets and feasting equipment (wine containers, salt cellars, vessels for cold and hot water, mixing bowls, candelabra and censors) and started to cremate their dead. The British elite was now aware that more powerful people lived lives of greater finesse within a culture they could hardly fathom. It must have brought unease and suspicion into their lives of a different quality than before; whether they also copied the Romans by reclining on couches to dine we do not know. One feels that they did not go so far for fear of ridicule or of being disloyal to their heritage, but it was only a matter of time surely. The Roman Empire itself must have perceived that this rough island had begun to be seduced, as so many other regions had been in the past; corrupted by luxury, they were ripe for plucking.

This period of trade and contact with the Romans continued for sixty years until Julius Caesar's abortive invasions a few years later, the last in 55 BC. He had now conquered a rebellious Gaul and some of the leaders of the revolt had fled to Britain, the foremost being Commius who was king of the Gaulish Atrebates, a figure hugely respected in Britain, for his name appears on the first British coins. But the war with Gaul had destroyed the trade connection with Hengistbury and the British economy must have suffered. It hurt when the luxury goods stopped. In 55 BC Caesar sent ninety-eight ships carrying two legions – ten thousand men – with cavalry and warships and attempted to land on the coast of Kent near Deal. But the British had been forewarned by Commius, and though they had been fighting among themselves before, now they buried their differences, met his ships in strength and fought. Caesar took hostages but retreated. The next year, in 54 BC he transported five legions in eight hundred ships with two thousand cavalry. Cassivellaunus, leader of the Catuvellauni, a tribe from mid-Anglia and Hertfordshire, led the British once more. Caesar fought his way through Kent and reached the homeland of his enemy, and then the British sued for peace. Caesar retreated bloodied but his honour intact; he had seen Britain and concluded obviously that the problems of adding such territory to the empire were too great.

Yet what had happened was that the centre of trade had now changed to the Belgic-Thames route. Within a few years Hengistbury declined, its coinage dribbled to a halt while the ports of Kent and Essex grew becoming industrious and wealthy. The Thames estuary was a convenient link to the newly established transport systems in Gaul which was based upon the Rhine; it was spacious and sheltered, the largest river nearest to the mainland of Europe. Londinium came into existence then; the Thames was tidal and ships could dock there, wharves and warehouses attracted traders, shopkeepers and cook shops opened on the dry island of Southwark.

Grave goods of British chieftains have been discovered of chain mail armour, Roman bronzes, furniture, and many amphorae. Later dated around AD 50, the grave of a British doctor at a Stanway site has been discovered with his set of medical instruments, scalpels, forceps, needles and a surgical saw, but with that he had some luxury goods, an amphora, a wine strainer, a pottery dinner service and a gaming board set out with glass counters. All these new and so desirable items that the British were now enjoying were products of the enemy, yet they must have felt equivocal about it all, for British traditions were disappearing: cremation was spreading, the ritual of throwing weapons into rivers had declined, neither did they now store grain in underground silos. The latter meant that they were no longer concerned with storing food for the winter as there was a steady supply if not from the homeland, but from across the channel.

The British elite now kept control of the trade routes and the rich burials of Essex, Kent, Hertfordshire and Bedfordshire display luxury goods, jewellery, gold and pottery. When Cunobelin, the great king of Britain, as Suetonius named him (Shakespeare called him Cymbeline) died in AD 40, the hierarchical system was weakened and the Emperor Claudius in Gaul could see an opportunity for a successful conquest. In AD 43 he landed and discovered that the south east welcomed him, for eleven kings joined Rome; the army of Aulus Plautius colonised the south eastern part of Britain with ease while the resistance led by Caractacus retreated fighting towards the west. Such is the power of luxury, such is the seduction of good food, fine wines and delicate, esoteric flavours, even to the untrained palate, yet greedy stomach.

Conquest

A writer as perceptive as Tacitus could detect this. In praise of the Roman governor, Agricola, he commented. 'Furthermore, he trained the sons of the chiefs in the liberal arts and expressed a preference for British natural ability over the trained skill of the Gauls. The result was in place of distaste for the Latin language came a passion to command it. In the same way, our national dress came into favour and the toga was everywhere to be seen. And so the Britons were gradually led on to the amenities that make vice agreeable – arcades, baths and sumptuous banquets. They spoke of such novelties as "civilisation" when really they were only a feature of their enslavement.'[18]

Contrary to popular belief though the Roman conquest did not bring civilisation and economic benefits to a backward nation, but only to a small number of British elite, 'to the officials and servants of the state (including the army) and to an influential minority of carpet bagging foreigners, many from northern Gaul.'[19] But because the food industry is such that it affects all classes, a new, rich and oppressive class with extraordinary demands must have instantly, if not enriched then benefited, many farmers, butchers, fishermen and merchants whose descendants would have flourished if they had stayed in the same trade.

With Roman occupation the same cereals continue to be grown, both bread wheat (*Triticum aestivum*) and club wheat (*Triticum compactum*). Oats and two rowed barley were grown for fodder and began to be cultivated in the north, primarily to feed the vast number of horses needed for the army. However, newly introduced are the parsnip, turnip, celery and the pea, but also a range of pot herbs, coriander, dill, fennel, mustard, parsley, rosemary and opium poppy, all were now commonly grown, though the last was certainly here in the Bronze Age. Pliny states that the cherry was brought to Britain, but cherry wood has been found earlier. The Belgae, a few hundred years before had already brought the vine as the leaf appears upon their coins. Figs, almonds, walnuts and the mulberry tree were all introduced as well as the walled orchard garden. Pliny mentions a domestic fowl, the Cheneros, as a specific British breed, but the Romans kept large flocks of geese and brought rabbit and pigeon farming. Pigs roam the nearby woods but return to the farm nightly for grain and whey, the sows are kept in for farrowing and a number of baby pigs are fattened up especially for the table. Olive oil was imported from Spain, from the Guadalquivir valley, pepper came from India, from Calicut to the Red Sea port of Berenice and cost a Roman soldier at Vindolanda two denarii. Garum also came from Spain and North Africa, a pottery container found in Carlisle was titled best quality while one from London contained 80 measures of fish sauce, which boasted that it was made from best quality tuna matured for two years.[20]

But perhaps the greatest difference in these years is the finalisation of the capitalist farming state. The operation of larger fields, deeper cutting ploughs, drainage ditches all require slaves, wage labourers and a tenant system run from afar by absent landlords. A system of feeding the populace that would continue until the present day. This created the great country estate with its exploitation of imported skills, knowledge and implements, the growing of fodder crops, controlled grazing and sown pasture, which constantly made inroads upon the common land. Very little has changed since then, 0.6 per cent of the population today, a tiny aristocratic elite, own 69 per cent of Britain's land, the same families that owned it in the nineteenth century.

The Roman system of administration was dependant on wealth; their hierarchical system began with the richest, so trade made it possible for Britons themselves to accumulate wealth and land could be bought and large estates acquired. Unlike in the past where land ownership was dependent upon the clan system and dynastic leadership. But this survived in Scotland and Wales where tribal meeting places possibly go back to the Neolithic and the third millennium.[21]

As the future of British food is partly dependent upon the character of the household itself, it is necessary to examine briefly the concepts that moulded the Roman one, for it was to have influence upon the Christian and medieval household which came afterwards. There was no word in Greek or Latin for 'family', the nearest '*familia*' meant all those that lived within the household or estate, who were subject to the *paterfamilias* which included slaves so this term could only apply to the wealthy and the free. In Roman law girls could be married from the age of twelve and their husbands would be quite possibly twenty years older or much more; marriage was expected to be monogamous and it is for the procreation of children, so a patrician was literally someone who knew his father or pater. Men, whether bachelors or not, were expected in the pagan world to express their sexuality outside the marriage, which could include homosexuality and pederasty. After AD 380 when Christianity became the state religion attitude to this very slowly began to change. It was Augustine of Hippo (died AD 430) who wrote at length on marriage and sex and who shaped medieval ideas on marriage, hence the household and its food. This led to our present concept of food, as being food for the family, domestic food for an inner circle of kin. A concept entirely alien to the Roman mind.

Food

Yet did British food consumption change that much after the Roman conquest? We should bear in mind that Roman rule was only effective in the lowland south east, that geographical diagonal from the rivers Exe to the Tweed. Though conquering and subduing the west and north was attempted, the terrain was too mountainous to ever be fully successful. The Roman army fought and marched on large amounts of bread, made palatable with olive oil, wine, salt, onions, garlic, radishes and water with a dash of vinegar. A diet not dissimilar to the Britons who worked the land to produce the cereals. They ate their bread in the same way and had done so for centuries, the grain as porridge, soaked in water or baked as a flat cake. It is likely that the Romans used some imported wheat grain which may have made slightly finer bread than the one the Britons were consuming. However, the Romans also ate meat and fish, though they did not delineate between the two and would possibly have eaten this far more regularly than the Britons, who would have supplemented their meal with cabbage, turnips, herbs and wild leaves like orache, fat hen, cress and mallow. While the Romans would certainly have brought both lentils and the fava bean and grown these, so that they had a supply, the fava bean had already arrived, as it was far too precious a food to stay within the Mediterranean area and it obligingly flourished in northern Europe. The physician Galen thought that 'legumes are those grains of Demeter that are not used to make bread'. Galen (born in AD 129) became physician to the Emperor, Marcus Aurelius and made many observations which he noted down: wet nurses gave babies skin diseases, because they ate wild plants in the spring, a young man could eat healthily for four years on a vegetarian diet, ditch diggers are strong and can eat bad food but die young.[22]

The soldiers knew that the poor man's dinner was bread, wine and roots, but a dinner of bread, wine and meat was special. But we must also not forget cheese, merely soured milk drained of whey and allowed to dry, what we now know as ricotta. This would help the hunger of both Roman and Briton. So there is little change in this basic diet for the worker, the soldier knew that the food supply was secure and by AD 70 we have increasing numbers of Britons who are also Roman soldiers. But the peasant farmer knew his locality, and where the wild things grew, so his diet and that of his families were always supplemented by bird eggs, game birds and small mammals, baby pigs and all the wild leaves, roots, tubers, the knowledge of which was always handed down from mother to daughter.

The Vindolanda letters, named after the fort built before Hadrian's Wall on the northern frontier of Britain, which have been discovered recently roughly date from the end of the first century and the beginning of the second, and tell us something of the food eaten in a garrison. Though these are scraps of thin wood written in ink, dumped old archives, shopping lists, letters and accounts, they all sound very familiar; a great deal of beer and chicken, also venison and roe deer, was consumed by the commander and one imagines the soldiers had a similar diet. The chicken and its eggs, which the Romans naturally brought from over the channel when they invaded, was to become a central part of the diet from now on. The commander also has a list of more exotic items to cheer such basic fare up which must have been ordered from afar, mustard, cumin, anise, grapes, nuts, potash and opium. The letters mention hunting, for hunting nets and dogs are also ordered and prize wild boars were sought excitedly, not only for their carcass, but also for blood games and entertainment. After all, the soldiers were supplied with bread, so they also had to have the circuses.

Forty-six different foodstuffs are mentioned altogether, one letter has a scrap of a shopping list, 'a pork cutlet, bread, wine and oil', another mentions a meal, 'beans, lentils, lovage and butter', yet another 'pork crackling, trotters'. There is one letter to a slave asking him to get 'bruised beans, two chickens, a hundred apples if you can find nice ones, a hundred or two hundred eggs, if they are for sale at a fair price, fish sauce and olives'. I imagine 'bruised beans' to be already soaked or possibly also cooked dried fava beans, our equivalent of mushy peas, when the dried peas have been thoroughly cooked and are sold from a tub.

The peasant farmer coming into the new towns like London, Colchester, Gloucester, Lincoln and later York (to use the names that we are now familiar with) bringing his few foodstuffs to sell, would have been suffused in the smells of cooking from the Tavernas (*Tabernae*) and Bars (*popinae*). At the first they drank wine and ate snacks, chickpeas, turnips and salted foods, while at the second they could drink, play games and also eat meals, grilled meats, sausages, fried sprats, stews of pigeon – there were pans bubbling on the fires always tempting people in the street. Here was the great temptation of the Roman cuisine for the British, to amble along the narrow streets inhaling the aromas.

The chicken and her eggs had been a part of Roman cooking since Etruscan times, roughly 500 BC; hens had always been raised in large numbers wherever the Romans went. We know too that they ate them because there were various ways of fattening the birds before slaughtering them as the vegetarian Plutarch (circa AD 100) tells us, criticising the cruelty of the method. Birds were fattened up in small cages where they could not move.[23] So I have little doubt that the Briton walking the streets of Colchester would have smelt roasting chicken as well as stews of dove or pigeon; he would also have smelt wild duck, deer and hare, for the soldiers loved hunting and the friendly owner of the popina would have been happy to have cooked the produce for them. Inside the popina there would have been several ovens of different sizes as well as hot plates and charcoal braziers, cooking equipment to amaze the locals.

But soldiers every now and again were restricted; Scipio got rid of the bivouac of tarts and soothsayers and limited each man's mess kit to a spit, a copper pot and a drinking cup. In the day they were allowed only raw food to be eaten standing up and at night meat must be either boiled or roasted. This banned stewing, obviously as it took time. It also introduced an element of Spartan austerity into military life which was never far away, and yet in Britain, once the opposition had faded away, life must have settled down to an almost cosy routine which the letters from Vindolanda suggest.

The Romans brought extensive flour production, milling done by animal labour turning the stones, and were slow to harness the power of water while they had cheap animal and slave labour. For the first time Britain had an efficient sanitation system, sewers, baths and an unpolluted water supply. Making their first appearance in the west are scissors, door keys, pumps and bellows. A great range of various iron pots and pans, as well as much terracotta, glass, enamel and bronze. There are silver spoons, ladles, strainers and that most useful culinary tool, a spoon with holes in the centre. The domed oven appears making great crusty loaves possible and for the first time we find that magician of the kitchen – the pastry cook – working his skills. While fermented ales are given a boost with the invention of barrel making and cooperage. The invention of pewter, when the Romans combined Cornish tin and lead from the Mendip hills, led to a form of tableware that fell in and out of favour until the seventeenth century when it suddenly became the smart dining ware.

Roman policy was to assimilate the conquered, to induce them to become an integral part of the Empire and this worked in a remarkable way. Yet that southern Mediterranean outlook where the conquered are always inferior, where in the Greek tradition, they are 'the other' was still within the Roman breast. A culture based on bread, wine, and oil was opposed to one based on milk, meat, butter and ale, though the Romans ate meat as well. But they would have said it was not the centre of the meal as it was with the barbarians. They, of course, insisted on meals only of meat and were content not to consume vegetables at all; while Romans proudly could eschew meat altogether for many meals and were content to eat bread, olives, cheese and wine. There was undoubtedly a difference and that difference still exists, and the Mediterranean mode of eating still possesses a moral authority, with its healthy sub-text, as it did then.

Tacitus goes on about the British weather complaining about how wet it was and saying that like Gaul, vines and olives would not grow here. But the Romans brought in many fruit rootstocks – apples, pears and plums – and Pliny tells us that cherries came in AD 46, both the sweet cherry (*Prunus avium*) and the acid cherry (*P.cerasus)*, the mulberry (*Morus nigra*) and the medlar

(*Mespilus germanica*) as well as the sweet chestnut and the walnut. Small, wild indigenous fruits which the Britons collected and ate like the wood strawberry (*Fragaria vesca*) or the wild raspberry (*Rubus idaeus*) seem to have been ignored by the conquerors, as were the currants and the berries. The Britons must have been somewhat relieved to have some foods that they felt were fully theirs to gather and enjoy. Blackberries were known, for the Greek, Theophrastus, writes of them, but these too were ignored. But as the Romans had cultivated the wild strawberry in Italy as early as 200 BC, I am sure they grew the fruit in the summer months within the confines of their garden, specially protected and manured. Cato discusses the growing of asparagus, while Columella describes the forcing of cucumbers in baskets of dung and we know that Tiberius was especially fond of this vegetable and had them grown from wheeled barrows which could be moved around in the sun. But vines must have been greatly more cultivated after the conquest, though they did not become common until the latter half of the second century when the Emperor Probus encouraged his troops to create vineyards. Unfortunately adding agricultural labour to military duties was deeply resented and the army mutinied and murdered the emperor.

Garden Produce
One must also thank Rome for bringing us the garden. The idea of a space architecturally designed, protected from the worst excesses of the elements, aesthetically pleasing, comfortable for people to relax, amble and recline in, filled with plants for perfume and taste, began in Babylon, was celebrated in Persia, Egypt and China and this heritage was brought to Britain by the wealth and stylish taste of their most important citizens. While Rome existed we copied it. Romans believed passionately in the garden, they cultivated gardens for each homestead or villa however modest, for the garden was the main food producer and it was expected to produce food all year around. More easily done in Italy than in northern France or Britain, however, but Romans always believed in success, they were not easily defeated. So gardens in Britain produced green vegetables such as cabbages, spinach, beet, tubers and edible bulbs, many different salad leaves, leeks, turnips, carrots, parsnips, garlic and onions as well as varieties of cardoon and globe artichokes. The gardens were near the house and walled being especially sheltered from prevailing winds and sited towards the south for maximum sun. The beans that they grew and valued highly were grown with the cereals as field plants, so were outside the immediate vicinity of the house in fields ploughed every year. Another area

would house the food animals, the chickens, geese and pigeons; peacocks were also raised on farms, while the wild birds were trapped with birdlime. Hunting and fishing were seasonal sports, there was no hunting in the spring and summer while the young were born and raised while fishing was banned in winter. The more wealthy Romans bred wild boar in farms on their estates and raised fish in hatcheries. Even in these households meat was considered a luxury, they were too close to the source, its slaughter and preparation, to just dismiss it as food.

But certainly for the first time a sophisticated cuisine existed in Britain. This of course meant elitist cooking, for the very few, the wealthy who controlled society, but ideas percolate through via servants and retainers to the community as a whole. Roman expertise, whether farming or culinary, whether recipes themselves or the culture of food were never to be completely forgotten and it became the basis of our culinary future. Even though a climatic change meant a cooling which followed the disintegration of the Roman Empire leading to rebellion, famine and plagues and a seeming sudden disappearance of this culinary culture.

There is little doubt that the Britons, if they became wealthy, would emulate the conquerors, as much as their income allowed, in every detail. We can often detect an estate and villa built by a Briton because among the buildings which are obvious Roman copies there are also stone-based roundhouses, the native vernacular form of building, as if for sentiment they could not resist building a bit of the old homestead. At the height of the Roman occupation, the prosperity of the island is obvious, population had risen and it appears to have reached around three million, which was comparable to that previous to the Black Death in the midst of the fourteenth century. Analysis of Romano-British graves show that males were 1.69 metres (5 feet 5 inches) and females 1.59 metres (5 feet 2 inches), they were on the whole well fed, there were even diseases of affluence, dental decay and gout and DISH (diffuse, idiopathic skeletal hyperostosis) an abnormal growth of bone in the joints, a pathology common among older, obese and diabetic men. The Romans also had imported new afflictions like leprosy, tuberculosis and rheumatoid arthritis.

Whether the Britons learnt that this was an aspect of high living is doubtful, for the high living was, as always, particularly astonishing, glamorous and highly appealing. The new servant lad who entered a large Roman villa at the time of a feast must have had his eyes on stalks. We gather a vivid impression of the food served from depictions on the mosaic floors, murals and reliefs throughout the Roman Empire. The servants would carry in huge platters of roast peacocks, cranes, fowl, and smaller game birds like woodcock, widgeon, partridge and pheasant, then there were suckling pigs, kids, oysters and lampreys, swordfish, tuna and sturgeon, pike and lobster, and arrays of vegetables with their sauces, which seem to be served with cakes and crescent-shaped rolls. They loved salads and especially shoots which they gathered throughout the year from constant sowings of peas, hops, grapes, borage, giant fennel and many species of cabbage and lettuce.[24] The range of spices which the Britons were familiar with must have extended to a large degree; as well as the ubiquitous pepper – desired everywhere – cinnamon, ginger, nutmeg and cloves were all top Roman favourites, but surely they would also have smelt grains of paradise, anise, cumin, asafoetida, silphium and galangal. Then there were the herbs, rue and lovage, oregano, bay, chervil, saffron and we cannot omit mastic (though the last is hardly a herb, but is an aromatic resin from a tree, *Pistacia lentiscus*). Then after the first and second course the floor would be swept, the table cleared and the dessert would be generally simple, nothing but fruit and nuts, but what a variety. The Britons who served would have been amazed at the range of grapes, peaches, apricots and figs which often travelled from the Mediterranean, though more and more would have been grown in carefully sheltered walled gardens in the south. Throughout the whole meal copious amounts of wine were drunk – unlike the Greeks, the Romans did not water their wine, at the beginning it all came from Gaul and Spain, but gradually vineries in Britain began to produce their own.

Asafoetida only became a firm favourite as a seasoning when silphium which Rome was addicted too finally vanished after the first century AD. The richest Romans of that era were the last people to taste silphium for by then the spice was rare, though it had always been expensive. Both Greeks and Romans loved this spice above all others, it was a large root with a stem as long as giant fennel and its leaf was similar to celery, it grew in Cyrene on the north African coast, but only in the wild and did not respond to cultivation. It gave out a resin, which was the valuable part that was collected, it was then mixed with flour and stored in jars and then transported all over the empire. As garlic was to traditional French cuisine silphium was to Greek and Roman; its flavour, perfume or even just faint resonance permeated every dish and it partnered both meat and vegetables. Archestratus, the great Greek gourmet (circa 350 BC), disapproved of its use with fish, though salted tuna was thought to need it. The Greeks first discovered it soon after 638 BC when they founded their colony of Cyrene which became rich on the silphium trade. Strabo, writing a century before it finally vanished, indicates how the end might have come;

there was a quarrel between the gatherers of the herb and those that marketed it – getting nowhere the former then uprooted and burnt the plants. Pliny tells a different story which was that when landowners noticed that the meat of sheep grazing on their land became suffused with the herb and could be sold for higher amounts, they allowed the land to be overgrazed, thus destroying the plant. Whatever the truth, human greed killed off yet another unique plant, another victim in our history of ignorance and folly.

But what of the food the servants and slaves cultivated and cooked every day for the extended family within the villa? What of the tastes in this new food, were they tastes which would remain with us, would become part of our gastronomic inheritance? Olive oil was exported from their Roman estates into the kitchens of Britain, crusty loaves baked on a bed of bay leaves, a great range of sausages, of all shapes, flavour and colour, and many diverse cheeses from hard to soft. We might well have begun to learn from that date how to make and mature good cheese, for it was an art which took many hundreds of years to master. As our cheese was always soft and in curds unless pickled in brine, when it became as hard as granite and tasted of nothing but salt. What a revelation then for the native retainers to take a slice of tangy, golden cheese upon their tongue and to experience such a complexity of flavour bound up within the creaminess. As to vegetables, the Romans grew chard and orache, asparagus, globe artichokes and cardoons, and lettuces in profusion, while they loved lentils, lupins, chickpeas, vetches, peas and broad beans. The Romans loved offal, which they marinaded, fried, boiled, poached in sauces, they loved small birds wrapped in stuffings or pastry, they loved sweet and sour sauces, bitter leaves and wine boiled down to an essence, but most of all the ubiquitous fish sauce or liquamen, which came in different strengths and thicknesses, matured to various qualities from the cheapest and coarsest to the most refined and subtle; all this would surely have filled Britons with awe and wonderment. Roman cuisine had embodied all the gourmet traditions in classical Greek and Persian cuisine, their cooks, chefs, bakers and pastry makers were enormously skilled in the kitchen, so much so that satires and parodies of the food, its preparation and consumption were fairly common, though we are perhaps only familiar with Trimalchio's feast in Petronius's *Satyricon*. These are chapters of a novel which contains a description of a feast given by a character called Trimalchio. The scene is thought to be satirical of the excesses of the nouveau riche – dormice rolled in honey and poppy seeds sounds enticing, but a roast hare fitted with wings to masquerade as Pegasus, a wild sow stuffed with alive thrushes are examples of gross tastelessness intended to be laughable.

The Greek gourmet tradition exemplified in Archestratos (circa 330 BC) who wrote a gastronomical travel guide, grading the best foods and exactly which area they stemmed from, emphasises the care taken in the selections of ingredients which continued throughout the Roman Empire. In Horace's Satire 11 (viii) the cold roast boar eaten had to be from Luciana and must be caught when a gentle south wind was blowing, while the apples had to be picked at the waning of the moon. The wine must be from Chios, only the breasts of the blackbirds are to be eaten, merely seared while a lamprey had to be pregnant and the Italian wine must be aged five years. And so it goes. It seems to me that this detailed fussing – though thoroughly sent up, we all know now people who are also capable of it – would have been shockingly new to a British sensibility, worthy of ridicule in the kitchen, yet would have marked their oppressors as singular but in possession of esoteric knowledge that might be desirable to have. While parts of those everyday meals would have been taken to our hearts and stomachs, like meat cooked with bay leaves, pies and sausages, the crusty loaf and the use of yeast, much of it too we might well have wanted to use, like olive oil and the craft in cheese making, but were unable to keep or grow.

Food Symbolism

But was there something else, one asks, which may or may not have taken hold of the British soul, the Roman philosophy of food, its symbolism and how that effected its consumption? Food, in the Roman mind, was divided between wild and cultivated, meat and vegetables, the cooked and the rotten, these distinctions were rigid and absolute. In the four hundred years that Rome ruled Britain (and indeed Western Europe) did the ideas of the partition of different foodstuffs, become absorbed by the British?

The symbolism within the food consumed and cultivated was every much as detailed for the Roman sensibility as it was in the Jewish dietary laws. The Romans first of all distinguished between foods that had been cultivated (*fruges*) and foods derived from animals (*pecudes*), the first came from the tamed land, the second from the wild, even domesticated animals roamed fields cropping pasture. This category also included fish, game birds as well as wild mammals, and they were husbanded by shepherds and hunters living on the fringes of their cities, who were like barbarians, for these were often slaves without wives or homes who were unknown and could be unreliable. Food from gardens and ploughed land seemed far more civilised, besides the sun had already partially cooked it, thus it could be eaten just plucked and raw. But cereals and beans came from less civilised land, not so well cooked as garden produce, so could not be eaten raw, yet grains remained alive capable of seeding new life, unless they were roasted, when they were killed and capable of rotting like animal flesh. So wheat was stored as grain and when needed milled and then used immediately and baked into bread. The suspicions that Pythagoras held about broad beans were also partially inherited by the Romans, who believed that the beans rotted more rapidly than wheat and the priests of Jupiter were forbidden to eat them. One thing was sure about Roman meals, the food was sparklingly fresh; indeed, if we consider Mediterranean food now and this is the area of the Roman Empire, the same is true today. It could be argued logically that this was simply because of the climate, that everything unless eaten at once, declined rapidly and rotted. But then surely all taboos and distinct regulations on food tend to be a reaction to the environmental and sociological context.

The Romans believed meat upon the living animals began to rot while they were still alive as everything is in gradual decay; once death occurred the animal declined quickly into a foul smelling liquid. To slow down this process the viscera was quickly removed and the carcass drained of its blood, then the viscera was roasted and with the hot blood offered up to the Gods. The meat was then eaten, but it was believed that it continued to rot in the stomach until defecation.

Bread, as we have seen, was central to the mythology of food and it was bread made from wheat that was essential, it was the food of the citizen-soldier, he consumed almost two pounds of wheat per day. Bread was hard and compact, shrank and became harder without rotting; like the soldier the food had stamina, it could resist the elements and do nothing but sustain. Bread, of course, was the staple and we have seen how the staple is a product of government and is used as a method of control. Juvenal's comment that the people's happiness rested solely on being given both an adequate supply of both bread and circuses must have echoed down the centuries with succeeding governments and is as true now as it was then, for today we appear to be happily compliant if given enough junk food and TV. Grain ships supplied Rome from all over its empire. In Imperial Rome the citizens erected a monument to their bakers in the shape of a colossal oven at Eurysaces. Bread itself, not just the grains that make it, had become one of the gods. As to what fuelled gastronomy, it was the greatness first of the republic that quickly merged into that of the emperor, whatever added to the image of his magnificence and power, while the gods had to be palliated with the usual votive offerings; luxury foods and their cooking, had become part of the trappings of state.

Perhaps the Roman mythology sounds somewhat bizarre to us, yet parts of it have become immersed within our traditions, and the following pages will explore what was jettisoned and what was kept and how it formed what we eat. But the symbolism which food carried suffered a series of severe shocks when the onslaught of invasion of the empire became a constant and insoluble problem in the 4th millennium. Roman writers had long described the 'barbarians' as living from the wild, so were feral creatures themselves – if they raised livestock it was in herds which they took with them, they did not cultivate fields and vineyards. The two cultures were separated by their foods, so the barbarians were despised and thought inferior and uncivilised for what they ate, they did not even hang their game before eating it, they ate milk curds and drank ale, they stank of onion, leek and rancid butter with which they dressed their hair, but how deeply humiliating and confusing when such people became the conquerors. All the more demeaning as this process was slow and in some cases almost arbitrary, this clash and merging of barbarian with sophisticated Roman, and in those parts of the Roman Empire which remained Roman for longer even greater emphasis was placed upon food mores. You find it in the writer, Decimus Magnus Ausonius when he writes about his estates in what would be Bordeaux, his love of good wines gives us evidence of large scale viniculture (there was no destruction of vineyards as is sometimes alleged[25]) and his detailed picture of the scenery and life along the river Moselle includes a catalogue of its many fish. It was people like Ausonius who kept the culinary traditions alive throughout the transition period.

I believe that the food symbolism of northern Europe is markedly different from that of southern, but throughout history the north has been constantly seduced by the ideas of the south, it is beguiled, then taken over but never totally. If you look at Britain today split into its class hierarchies, it is clear that one of the markers that signify the differences is food. The difference is exactly similar to the one of two thousand years ago that marked the Roman world from the barbarians – meat opposed to vegetables. Broadly speaking, the world of fresh fruit, salads and five a day vegetables today tends towards affluence, culture and higher education, while the world which negates all that food is working class and meat orientated.

Yet these sociological differences are always in a state of flux and at the time of the Roman Empire's decline something quite new and radical was growing within society, something which would save the old symbolism, in fact, reinterpret it, raise it even higher still, so that what we now call the Mediterranean diet would have a new resonance, and become even more sacred and ritualised.

CHAPTER FOUR

The Crucial Era

We have come to what was once called the Dark Ages (mainly because we knew very little about it) but which now is referred to as early medieval, as we now know a lot more. I have named it as crucial because so much of what we call English as opposed to British began to take form then, including pertinently its name, the stronghold upon society which the Christian hierarchy began to have, and the beginnings of the middle classes.[26] The last are particularly significant in the history of our food, as they foster, generate and improve on certain root traditions that dominate a nation's tastes.

The Prize

Once the Roman Empire weakened and began to decline from the midst of the fourth century, the world as people knew it was in ferment. As industries failed to produce, roads needed repair, the structure of society collapsed, there was no overall authority, no taxes and no law, so the coinage dribbled to a halt. Britain became a magnet for the tribes of Europe who began to invade. We should ask ourselves why. Certainly the tribal frontiers had broken down, now everything was in flux, there was no restraining military overriding where you went or what you did. So much was up for grabs and Britain seemed to be very well worth having. One might also ask what happened to the food at such times; one can only speculate, but most of what was eaten before, what was grown and harvested would have continued to be eaten, yet as the old masters gradually died out or fled, one can imagine that standards fell, that meals became a spontaneous act; eating on the move, grabbing what one can could to stave off hunger must have been the order of the day. The favourite foods that the Romans had brought to the land and culture must have continued to be cooked, perhaps even some recipes written down, but the food that was integrated into the fabric of society would have been changed radically, its southern roots, its Mediterranean heart buried beneath this northern climate.

The fact that Britain was an island must then have had obvious attractions – it had not escaped notice that the island even took the Romans over a century to invade and master; that strip of sea that divided us from the great land mass looked ever more desirable as a natural frontier against an enemy. It was also bound to have been registered that the land was fertile, that cereals grew abundantly, that within its rocks were valuable metals, which were being mined, and that under Roman rule the society had been prosperous and peaceful. It would have been remembered also that as late as AD 359 the Emperor Julian filled 600 of his ships at the mouth of the Thames with supplies of grain for his beleaguered garrison in the Rhineland. A country so overflowing with food, wine and arms could not lightly be ignored. So by AD 364 the invasions had begun, Saxons on the east coast, Irish on the west and Picts in the north, they came silently in ships just before dawn, landed, killed, fought and stole, staying sometimes for a few days or weeks until their lookouts warned them of armed forces about to arrive. Until the time came when there was no rescue parties. The tribes met and co-operated, together they launched an attack in AD 367, the Romans named it '*barbaraca conspiratorio*' and could do little to stop them over running the country, looting villas, killing and taking hostages and slaves. The Romans built forts and watch towers and on the east coast these were known as the 'forts of the Saxon shore'.

Perhaps it is just that all invaders are barbarians; after all, St Jerome himself was not flattering on the eating habits of the British invaders in Gaul. 'I myself, as a young man in Gaul saw that the Attacotti, a British tribe, eat human flesh and, even though throughout the woods they might find herds of swine and oxen and cattle, it is their custom to cut off the buttocks of the herdsmen and their wives, their breasts too, and to judge these alone as culinary delicacies.' Is this the usual tall story that emanates about the enemy in wartime? After this date there were Attacotti serving in the Roman army, so they had quickly changed sides, perhaps the attraction of a better diet? For the clash between invader and Rome was further exemplified in food, with stories being told of the prodigious amounts of meat consumed by the invaders at a single sitting. Maximinus the Thracian, the first emperor to be born of barbarian parents was thought to eat between forty and sixty pounds of meat a day, while an earlier emperor, a Roman, Didius Julianus, was happy to eat vegetables and pulses without any meat at all. The symbolism of their different diets was highly apparent, no question who was civilised and who was not, meat and a prodigious quantity said it all. Yet, generalisations about their nature are bound to fail, as the particular example always engenders others that contradict the general impression. Vinidarius, an Ostrogoth, who flourished in the fifth century, made up a catalogue of spices for the well-stocked larder necessary for any important kitchen, while also gathering together a small collection of recipes which purport to be those of Apicius, but which bear little resemblance. However, barbarian cooking appears to our eyes to be every bit as sophisticated as the old Roman cuisine.

There is much use of asafoetida taking over silphium's role as a favourite flavouring, as well as the berries of bay, myrtle and rue, poppy seeds, celery, fennel, lovage, rocket, coriander, anise, parsley, spikenard – these are but a selection. The recipes given treat chicken, beef and fish with many of these herbs mixed with honey and vinegar, the sauces thickened with rice flour and yolks of eggs. There is a dressing for spiny lobster that uses pepper, lovage, celery seed, and vinegar thickened with the yolks of hard-boiled eggs. Another dressing for roast fish is fig with dill, honey, oil and egg yolks. Admittedly this was all in southern Gaul and not Britain, but it serves to show that the title of barbarian was hardly an apt one for the new peoples that were taking over from Rome.

Yet as the invasions spread through the declining Empire another restraining force was rehabilitating it. The new religion – Christianity. Firstly, they preserved the language – Latin, and all that knowledge contained within it, not all of which they might want to keep. Secondly, one has only to glance at that central pivot of culture and sustenance – the garden – to see it re-emerging, as an adjunct to the newly built monasteries. By the end of the third century the conversion of the Empire to Christianity was complete; in AD 390 the Emperor Theodosius outlawed all pagan worship. But in Britain Christianity took many more hundreds of years to become established and some would argue that paganism has never died.

Dietary Changes

That sharp difference between the Mediterranean world and the 'barbarians' began inevitably to blur and merge. Christian missionaries were adept at taking pagan festivals and rituals, and by referring to them with Latin names they changed their nature and converted them to Christianity. So with the food; it is no coincidence that bread, wine and oil became central to the Christian liturgy, the symbolic food of the old elite becoming sacred. The newly appointed bishops and abbots began to plant vineyards and wheat fields around their churches and monasteries. This oasis of cultivation became a magnet to the curious who were becoming bewildered by the growing wildness of the countryside, as woodlands took over previous ploughed fields and the once domesticated herds of animals were depleted by their foraging further into the newly wild areas. The barrier between wild and cultivated was blurred, food was very much what was at hand, and the diet was an amalgam of both and all the better for it.

Dense woods and forests, however remained a rich larder for the peasant family, whether they lived within them or on their outskirts, and these areas were especially significant at times of violent change in society, for then the dense forest became a refuge and a hideaway. There was another reason also why woods were treasured; they were central to religious belief, all woods were sacred, and they were magical places where spirits lived, appeared and wrought wonders to mere humans. The tree was hugely significant, for people could live in its branches or beneath its shelter, they could build with its material and cook their food with its help, besides it actually produced fruit and nuts for them as well as feeding their pigs which ran and foraged beneath the beech trees. But perhaps the most significant aspect of the tree was that it became an infinite resource of weaponry. Ash bows found in the bogs of the Stone Age could shoot goose-feathered arrows for 150 yards. They were no doubt about it, skilled hunters. Yet in a forest such weapons were of little use, dense trees called for sling shot or catapults, or most effective of all, snares and traps. People familiar with their neighbourhood woods were also acutely aware of animal tracks and the paths worn by them.

However, the forests in Britain which were at all near the cultivated triangle (the line between the Exe and the Tweed) were all managed woods; they were constantly coppiced, for the need for wood was constant, for building, for ships, for fencing and weaponry, for cooking and heating and also for gathering honey. But also the stretches of wild woods, not so heavily eroded and managed, were much desired by the nobility and the monarchs themselves for hunting. So this natural larder for the peasant was always at risk. There were agricultural areas, though, far away from woods where another fuel existed, East Anglia for example relied on turbaries (peat diggings) and such pits that were gradually linked became so extensive around Norwich that they became inland lakes and we know them now as the Norfolk Broads.

The merging of the two worlds in one diet was partly because the so-called barbarians were fascinated by the Roman model, they wished to ape it, the sophistication, the style, the very intelligence that permeated it, was attractive to many of those who had been born outside the empire. But the fact that Christianity had now made bread, oil and wine into a sacred part of worship, added another level that pulled the new elite in. When they saw the new abbots and bishops planning, planting and propagating vineyards and olive groves, while their domains were filling up with fields of golden wheat, they felt Elysium would now arrive as the new faith promised. Then, even though the exploitation of forests and woodlands by the barbarians had once been condemned now it was approved, though no longer thought of as exploitaton but as cultivation. Forests were regarded as productive and were managed by woodsmen and their serfs. The pig being still the most popular of all meats, the swineherd tended to be valued the most highly among the serfs. But the population was declining, peasants without Roman rule tended to gravitate either to the towns or to faraway rural hideouts where they could live a simple life grubbing around for sustenance, but away from all authority. So large parts of the country were now also deserted.

The basic diet was true of all social levels, the staples were the same: cereals, pulses and vegetables but integrated with them were the few domesticated animals still kept, sheep and goats and from the wild, game and fish. The sheep and goats were far smaller than our animals now – about half the size – and they were kept largely for their wool and the milk; these small animals represented 80 per cent of the livestock. The pigs too were small, reddish, bristly with a pointed muzzle and tiny tusks. Farmyard poultry, ducks and geese were kept for their eggs and also eaten. Farming fish, part of the Roman heritage, was also kept alive by the Church, who with its rising number of meatless days needed a steady supply of fish for the devoted to eat. The milk from the sheep and goats was not drunk, as this was a sign of being a barbarian, it was made into cheese, simply being left to sour and drain.

But in a lawless community the Church was not yet powerful enough to keep the peace; there had to be a strong secular structure which would reform itself after Rome had collapsed. When coinage has disappeared (indeed the metal that makes the coinage has stopped being mined and the person who owned the mine and paid the wages has either been murdered or has fled) a more ancient trade has to replace it – bartering. Hence, goods were exchanged – cloth, cattle, herrings, spices, especially pepper; any desirable goods were traded giving this age old activity a boost. At the same time the rise of Islam divided the known world and as Arabs conquered the south Mediterranean coast and a great part of the Near East precious supplies of gold and silver, which the Romans had relied on, were for the moment out of reach.

Farming

It is now thought whilst that the invasion of Angles and Saxons from north Germany was fairly small in number, between ten to twenty-five thousand over a few decades, DNA evidence and bone analysis points towards the fact that the invaders settled and inter-married with the Romano-British. The first Anglo-Saxon settlements occupied good agricultural land, which had been tilled for many centuries; these were in the Thames valley, East Anglia, Kent and Sussex. Our language is strong evidence of what happened, as its roots are Germanic, developed from the Old English spoken by these Anglo-Saxons. Once settled for a few generations, they expanded in the seventh century north and west. They built in wood, ignoring the crumbling Roman stone remains; it is conceivable that in their total rejection of Roman villas and towns they feared them, seeing these extensive stone remains as the reason for the destruction of the people themselves. They had worshipped the wrong gods and suffered because of it. But there is strong evidence that after the first few decades their ideas changed and a new respect crept in for the crumbling ruins; they had used the straight Roman roads so why not the foundations of their villas, nor did the settlers now build in wood only, as we see from illustrations in manuscripts written by chroniclers at the time.

The Anglo-Saxon long halls are impressive buildings, both in height and length – 25 metres long. The most impressive is at Yeavering in Northumberland, a seventh century royal residence of King Edwin, where the great hall stood on a plateau above the river Glen. From excavations at Sutton Hoo and Prittlewell and the recent Mercian finds we know that this was a time of many kings, who were buried with gold and bejewelled armour, buckles and belts of exquisite workmanship. These kings rarely stayed in one place, they travelled in as much grandeur and pomp as they could muster within their realms, feeding from their people. Hearing the sound of drums and music from afar with the clatter of hooves and the chink of armour, the peasants and their Lord must have succumbed to mixed feelings, knowing that the King, his family and court, like one of the plagues of Egypt would speedily go through all their stores and consume the lot. Later, we have accounts of this effect, where the prices of food went up so that the poor had to do without bread, as all the stores went to the royal palaces to feed the monarch and his guests, such an event meant famine and children wailing and weeping, and eating dirt for something to put in their bellies.

The new social structure that would appear in these Anglo-Saxon kingdoms had many elements of the old pre-Roman society – feudalism, from 'feu' to mean a tract of land held by a vassal to his lord paid for in the produce it grows.

This structure could only work on the land that had been easily conquered, as here the agricultural worker became a vassal of the lord, but there were also plenty of free peasants living out on the mountainous, hilly regions, on the difficult terrain that remained inviolate from the new masters. They would, these people, for a thousand years be a thorn in the flesh of the conquerors, causing endless strife and bloodshed and when not fighting scraping a living from the wild.

But down in the valleys, roughly in that south-eastern triangle from the river Exe to the Tweed – where land was fertile and sought after – waves of Saxon invaders settled, intermarried, built farmsteads, occupied great tracts of land, sometimes by force, sometimes by purchase, but by whatever means they became an integral part of the land, and life resumed a pattern not so unfamiliar to their peasant ancestors living under the Romans. The land that they tilled had been often taken by force and held by force from whoever had owned it before. The land and everything it contained, whether it be river estuaries, tin mines, great forests or stretches of sea coast. The peasants that tilled that land would have been allowed to stay as long as they paid their dues in the food the land produced, whether cattle and all their produce or cereals. This is no different from having a Roman living in his great villa demanding your tax. As long as in return you were protected from robbers and marauders it was a system that in times of plenty must have seemed mutually beneficial. But land was too valuable, the age too violent, and the agreement too fluid, for the weaker partner to benefit. The agricultural peasant for the next thousand years or more had a wretched existence, full of hard labour and a meagre diet. But in the fifth and sixth centuries[27] there was one minor hopeful sign, that the peasant may have been aware of – there was a general decline in the population, so his value as a labourer was greater, and sought after.

Also, farming techniques were changing slowly for the better. In the Roman era there were square fields walled with dry stone, but from the sixth century a change slowly crept across western Europe which came to Britain – strip cultivation, so the areas could be better drained while one third was always left fallow, while the plough now had a mouldboard dragged behind to plough the fields into a markedly ridged form so that seedlings never dried out and were protected. This was simply a wooden board which pushed the freshly dug earth up into a ridge. In the tenth century there were improvements to the harness which enabled horses to be used for ploughing rather than oxen and there was now enough fodder grown with the three course rotation to keep more horses.

The Founding of the Village

This improvement in the food supply was due to an entirely new and fascinating development during which the foundations of modern Britain came about. Though there were already plenty of small communities and villages scattered over Britain, now, whole farming families, from isolated hamlets and farmsteads all over the agricultural triangle but also affecting the coastal strip of Eastern Scotland, came together in new villages, and these emerged in the tenth, eleventh and twelfth centuries. Such folk abandoned their homes and whatever land they had tilled and created a farming community, which had the same pattern throughout the country. There was a cluster of dwellings around a central road next to a river, the buildings were packed quite tightly together, but also had small strips of land around them. But the main small holdings were in strips which divided up each field around the village, there was a limited area of pasture and meadow, each strip was 46 furlongs (called an acre) and each household had a collection of them, a standard number of 15 or 30 acres and all of them abided by the rules. These were that up to half of the land would lie fallow each year, which ideally would form one block of land, so that all of the animals could use it for pasture and fertilise the land for the following year. Also that permanent grassland was available for everyone and the number of animals had to be limited as over grazing would have been a great error.

The isolated hamlets of Northamptonshire were abandoned soon after 850, which appears to have been the beginning of this movement. But what, one wonders, could have instigated it, for it is apparent that these new settlements are economic and logical. The villages were planned, the houses built all around the same time with generally a church built as well; the houses and the plots were identical in size, there is a sense of common justice, wisdom and foresight about the whole project. For all peasants were treated equally, they shared the best and the worst land, which ensured that no one of them could become very rich but no one would starve, they were all committed to the common land, all shared the same advantages and disadvantages of the village site itself with its supply of meadow, fresh water and forest. Over the centuries villages, of course, grew so that they spread either by plots being sub-divided or by the lords granting out more land and sometimes the villages split in two, so that the names are changed to Great or Little, Upper and Lower, East and West.[28] So the amount of land under cultivation grew but always with the same rules attached. It was a highly efficient method of growing food for a small nucleus of people; the dwellings could be any number from 15 to 60, but paying their rent in food was a necessity. They paid in grain, wheat, barley and rye, cattle, sheep, pigs, butter, ale and honey, they paid in bushels of malt and oatmeal, they paid in sides of bacon and cheese. It is thought that the first movement towards these villages (and the central core of today's villages and towns were these very ones) was instigated by the people themselves. It would seem from the dates that this was basically a defensive measure against invaders, that by coming together the people stood a greater chance of survival than remaining in isolated farmhouses, yet the villages never built defensive walls, though they often were positioned with natural defenses, on hills or behind rivers. After their creation the elite, the landowners or those that came to rule by stealing the land from others, saw the economic wisdom of such habitats and encouraged their existence and prosperity. Part of the rent they took was also in labour, the peasants would spend some of their time tilling the lord's domain and caring for his livestock and holdings, for as well as food, they had to grow flax, hemp and dyestuffs for a growing trade in wool and cloth.

The lord, of course, had his own land for his exclusive use which the local peasantry and his slaves worked for him. In these centuries (the ninth, tenth and eleventh) slaves were common, and most estates had twelve to thirty men; they were listed in wills as part of the livestock which could be bought and sold, the price of a man in the tenth century was £1, eight times that of an ox.[29] Their main job was as ploughmen, a particularly gruelling labour which required two men for the one that held the plough guiding it, but they also worked herding the sheep, cattle and pigs, while the women slaves worked as dairymaids. But they were allowed to marry, which was encouraged for the children of slaves also became slaves and even owned land and in the tenth and eleventh centuries they began to be freed, for though churchmen kept slaves it had gradually become an issue where there was growing moral disapproval. As they were freed they were also given tenant holdings so they swelled the ranks of the peasantry.

In the fields of the south the farmer grew the cereals, wheat, barley and rye, while in the north it was mostly oats as they flourished in the colder climate. But there were more obscure plants the peasant also needed, knot grass (*Polygonum aviculare*) which is related to dock and buckwheat and was used in porridge and for distilling, gold-of-pleasure (*camelina sativa*)[30] for producing oil used for eating and lighting, spurge, flax, horse beans, woad for making blue dye, garden orach (*Atriplex hortensis*) and Fat-hen (*Chenopodium album*) which is related to quinoa and very high in protein and Vitamin A – every part of this plant could be used from the first shoots to the black seeds. Also more familiarly, beans, lentils and grey peas, while in smaller plots around their dwellings, onions, leeks, shallots, garlic and radishes were grown. At an excavation at a hamlet at Wicken

Bonhunt, Essex, the bones of 295 fowl were found, mainly geese, but also ducks, doves and a peacock. The other most common food seemed to be pig.

This might seem a small range of foodstuffs but the peasant also foraged in the wild, gathering chestnuts and acorns, asparagus, watercress and mushrooms, searching for edible tubers, leaves and fruits, many of which, like wild garlic, mustard, sloe and damson, were intense in flavour and would have been a pungent and welcome addition to his diet. Fruits were dried for the winter, threaded on hemp or nettle fibre, apples, pears, apricots, and crab apples were made into cider as they had been for over a thousand years. At this time the peasant and his family had the freedom to roam the countryside and especially the huge tracts of forest that became inevitably his larder. It was when he was marginalised and confined to the fields that his real suffering began, but this was not until the eleventh century.

Anglo-Saxon Dining

Before looking at what they ate let us first glance at where they ate it, as the context of the dining area tells us much about the food and its importance. We have foundations of halls of impressive dimensions as well as constant references to them in ballad poems, but there is one full drawing which exists of an Anglo-Saxon house from a ninth century manuscript.[31] We have seen how the village (that we know and love) originated, now we can see also how the great estate or hall emerged, beautifully sited on a hill within its own grounds, perhaps overlooking a river in a winding valley, and here is a collection of rather grand buildings, a pillared porch and portico, a chapel to one side, a tall building with a tiled turret, another one with high arched windows, there are retainers with spears and shields framed in large doorways, there is a rich family giving away clothes to the naked and poor. There is also a fire outside with a large cauldron bubbling away. The whole illustration shows in a striking way that the ideas and traditions of the old Roman Empire have been inherited and built on in their own style. This is not one huge wooden hall as at Yeavering where Beowulf was declaimed around the central fire, this is a collection of buildings, which could easily have been built above the foundations of an old Roman villa; what is more, the foundations and bottom half of the walls are made from stone and perhaps only the top made from wood, yet that could be stone too, certainly the roofs are all slate, some curved, others flat.

Aelfric (955-1010) a Benedictine English abbot and writer who was at Cerne Abbas in Dorset, wrote a Latin primer which described all the trades and occupations of the time, from which we learn much about how people lived.

From Aelfric's Colloquy we know that the word 'steep' is applied to a roof, that halls are nearly always referred to as lofty, but also that it is the carpenter or wood worker who builds houses, so we know that most were built from wood and that fire was a constant hazard which needed precautions taken, especially when cooking. A variegated floor is mentioned in Beowulf which is a paved one with coloured stones or marble, another Roman inheritance; it is thought that all the buildings were one storey, but in the illustration some of the rooms look tall and there is an interesting story in 978 of Dunstan's council at Calne in the Saxon Chronicle. Dunstan, later made a saint, was Archbishop of Canterbury and met the ruling council in a two-storey house to persuade them to accept the church reforms he wanted, namely to replace priests with Benedictine monks and to halt the wealthy from stealing church land. Getting nowhere Dunstan called on God to help him, whereupon the floor gave away and his opponents fell, Dunstan himself clinging onto a beam. He got his reforms. The word 'house' was used for all residences, great or small, but as the dining area was always referred to as the 'hall' this came to be the term used for all large houses. The Ramsey Chronicle in 991 from the abbey at Ramsey in Huntingdonshire in describing the beautiful position of the mansion at Schitlingdonia (Shitlington) in Bedfordshire, noted that 'the surrounding country lay spread out like a panorama from the door of the hall.'[32]

The hall itself was the scene of hospitality, where people were entertained, where the family and retainers gathered around the lord and provider, and the walls were covered, with plain and coloured cloth and if the lord was rich then embroidered and richly ornamented. Aldheim in the seventh century speaks of the hangings or curtains being dyed purple and ornamented with images, and we find in Saxon wills that there are bequests of 'heall wah-riftas' wall tapestries and on some festivals special tapestries were taken from store to be hung. There were pegs and hooks upon the walls to hang armour, weapons, and even musical instruments. The fire was for the safety of all lit in the centre and there is obviously in the illustration a louvred projection in the middle of some of the rooms; there are Saxon words for tongs, bellows, coal, cinders, fire shovel and hearth. The hall was furnished with benches, which could be covered with carpets and cushions; these are also left as bequests. Poems speak of the halls being adorned with treasures and these are likely to have been taken out of chests and displayed when a feast was being held.

From a recent finding in 2009 of the Staffordshire Hoard[33] of war booty numbering three and a half thousand pieces of gold and precious stones, we know how astonishingly beautiful and magnificent their art was. The jewel craftsmen of today say that their technique was as great as theirs. What makes their art so unique is the fusion of pagan and Christian motifs. It was in AD 597 that St Augustine landed to convert Britain to Christianity; it took well over a hundred years and afterwards it was still piecemeal, and in all this time prayers and invocations were made still to Odin. As the Anglo-Saxons had to fight off waves of invaders it was a harsh and brutal age, the naked yet bejewelled warrior still went into battle believing that glory was his in death when he ascended to Valhalla where for eternity he would feast and drink. His gold buckle, sword hilt, shoulder clasps, helmet and torc would be studded with garnets and amethysts in intricate designs of serpents, birds and the horned god, Odin. The jewel found near Alfred the Great's refuge, the abbey at Athelney, Somerset, with the inscription 'Alfred had me made' has a decorated gold back plate enclosing rock crystal over a figure in cloisonné enamel, that could in its perfect workmanship have come from Fabergé. The Fuller Brooch (ninth century) is silver incised with niello which celebrates the five senses, sight in the centre and then touch, smell, taste and hearing around the sides, hardly pagan or Christian, but a beautiful celebration of human awareness. But by the tenth century one finds the most exquisite ivory figures on a crucifix reliquary mounted on gold (in the Victoria and Albert Museum). Though the rich loved gold most of all, they used walrus ivory and whalebone to carve in; such intricate designs are best appreciated in the amazing illustrations to their manuscripts. At a great banquet then we can expect the walls to be hung with golden weapons, while the gold and silver plate would have been displayed for all to see.

The Anglo-Saxons have a word 'heah-setl' which literally means 'high seat' but could refer to a dais at one end of the hall where the lord and his family might have sat, which was the pattern in later medieval dining and which is still continued in Cambridge and Oxford colleges. Their tables they referred to as 'board' a term still in use which was brought out and placed on trestles. They had a charming way of making inanimate things speak with their own character; an Anglo-Saxon writer, Tahtwin wrote riddles that were popular in the eighth century. One of these states that 'he' is in the habit of feeding people with all sorts of foods and while doing so is a quadruped and is adorned in handsome clothing, but afterwards he is robbed of all his apparel and also loses his legs. In the illuminated manuscripts the table is covered in a rich cloth and the general laying of this table was always referred to as 'laying the board'.

They had three meals each day, they broke their fast at nine in the morning, having risen at six, then at the canonical hour of noon, our three o'clock, they ate their noonmeat; then in the evening, their repast, food or meat (they used all three words) was a moveable feast. If strangers came to the hall door they divested themselves of all arms and left them with the porter, then they were welcomed, whether known or not, and invited to sit and eat. Such customs did at times lead to tragedy. King Edmund in 946 was dining at his manor in Pucklechurch, Gloucestershire when Leofa, a bandit whom the king had banished disguised himself and turned up at the dining table and was asked to sit down. Though the King recognised him and rose to expel him from the hall, there was a fight and the King received a fatal wound.

There are several illustrations of meals in manuscripts, all of them with men and women seated at long tables, but there is one where they are seated at a round table which is tenth century. It is covered with an embroidered cloth but this is no trestle table, for the bottom of the legs are showing and they are carved and ornate, while the cloth has been draped and pegged in the most decorative manner. There are three men served by two servants who are kneeling while serving the men with roast meats pierced still upon the spits; the meats look uniform as if either they have been minced and rolled first before being roasted, or else they are a fillet. A round table appears again in another illustration without a cloth, so that one can see the ornate carved legs, at which the company is eating without knives or spoons and seem to be celebrating rowdily.

Anglo-Saxon Food

But what of the peasant, the one that toiled in the field and produced the food, how did he fare at this time? There was one major difference between his diet and his lord's and that was how meat was cooked. The peasant boiled what meat he had, cooked it slowly over a low fire in a cauldron, thus able to extract from the carcass scraps every ounce of goodness. Meanwhile in his lord's kitchen the meat was roasted, exemplifying the atavistic link between the roasted carcass and the warrior, meat eating and physical strength. The Romans believed and medical writers endorsed it, that meat was nutritionally the richest food for a man's physique, and that it encouraged his muscular strength which is why they respected it and ate it in moderation.[34] Meat, even in its symbolic stature, must be kept in proportion, so it could be a small percentage of the foods eaten, the bulk of them being vegetal.

Meat then was identified with power (indeed it always had been in antiquity as we know from Homer where the only food the heroes eat are great roasted haunches of beef) so that every form of punishment took the complete omission of meat from a diet as punitive, though bread, the staple was left in the diet, even if it was always of the worst quality. The meat that the peasant ate would always have been game.

The lord encouraged him in armed warfare for the peasant was also at this time his military force. They could be taken from the land at a moment's notice (the tilling and cultivation left to the women) and marched off to fight, not always to protect the lord's domain but to invade. So the peasant was a skilled archer, though while stalking deer through the forest he would have been more likely to have used a catapult, stunning the deer then dispatching it with a knife. Of course, the lord too ate plenty of game and spent much of his time heading hunting parties, but he also roasted whole sheep and goats and occasionally an ox. But these were old labouring animals, killed after six or eight years and their carcasses were hung and beaten before being cooked, as the meat was too tough to eat straightaway. They were not popular because of this, sheep and goats were much preferred but the peasant is likely only to have eaten those parts that the lord's kitchen threw out for the dogs.

It has been estimated that the peasant at this time ate around five pounds of bread, washed down with a gallon of weak ale per day, which was food supplied by his lord in return for his labour. It was supplemented by any cheese he made from the milk of his own goats or sheep and a few eggs from his hens; he also had around a bushel (56 lbs) of both peas and beans, another allowance from his lord, to see him through the year. The bread the peasant ate was of inferior quality from dark and mixed grain, barley, rye and spelt. The fat they used was lard rendered down from the pig. Cheese was only eaten as a substitute for meat. But the heart of their sustenance was the harvest; if it failed, they suffered, and some years it rained unceasingly and the harvest rotted in the fields. They had to pray that their lord could buy grain from elsewhere, that supplies would arrive down river; in the meantime, they had to forage from the wild, fall back on making flour from dried peas, beans or chestnuts, but these also were quickly exhausted.

Hunger throughout history has been a spur to invention on all levels, certainly in cooking and in the use of all parts of the carcass. So salting, drying and powdering meat was always done; so done it kept well and could be reconstituted in water, then a little used for flavouring wild leaves and roots. While fish could always be smoked, salted and dried; if the latter then soaking in water overnight before being cooked was essential. The sausage was the great standby going far back into antiquity and common to every land. The Romans used ground meat, fat and flavourings for stuffing the stomach and guts, but fine cooking insisted on high quality cuts of meat for such purposes. The peasant used scraps, but these inevitably had a high fat content. He was also concerned always to provide for those winter months when there was little that could be gathered from the fields, so many of these scraps, well ground and flavoured with herbs, that could be stuffed into intestine or stomach casings would be hung up in the rafters and smoked. Salt was a necessary ingredient in the life of any kitchen, known as a preservative since Neolithic times, but in the peasant's home throughout a merciless cold winter it spelled survival. If you were not near the coast where there were salt pans, or near salt licks (exposed rock salt which animals had found) then you relied on the salt pedlars who travelled the country. So not only were the sausages preserved by salt as well as smoke, so would have been a barrel of meat off cuts, bits of carcass from pig or ox, heavily salted, which when needed would have been added to a stew of cabbage and beans. We think of such food now as 'comfort' food, I wonder if this is an atavistic response to the one daily dish that spelt survival for our ancestors.

We know much about food and feasting from the scraps of ballads and poetry which were written down in the early medieval period. The staple continued to be wheat and various breads, biscuits and cakes made from it, but rye, barley, acorns, oats and beans were also used to make a meal out of, the daily bread tending to be flat breads or sough dough mixtures, but there were small rolls as well as flat loaves. There was more gender equality in Anglo-Saxon society than before or afterwards until the twentieth century, so there were women bakers. The loaves could be flavoured with seeds, dill, caraway, poppy, fennel or sweet Cecily. These people were great herbalists and they noted and used for medicinal and culinary purposes many more herbs than the classical world did. They also made a brioche-type bread, using eggs, cream and curds which was beaten into the dough and cooked on hotplates or in pans, like scones or pancakes. It is a puzzle why these peoples from the Jutland peninsula should have acquired such herbal knowledge – the flat terrain and windswept land they left lying between the North and Baltic seas was hardly a lush and fertile earth to survive upon – yet most herbs are salt resistant and even thrive in poor soil, so perhaps the fact that so many flourished there was a good enough reason for their use and study.

In the Latin teaching text, Aelfric's Colloquy, the fisherman boasts that he sells eels, pike, minnows, turbot, trout, salmon and lampreys. One questions the minnows, wondering whether there was some dish not unlike our dish of whitebait where 100 minnows were deep fried. He also goes out to sea and brings back in his nets, herrings, porpoise and sturgeon, oysters, crabs, mussels, winkles, cockles, plaice, flounders and lobster. Anthimus, writing around AD 528, instructs us that eels should be cut into chunks and grilled on a skewer, far more suitable than boiling, but they should be basted with brine while grilling, small young trout should be baked, scallops can be boiled or baked in their own shell, also oysters are better if baked in their shell, plaice and sole should be cooked in oil with salt and salmon must be fresh if eaten at all. He worries that sick people might find sturgeon too strong, while salmon skin that is fried is extremely harmful. His letter on the Observance of Foods, though written in the midst of the sixth century to Theuderic, King of the Franks who he was physician to, is pertinent to any food eaten at royal courts across the channel. Among the inheritance from the ancient world was the use of a wine reduction, sweet and sour mixtures, the eating of runny eggs and whipping egg whites into a froth. He gives an amazing recipe which sounds like the food of the gods (and might well have been as it must have been served to monarchs) which was called in Greek *afrutum*; it comprises chopped chicken tossed in egg white with scallops piled on top of a sauce which is then baked, cooked in the steam of the sauce, then served with another sauce made from wine and honey reduction, poured over it.

Meat and vegetables were dried, pickled, salted and smoked; mushrooms, crab apples, herbs, seaweeds were dried in the hot days of summer, then brought inside and hung in the rafters to be smoked by fires. They salted both meat and fish, butter and cheese, pickled vegetables in brine and cooked fruits slowly to make a glutinous paste to be stored in jars. Of course, the high salt content of the medieval diet must have been a great hazard to their health, but then life expectancy was low.

The hearth was a stone-lined pit in the centre of the communal hall, but when the weather was good cooking happened outside; a bar fixed across the fire pit would hold a cauldron filled with boiling water (stones were heated and dropped into the liquid) in which the poorer cuts of meat would be cooked with bits of dough added which they called 'apples' which we now call dumplings. For feasting the carcasses of meat would always be spit roasted over the open fire, with fowl, chicken, duck and goose also roasted on a separate spit. Fish was an important part of their diet (fish weirs that date back to this period have been found in the Thames) eels were a favourite food as well as all the shellfish found on the coast. They picked and used many different varieties of wild leaves, so salad was a favourite dish in the summer.[36] They valued bees for both their honey and their wax, hunted wild birds, deer and boar, gathered wild nuts and berries.

They drank beer, wine, ale, mead, buttermilk, whey and milk straight from the ewe or cow, and though their villages and towns would be carefully sited for an abundant source of fresh water, they were naturally suspicious of its purity. Ale was the daily drink for it came in different strengths, it could be stored in casks where it had undergone a secondary fermentation, it was flavoured with either rosemary, bog myrtle or yarrow; the longer it was kept the stronger it grew, though it then turned vinegary, so had to be watched. Though the word 'beer' is mentioned, it is thought that this was a fruit-based alcoholic drink, possibly cider, which could possibly also have been flavoured with berries or cherries. My own guess is that it was based on crab apples, as they had been used since the earliest times in northern Europe, as they were the most common and hardy of all fruits. Both wine and mead were kept for feasting and were only drunk by the elite, but it was mead that was the quintessential Anglo-Saxon drink made by fermenting honey with added flavourings. It was expensive and so had a high status, but a poorer version could have been made from the discarded bits of honeycombs, while another drink, Bragot, was a mixture of ale and honey. It was originally thought that hops were first used to flavour ale and turn it into what we call beer at the beginning of the sixteenth century, a style which came from Flanders. It is now felt, however, that the invention of beer using hops as flavouring was begun by the Benedictine order in the Carolingian period in the ninth century. Whether it came to Anglo-Saxon England soon after we do not know.[37] One realises the importance and the great significance of fermented drinks by the fact that there are over a dozen words for drinking vessel, which describe several kinds from cup to chalice to beaker and the same number to describe kinds of flagons, pitchers and urns.

As to cutlery (they used iron, wood, horn and silver) there was the eating knife, no more than 6 inches in length and very similar to the ubiquitous tool carried everywhere and used for every job, but spoons were also indispensable, as was a shallow, oval bowl, good for scooping more than ladling, though they had ladles too as well as meat hooks. A fascinating discovery at Sevington in Lincolnshire showed a double-ended spoon, bowls of different sizes and a spoon and fork combined, both decorated, which would have made an excellent travelling kit; indeed, eating utensils were carried with one hand for eating on the road. Spoons made out of bone, horn and silver have also been found.

Plates, bowls and dishes were made from wood, the skill honed over the centuries and turned wooden bowls were the most common form of food receptacle, though bowls made out of soapstone have been found which were imported from Scandinavia. Monarchs, of course, had their tableware and cutlery specially made from silver and all that have been found are of great beauty and intricate craftsmanship.

A peasant's life expectancy at the beginning of the Anglo–Saxon period was 33 years for women and 34 for the men which rose in the middle period to 35 and 38, but 71 per cent of the women died in childbirth between the ages of 17 and 35. This must seem shocking to us now, but it was a rise of a few years from that under Roman rule. Life expectancy would continue to rise slowly; the figures for the nobility were quite different adding ten or fifteen years to the expectancy of peasants. Of course, the nobility were not so dependent upon salt meat and dried fish for their protein, for they had copious supplies of freshly killed meat throughout the year. So we must consider that the high salt content in the peasant diet was a major factor in their brief lives.

There is a scrap of an anonymous letter[38] (circa 890) where the author complains of the behaviour of women who were in a communal loo both busy defecating while also eating and drinking. They were women of the Danelaw, (when England was divided into the eastern half ruled by the Danish kingdom and the west by King Alfred) so it was a racist diatribe, but drinking and overeating was thought to portray moral laxity in Anglo-Saxon literature.

But what stays forever in the mind is their art, their jewellery, their working of metal, the staggering beauty of the grave goods found at Sutton Hoo; the intricacy of the decoration in altar crosses and clerical ornaments and clasps take the breath away with their skilled artistry and beauty. It was a rich life for some in a land abundant with food, in a temperate climate, so attractive that it appealed to others searching for fertile land, where to be isolated in a cold wild sea was no protection at all.

The Vikings

What then happened was to electrify Christendom. According to the chroniclers it caused an immediate famine as well as 'immense whirlwinds, flashes of lightning and fiery dragons' such was the ravages of the' heathen men' who had destroyed 'God's church on Lindisfarne'. In AD 793 during the first Viking[39] raid on the English north coast, they stole precious church relics and murdered anyone who attempted to stop them. They had chanced on islands off the coast with large abbeys, containing enormous riches which were easy pickings. They continued to raid – Iona in 802, then Lindisfarne and Jarrow, taking treasures and livestock, they crossed the north sea and descended upon these great landed estates which the Church owned, without warning. These were not places of spartan and ascetic devotion; in 786 the English Church Council had inveighed against nuns for their 'elaborate dress dyed with the colours of India,' and for the richness of their food. The

Venerable Bede also criticised the nuns for their rich clothing and making friends with visiting men. Were the monks so above reproach one wonders or was this early Church misogyny that was never far away? The abbesses were quite often members of the royal family, so the cleric who criticised them had to be brave and powerful in his own right. For these great estates seemed untouchable, so packed were they with richness. The Anglo-Saxon Chronicles bemoan the terror of these raids by Northmen from 789 to 864. The raiders grew to know the Christian liturgy and the dates on which there were the great feast days, so they timed their raids with these, so that they could catch the priests celebrating with golden, jewelled-encrusted chalices, reading from the Lindisfarne Gospels or the Book of Kells.

There are a few accounts of the food that churchmen ate, they were certainly not spartan as the early Church fathers had recommended. On fast days, though meat was banned, the most expensive fish were served, with elegant sauces and eggs, which were supposed to be banned throughout Lent. Saint Bernard of Clairvaux inveighed against eggs and the 'pain and care taken to disguise them, to turn them, to make them soft, to make them hard, and to chop them. Here they are fricasseed, there they are cooked over the fire; they are stuffed, they are scrambled, and at times their parts are separately served.' But then St Bernard's monks at Clairvaux endured a strict dietary regime, no meat or fish ever and no dairy products at all including these wicked eggs, just two daily meals of coarse bread and vegetables with oil.[40]

Alcuin of York at the court of Charlemagne was so horrified at these barbarian invasions, that he wrote immediately among others to the Archbishop of Canterbury, the Bishop of Lindisfarne and the King of Northumbria, but alas, poured blame upon the victims, as they considered such raids were ordered by God as punishment on their wickedness. In 837 sixty longships carrying three thousand Northmen invaded Ireland along the Boyne and Liffey, and there was warfare from 'Shannon to the sea'. But the raiders had seen the attraction of such a fertile green land and by 841 they had ports upon the coast at Linns in County Louth and at Dublin. The islands of Orkney and Shetland were of such strategic importance to them as stopping places on their journeys west across the Atlantic that they too were soon colonised. We know from the late eighth century to AD 900 that the Vikings had colonised parts of North America, Greenland and all the islands in between and this included parts of the British Isles. One of their foremost features was an active acquisition of slaves from every raid which were exchanged with Islamic merchants. They used Dublin as a base, even bringing black slaves from Africa, and they were not outstanding at this time. Buying and selling slaves was commonplace. The Pope, Gregory the Great, records that Jewish slavers were at work in northern Gaul, Bede records stories of slaves, under Kentish law criminals were often punished by being enslaved, and the Bristol Channel was used as a centre for slave auctions by the Vikings. The Church was adamant that no Christian should ever be sold into slavery but many of their churchmen were slave owners.

Viking Food

Yet what of the new foods that the Vikings surely brought to these shores? We can construct the diet partially from finds made in York after they had settled, also from a knowledge of the food available in Norway and knowing also they would have forged a diet especially made for long sea crossings, which would have been basic, but highly nutritious. Let us examine the latter first. It consisted of a hard baked biscuit made from rye and oats, which could be softened in whey, for there would have been a barrel of fermented fish in whey, or in sour milk. There would also have been a barrel of weak ale flavoured with herbs and washed honey combs or even, as we have noted, hops. What meat they had for the voyage would have been dried in strips and could have been wild boar or reindeer. They must also have caught fish on the way over, then filleted it and cut it into strips, salted, pickled and dried. They also took with them sacks of dried cranberries and nuts. But what of the food they left behind?

A porridge of oats mixed with sour milk or buttermilk. A sourdough bread made from rye, barley and oats, a bread that may have contained other flours too made from nuts, beans or peas and a bread flavoured with seeds and herbs, also made with buttermilk. They made butter and preserved it by heavy salting, they drank whey and they ate the curds and cheese. They not only used the milk from cows, sheep and goats, but also from horses, but only in the spring when they were lactating. At home in the far north they could hunt for seal and even polar bear, as well as reindeer and smaller game like hare, boar and squirrel. They were rich in both fresh and sea fish; they already had a flourishing trade in cod and herring. They smoked salmon and salted bacon. What they were not rich in was fertile land to grow vegetables, and what land there was grew cereals for their bread.

Once settled in northern England they obviously enjoyed a wider range of foods, they ate the meat from red deer, beef, mutton, lamb, goat and pork. The poultry they chose was chicken, geese, duck, and from the wild, golden plover, grey plover, black grouse, wood pigeon and lapwing. The freshwater fish were pike, roach, rudd, bream, and perch; while from the seas they dined from herring, cod, haddock, flat-fish, ling, horse mackerel and smelt; from the estuaries, they gathered oysters, cockles, mussels, winkles, smelt, eels, and salmon. They soured their milk, made cheese and butter and gathered wild bird eggs, as well as eating the eggs from their domesticated poultry. But surely one main reason for settling in Britain must have been that the food in their diet was so much more varied and interesting – imagine the vegetables which they could now eat. Broad beans as well as carrots, parsnips, turnips, celery and spinach, but I daresay they still served cabbage. For that was the only vegetable they might have eaten at home which would have been preserved as sauerkraut. They now ate more wheat products as well as the oats, rye and barley. The fruit they had were many: sloes, plums, apples, bilberries, blackberries, raspberries and elderberries (*Sambuca nigra*) as well as hazelnuts and walnuts. They used herbs and spices as they had done before, dill, coriander, henbane and agrimony, the last two being medicinal. They cooked with linseed oil, hempseed oil and honey. They drank ale and Rhine wine.

There would not have been much for the Anglo-Saxons that was foreign and new in this diet of the invaders, but the fact that all types of fish or meat could be salted and smoked might have been intriguing. They may well have introduced the concept of a 'kettle of fish' or what we know of as fish stew or soup. For the fish stew or 'skause' seems to have been a favourite if not a daily dish, made with sour milk and flavoured with dill.

The Vegetable Garden
We cannot omit from this time a description of the monastery garden or what has come to be known as Charlemagne's list. Both are impressive in themselves and set a high horticultural standard as the kingdoms of Charlemagne and Britain were closely linked and as Charlemagne was known to admire British monastic scholarship and its art, we can be certain that his horticultural list would have had a following; church life, law and ideals knew no boundaries as it grew and flourished throughout these years, so undoubtedly the list had an influence in the British monastic garden too. It was written down in the late eighth century when Alcuin was at the court starting his theological school. The list of plants was officially promulgated throughout Charlemagne's empire, the decree laid down that every city should have a garden planted with 'all herbs' numbering 73 in all, and 16 fruit and nut trees, but there were apple and pear varieties as well as several sorts of plums, cherries and peaches.

Imagine a government decree that rules which plants one might grow in one's garden. Such decrees when they happen are always wise, the last one happened in the Second World War, when we happily pulled up flowers and shrubs and planted vegetables which were enthusiastically welcomed in the kitchen. Charlemagne's list was far more comprehensive. There were several varieties of cucumber, melon, gourd, lettuce, endive, beet, carrot, parsnip, orach, kohl-rabi, kale, onion, leek, radish, shallot, broad bean, pea and chives among others. Both madder and teasel were grown for the cloth industry, while lilies, roses and flag irises were there not only because they were decorative but because of their religious significance. Even if the emperor's decree was not fully carried out, half the amount of plants cultivated in every city in his empire would have been impressive, but advanced horticulture must have been inspiring at this time. For soon after Charlemagne died in 814 a plan for the ideal monastery garden was made at St Gall in Switzerland, a plan which has been preserved over the centuries.

There are three gardens, one of medicinal herbs next to the house of the resident physician, a kitchen garden beside the poultry yards and the monk's cemetery which is treated as an ornamental orchard arranged around a central cross. The physic garden contains 16 beds each containing one plant: beans, savory, rose, mint, cumin, lovage, fennel, tansy, lily, sage, rue, flag iris, pennyroyal, fenugreek, mint and rosemary. While the kitchen garden has 18 beds containing: onions, garlic, leeks, shallots, celery, parsley, coriander, chervil, dill, lettuce, poppy, savory, radishes, parsnip, carrots, coleworts (kale), beet and black cumin. Both gardens had flocks of hens and geese, the last not only kept for its eggs, feathers and quills, but also for the fact that geese love all the garden pests and would happily consume the worst offenders.

Both of these must have had considerable influence throughout Christendom for the monastic gardens grew in number and size; as their communities grew, the amount of food needed to feed them all needed a productive garden, a large poultry yard, ponds for farming fish and much labour throughout the year. Yet we also find that gardens were stimulating the likes of monks such as Wandelbert, a monk of Prum, between Aachen and Trier, and Walafrid Strabo, a tutor to Charles, the son of the Emperor Louis, to write poetic descriptions and a gardener's verse calendar. But in Britain we know the Abbot of St Albans (936–946) became a hermit and tended gardens. Moreover in this warm period the vine had returned to these shores and King Alfred provided compensation for damage to vineyards. Even the Vikings became gardeners for the plants grown around York show that fruit and nuts were eaten on a substantial scale, flax and nettles used for weaving cloth, hops and coleworts (they could not do without this tough brassica which withstood the coldest winter) were cultivated and medicinal herbs like chickweed, groundsel, mugwort, scabious and sorrel were gathered.

The Anglo-Saxons loved apples and created apple orchards wherever they settled, the tree they called an '*apulder*' and the only varieties mentioned are a sour apple '*surmelst apulder*' and a sweet apple tree, '*swite apulder*'; they made as we have noted a fermented drink which they called apple wine '*appel-win*'. They also had pears left from the Roman occupation and also from the same source, cherries, peaches, mulberries, the chestnut and possibly the almond, but they would have found that our climate was too cold for the nut to ripen; in sheltered parts of their gardens they grew figs and the pine, but it is doubtful that either fruits would have been edible. But they also grew plum trees, the medlar and the quince, which they called a '*cod-appel*' and they called the olive tree the oil tree '*ale-beam*'; the vine was also well known to them, called the '*win-treow*', and they referred to grapes as wine berries and a bunch of grapes, a cluster. They had no words for gooseberries or currants but they were well acquainted with the wild strawberry and the raspberry – they certainly used all the fruits for desserts and ate them with a brioche-type bread which was allowed to soak up the juice. It sounds remarkably like our version of summer pudding. There are some things that never change, or change very little, in this world.

Danes, Taverns and Bakers

But by now Anglo-Saxon England was decimated, for in the mid 860's a great Danish army had crossed the country and shared out the lands among themselves, all except the south west and when the young Alfred became King he fought back and defeated the Danish at Eddington in Wiltshire in 886. Alfred then forced the Danes to sign the Treaty of Wedmore which established the boundary between Wessex and the Danes. The continuous threat of the invaders had forced people into defensive towns, which encouraged urban life and settlement; some of the towns chosen on the Wessex borders were old Roman ones revived into life because of their defensive walls and ramparts which could now be strengthened.

Danish presence in the whole of eastern England must have strengthened the Scandinavian food tastes which had already been started by the Vikings, so that preserved fish, whether smoked, salted or pickled with an emphasis on herrings was likely to have been a staple. One wonders, because foods take on the character of the people whether among the English in Wessex and further west there was not a resistance against such food, as it was associated in their minds as the food of the enemy. Even today, people can be divided into those that are devoted to these foods, who fall upon them with delight, and those that are repelled by them.

Because these centuries were full of violence and change there were only relatively short intervals of calm, when for example a strong ruler like Alfred created a stable social structure, hence the economy and agriculture which was so wedded to it, suffered. The state could rarely accumulate capital, though the Church could and did, there was never any surplus of food, and though society was full of hard working people, committed to many different kinds of work, the rewards were minimal, little more than survival. When the working farmer had to leave his fields and fight, when babies died in the womb or at birth, when his existence numbered less than forty years and it was commonplace to die violently in your twenties then existence was hard and such that we in our age are barely able to envisage. However, there were two trades attached to food that survived, helped by the greater urbanisation of society in the eighth and ninth centuries, though one could argue that both trades, tavern keeper and baker, had never suffered any neglect.

Tradesmen, clerics and soldiers, clerks and servants all used the tavern to drink and eat in. There they could drink wine, barley beer or mead, eat bread and cheese or roasted birds on the spit, stews of fish or chicken, meat pies and fat sausages. Soon taverns would be built at cross roads, within the walls of fortifications, close to monasteries and at the gates of big cities. Becoming a baker was a highly skilled craft which had to be learnt over the years as an apprentice for the ovens needed great fires which could easily get out of control. There was a distinction between the role of an oven tender, one who lit, fed and controlled the fire and the baker who made the dough, knead it and then baked the bread.

For agriculture to work efficiently, that is to feed a large population continually, through declining weather conditions as well as stable ones, there has to be a strong social system that supports it at all levels. Not only at the level of labour and cultivation, but also that of marketing and distribution, which has been singularly lacking ever since the end of the Roman Empire. The Church itself had a strong system, a hierarchy which they imposed on society and in their use of Latin and their refusal to translate the Bible into the vernacular; they gave Christianity and their own existence a mystique, an otherness, which preserved them as creatures apart. Their food, of course, was always akin to that which the nobles ate, but the moral strictures and the picture of the afterlife was full of terrors. This life for the working peasant was unremitting; hard labour with at the end of it a reward in paradise if they were free of sin. The

Church did not invent the system of indulgences until the late thirteenth century, so there was no way they might buy themselves out of sin.

However, what the Church did bring was education, vital to a growing and flourishing society, where people were determined to improve their lot. Another aspect of education is that a cuisine which develops over many generations needs literacy and a middle class to foster it. Both begin at this time. Aelfric, teaching at Cerne Abbey in Dorset, produced around the 990s the first known Latin textbook, which was widely used in England for many hundreds of years. But attached to church or minsters there had been schools in Anglo-Saxon England since the seventh century and surprisingly the Church did not insist that such schooling was just for boys and girls intending to be monks or nuns. Both bishops at the time of the Venerable Bede, Aidan of Lindisfarne and Wilfrid of York, had lay youths in their households as well as clerics. Women also learnt to read, King Alfred's daughter Aelfthryth read books in Latin and English. By the time of the Norman Conquest there were many schools attached to abbeys, minsters and cathedrals, but also in some royal and noble households. Both the Church and the secular elite now knew they could not administrate society without a staff and retinue that had literate skills. Scribes, linguists and mathematicians, herbalists and doctors, architects, designers of ships and machines of war and many more all had to be literate and paid a sum for their services in recognition of their skill. Counting up the number of educators in these last three hundred years up to the conquest, is the surest indicator of a rising middle class, for they would count among them all the merchants and traders, the bakers, innkeepers, the oenophiles and gourmands, as well as the lesser clergy with their mistresses or families. For celibate discipline was not treated always with great respect.

The Naming of England

In the late tenth century a chronicler, Aethelweard of Wessex wrote that the name England was first used in its Latin form of Anglia when Britannia had previously been used. He goes on to say that the word stemmed from the invaders, the Angli, and the land was also known as Britene and Albion. The first incarnation of its new name was Engla land.[41] By 1020 the scribe of the Anglo-Saxon Chronicle has plumped for Engla land even though a Danish king was ruling the country, but he also chose this name for his letters, laws and charters which formalised it; these were all addressed to the English people and were written in their vernacular. Distinguished churchmen were the first to use the name even before these charters, both Abbot Aelfric of Eynsham who became Archbishop of Canterbury and was a prose stylist used the term at the end of the tenth century followed by his disciple and friend Abbot Wulfstan of York (he was the author of the Oxford law codes of 1018 and the Winchester Code of 1020) and had much influence with Cnut. A glance at both of their surviving writings shows that they follow St Bernard of Clairvaux in their rigorous distaste for bodily indulgences of any kind but food being uppermost, no doubt well aware of the excess that befell the Church too often. However, from thence on whatever was consumed was thought of as English food, and even though the diners might be speaking in Danish or later in French, because they were dining in England it was English food upon the table and not British.

There was another aspect of being English and expressing it in food of the highest quality, which drove its cuisine always to find the most rarefied and exquisite dishes, which was the incarnation of its kings into the sacred realm. England remained a country of "holy sufferers", men and women who were high-born and whose styles of life and death entailed the trauma of inner (spiritual) or outer (fleshly) martyrdom. This tradition was of great antiquity: the imprint of the cults of royal saints had been made long before the Norman Conquest. It was deep and persistent and its main representatives were typical: kings or princes who attained physical martyrdom (notably Edmund of East Anglia (d.869) and Edward the Martyr (d.978)... 'Edward, named the Confessor, to distinguish him from Edward the Martyr, displayed the style of sanctity of the inner martyr, based on the privations of chastity.'[42] Gastronomy for this period was touched and motivated by the zeal of the divine fused with the concept of kingship; one honoured here both the state itself as well as the god within the king.

But England so soon after being christened was to undergo another great defilement and humiliation, no invasion before had ever inflicted so much suffering on the people. For the first time the suffering fell on noble and peasant alike and perhaps the former suffered even more. The peasant's life for the last three hundred years had been freer then than it would be from the midst of the eleventh century, when they were cruelly oppressed, for the Normans brought a system with them, which like everything else they imposed with gruelling severity.

CHAPTER FIVE

A Conquered Island

Ten sixty-six is a date branded into the national consciousness; today, almost a thousand years later, the British have become such a racial pot-pourri, yet still most of us must have traces of Norman ancestry. I have certainly as my surname was brought here with the Conquest, something that I feel equivocal about when I examine the ferocity of Norman rule over subject people. We have long forgotten, it would seem, the devastating change, the enormous humiliation, the slavish oppression that began in 1066. Then as the English King Harold marched down south after defeating the invasion in Yorkshire he must have thought that Duke William's landing at Pevensey was yet another outrage that would inevitably be repulsed. But he was killed (a spot is marked at Battle Abbey) and the exhausted English army, after a harrowing and long battle, defeated.

Dispossession

What happened afterwards was horrific, every bit as barbaric and inhumane as it would have been if the Nazis had won in 1940. All the English landowners were murdered or they fled, between four to five thousand estates were redistributed from the English to Norman nobles, then six thousand smaller landowners were turned into tenants and made to pay for the land they had previously owned. The Church too was purged of native English, and by 1080 among the 16 bishops only one was English. The Normans built large fortifications at every key point all over the country and any sign of rebellion was brutally put down. As Duke William, quickly crowned in Westminster as King, was pious and devout, the Church blessed his actions. It is interesting to note that the bulk of papers which documents the period immediately after the

Conquest are all about the transfer on land, the right to hold it, to hunt on it, or the conditions of which such land must be held – and the only names that appear are those of knights, churchmen and nobles, all of them Norman.

One catches a glimpse of the virulent hatred that the Anglo-Saxons felt for the Normans when one realizes that thousands of them exiled from their country became mercenary soldiers eager to fight for anyone who wanted to kill Normans. In the Battle of Durazzo 1081, the Normans led by Robert Guiscard, Duke of Apulia, fought against the Byzantine Greeks who employed the imperial Varangian guard which consisted largely of Anglo-Saxons exiled after Hastings. 'Many of them had been waiting fifteen years for the chance of avenging themselves on the detested Normans and they attacked with all the strength and vigour of which they were capable. They fought on foot, since the huge two-handed axes that were their principal weapon were far too heavy to be wielded from the saddle. Swinging these round their heads and then slamming them at horses and riders alike, they struck terror in the hearts of the Apulian knights, few of whom had ever come across a line of foot soldiers who did not at once break in the face of a charge of cavalry. The horses too soon began to panic and before long the Norman right had turned in confusion, many galloping straight into the sea to escape what seemed to them certain massacre.'[43] I find it impossible not to feel sympathy for these mercenaries in their intense and burning rage and a sense of jubilation that the Normans were defeated.

But how did all this affect the subject of this book? Partly because of the land, for it is the land which produces the food and most importantly because of what the Normans were colonizing elsewhere, bringing once more a taste of the Mediterranean into this northern isle; so the British diet changed as radically as the rest of life was altered and in a most unexpected way, it was almost as if the Roman experience had prepared us for a taste of the exotic which we now fell on avidly.

A quarter of the English had already got Viking blood running in their veins and the Normans were Vikings who had settled in France, so these invaders were not as foreign as they appeared. They brought with them, possibly not even detected at the time by the English, Moorish influences. Various relations of the leading Norman knights in England, brothers and sons, had also been fighting in southern Italy, Sicily and in Aragon, from which parts of the Mediterranean shores they brought singers, musicians and cooks. William VIII, Duke of Aquitaine, had captured Barbastro in Aragon from the Moors and had taken several thousand prisoners; some of these came to Normandy and thence onto England, and were thought to have been directly responsible for the son and heir of the Aquitaine duke for becoming the first troubadour making use of Arabic stanza; there also they learnt the ingredients and sauces in Moorish cooking, the skills and style of which all came originally from Persia, where Roman cuisine also originated.[44] So the cooking of the elite, that is the court and the immediate retinue of the most powerful barons, was transformed into something far more rarefied than it had been before, though it was dictated by the demands and character of the monarch himself. But not much of this percolated down in the first few hundred years of Norman rule. Unlike the Roman policy, there was little intermarriage and no mixing of race in the administration of the kingdom, or within the extensive military machine which the Normans forged so efficiently. Anglo–Saxon and Norman kept apart and used their own language.

An early writer of the period, William of Malmesbury (c1080–1145) son of a Norman father and English mother (a notable exception in the avoidance of miscegenation) was highly critical of the Anglo-Saxons. He thought that their nobility had become luxurious without refinement, that drinking in parties all night long was a common practice; he complained of their dress, their short garments, the gold bracelets upon their arms, their tattoos. But then William complained even more volubly about the behaviour of the Norman nobility under William Rufus and Henry I (the Conqueror's sons who succeeded him); in their reigns young men were to rival women in delicacy of person, 'to mince their gait, to walk with loose gesture and half naked.'[45] He also tells us that the nobility ate garlic with their goose which seemingly he does approve of.

The Normans brought with them from the continent the manorial system of food production; this fitted their legal mind (they had embraced the French legislature wholeheartedly) and need for efficiency in enslaving the English people. The land owner did not farm the land himself (he was generally away fighting) but had farmers who were subject to his will, who paid rent which was the food itself given to the lord and a further percentage of produce was given to the Church. This system was known in England before, but had only worked spasmodically in times of brief stability. Now it spread over the whole country; as the Normans conquered new territory so the agricultural worker was chained down to a system. Once the Domesday Book had been compiled it was known who owned every tract of land in the kingdom and the economic worth of it. The peasant knew very little of the world beyond his strip of land, only when he travelled to give his produce to the manor did he observe strangers other than the peddlers and beggars that passed his home. He might have gone further if his lord had two or more manors, in which case, he would have had to travel with the produce to deliver it wherever the lord and his family were. He brought the wine or ale, the cheeses, the wool and hides, the eggs and fish, either across the land or very possibly by boat up the wide rivers that were commonly used for transport across Britain. If he and his family were slavish in demeanour, did only what was expected of them, he was untroubled, too necessary a cog in the system to be harmed, and so his life though unremitting hard labour was uneventful, little difference there from what it had been a few hundred years before.

He lived with his small family around a source of running water, generally a small stream where a settlement had been for several hundreds of years, in a thatched dwelling made from wood, lath and plaster, wattle or mud, which in design could not have changed for that length of time either, though by its nature it would have been constantly renewed. A single room structure of timber tree trunks, all sides, except the entrance, filled with wattle and daub, roofed with straw or reeds laid over branches, there were no windows, no chimneys and the floor was beaten earth. At night any animals they had, hens, pigs, sheep, shared the space with them. They had a simply made table, possibly a bench and some stools; they made their own clothes and footwear from home-spun wool and home-tanned skins. They cooked outside, except for the depths of winter, on open fires in terracotta pots, with large earthenware jars being used for storage of grain, beans and peas. Soup was the staple, made with dried beans or peas, kale, herbs and any scraps of wild game – a ham bone addition would have been a yearly treat. With the soup they ate bread; in fact the soup would have been spooned onto a trencher of bread, made from a coarse flour, a mixture of wheat, barley and rye with possibly the addition of pea and bean flour to eke out supplies. They drank ale, a weak brew made from fermented barley. This seems a nauseatingly monotonous and dull diet, but knowing human nature I am certain in those few hours the peasant had from necessary labours, he had trained his children to forage and gather and led them in the hunt for all sorts of wild foods.

There is no doubt that the land itself was rejuvenated, it was given the kind of order, structure and consistent attention it had only had before in passing. In 1086 in the southern counties from Essex to Gloucestershire 38 vineyards are mentioned, even as far north as Cheshire there is a note of a timber church with vines climbing over it; Geoffrey de Mandeville had used purloined land at Smithfield and turned it into a vineyard. A little later in the century we get a glimpse of a new abbey building at Crowland in Lincolnshire being carefully planted with ashes, oaks and willows, close by were 12 acres of orchards, under planted with herbs, flowers, mint and fennel. Henry, Archdeacon of Huntingdon, who wrote a history of England, and was a poet and literary theorist also wrote a work in eight books on plants, perfumes and gems (*De Herbis, de Aromatibus, et de Gemmis*) which is sadly lost to us. The book dealt with medicinal healing from these three sources and he died in 1154 revising his history to the last. The book's existence shows what a central part in people's lives horticulture was in a way quite unimaginable today where we are so removed from its cultivation. A contemporary was Robert, Abbot of Malmesbury who was surnamed 'de Venys' (of the vines) because of his skill in viticulture. At around this time we have the first mention of the wheelbarrow; this deep tray on wheels had been in use in Roman times and then vanished into obscurity, now it re-emerged, perhaps because of cheap labour and after a few decades changed its design to the one we are familiar with.

Mealtimes and Kitchens

In the towns the food trades grew and multiplied in number, tavern keepers were always popular as were bakers, but also butchers, fishermen and fishmongers as well as the merchants who traded in spices and sugared comfits, both of which were considered medicinal. Local gardens provided eggs, chickens and other fowl as well as vegetables and salads. All the trades were tightly controlled by the guilds, and fines and punishments given for selling rotting or fake foods, that is foods pretending to be something else, an ox cheek posing as venison say; further, itinerant peddlers were only allowed to sell certain foods and not others, the egg man might be allowed to sell cheese but not spices.

The guilds were a remarkable system. Skilled craftsmen would group together to protect themselves, they would insist the product they produced was faultless and ask a fair price for it, they would accept apprentices from the age of twelve, their parents would pay them a fee for their son's tuition and after some years he became a journeyman and was paid a wage. Cooks, of course, had their own guild and were highly skilled having trained since young. There is no doubt that the guilds advanced each particular trade and if you take cooking, the Anglo-Norman kitchen was one which, if we could be transported back there, would astonish and impress us with its huge range of culinary skills and equipment. The patisserie alone would equal anything we could contrive since. Then there is the huge variety of kitchen equipment which tells us much of the dexterity and technical skill of the cooks. Punched iron discs for skimming, perforated earthenware bowls for straining and horsehair drum sieves, wooden rollers, wooden mortars, brass and bell metal mortars. Pie peels, oatcake spittles, dough scrapers, ridged rolling pins, grooved riddle boards, sugar cutters, salamanders and much else show a passionate artistry and love of gourmet cooking. Of course, none of this would have been possible without a huge pool of very cheap labour that worked in hellish conditions; just keeping a huge fire going would have been a formidable task. The kitchens kept their cheap labour because the scraps of food that was thrown away kept the staff well fed as well as their families and that, in this age, was the first struggle over.

Mealtimes and their character changed over the centuries; people rose early throughout the middle ages and went to work, or out to hunt, at the first glimmerings of dawn. They possibly grabbed a crust, drank down a flask of the weak ale, but took nothing else at that hour, as the Church advised that no one should even take a crumb before hearing mass. Later, Andrew Borde advised to his more affluent readers that they should walk in the garden or in the park before then serve God in prayers before going to the refectory. He thought a gentle exercise – 'playing at the tennis or paysyng wayghtes or plomettes of ledde' – opened the pores and kept you healthy.[46] It was thought that eating late the night before led to gluttony and that the sleeper woke hungry and needed a snack to rise at all.

The Normans were imbued with moral righteousness (not unlike the Victorians) and rising early was one aspect of it. There is a Carolingian romance (which must have been part of the Norman education) where the feudal lord of Mayence exhorts his sons to rise early preaching at them, 'he who sleeps too long in the morning becomes thin and lazy, and loses his day.' Later two of the heroes, Doon and Baudouin, rise with the sun, dress and wash, say their prayers, then their attendant, Vaudri 'placed between them a very large pasty on a white napkin and brought them wine, telling them: "Sirs, you shall eat, if it please you, for eating early in the morning brings great health and gives one greater courage and spirit." They settle down happily to demolish the pasty. This feels like a reflection of reality and not a moral tale.

It was, of course, the Church which gave the structure to the day, ecclesiastical law laid down that devotions should be sung at certain times throughout the day and it was the monasteries that rang the bells to mark these devotions. You were never very far away from that reminder of God's demands upon you; people in the medieval world must have lived through a haze of guilt, through a fog of self abnegation, always reminded of how worldly they were laden with such fleshly demands as hunger or a perpetual itch for fornication. But to stop to say prayers would erase the devil within and if it didn't then you had not prayed hard enough. The Hour of None was the ninth hour after daybreak and marked the main prayers of the day. It ran from around noon to three in the afternoon and it was thought suitable to eat the main meal before the prayers, though with many retainers serving, the meal was split between some that ate before and the others that ate later. In monasteries they always ate after prayers. The word 'noonmeat' became a word for dinner or meal, while none changed to our present word noon, twelve or midday was the designated time to eat and this has hardly changed in a thousand years. In the middle ages depending on the type of meal eaten then, whether banquet or a single dish, whether for the workmen or the baron, this meal could take as long as half an hour to five hours. It might on a fast day be a poached fish in a sauce or a crust of bread with water, but it would still be eaten around noon. This meal could be termed, except it wasn't, breakfast, because as the Church stated this was when the fast throughout the night ended, but as we have seen few people, except the exceptionally pious, could quite manage to not eat a thing when they had risen with the lark and worked for so many hours, so sometimes in some households, the main meal of the day could be as early as nine and it might happily stretch to noon. Whatever the Church said there was in the human spirit flexibility, a way to get around obstacles, which intruded on comfort and pleasure. Courtiers, for example, might begin eating at nine, so that they were free to wait upon the monarch's table at ten. It was said that the right time for dinner for a rich man was when he will, but for a poor man it was when he may.

It was thought proper that there should be only two meals in the day, dinner and supper and the latter was eaten by sunset. Again it was the early church fathers that laid down these rules, stating that the last meal of the day must be eaten in daylight; this was agreeable to all but the very rich because it was economical on tallow, oil and heating. Supper was a modest meal, light and highly digestible or should be as the Church saw it, preparing a soul for more prayers and a deep restful sleep. But people felt differently after working all day and wanting to relax, they lit too many candles, drank too much ale, ate far too many pies and meats and then slept on until noon the next day. Two meals a day was the proper idea for many centuries, but a different picture emerges from poems, ballads, stories and paintings, where people eat informally, they picnic and snack, drink wine, pick salads, eat fruits, and realize fully the pleasures of food as one of the supreme enjoyments of life.

Dinner

Alexander Neckam (1157-1217) the English scholar and teacher, who shared a wet nurse with Richard I and lectured later at the University of Paris, waxes enthusiastically about food and we catch a glimpse of Norman tastes in the twelfth century. Pork, roasted on red embers required no other sauce than salt or garlic, a capon done in gobbets should be well peppered, a goose roasted on a spit required a strong garlic sauce mixed with wine or a green sauce made from unripe grapes (verjuice) or from crab apples, a hen boiled must be seasoned with cumin, but if roasted should be basted with lard, might be seasoned with garlic sauce, but would be more savoury with a simple sauce, fish should be cooked in a sauce composed of wine and water, then served in a sauce made up of sage, parsley, dittany, wild thyme, garlic, pepper and salt.[47] The fruity but sharp juice made from crab apples or unripe grapes was a fundamental flavouring in our cooking, as in our climate grapes often failed to ripen while the crab apple was an indigenous tree which had been flourishing here since the glaciers retreated. Our partiality to this flavouring was no doubt helped too by our liking of the citron when we travelled east.

There is no doubt that dinner, the main meal of the day, was celebrated by the rich as the most significant entertainment of their day; both church and court, decorated dishes, had music playing and acrobats somersaulting and the monarchs themselves insisted on a service with much ritual. We have only to note Edward I's gift of plate to his daughter Margaret on her marriage to the Duke of Brabant to understand how spectacular her dining table would become. It consisted of forty-six silver cups with feet for drinking, six wine pitchers, four ewers for water, four basins with gilt escutcheons, six great silver dishes for entremets, one hundred and twenty smaller dishes, a hundred and twenty salts, one gilt salt for her own use, seventy-two spoons and three silver spice plates with a spice spoon.[48] When not in use this plate would have been arranged upon a dresser or dressers at one end of the great hall. This furniture with the trestle tables would have been in the charge of a groom.

Except on fast days meat was thought essential to be eaten as the main course at dinner. The meats were roasted, broiled on a gridiron, fried, boiled and stewed; for more subtle cooking they could use portable chafing dishes over charcoal which could simmer, poach or steam. They loved jelly; making gelatin from both animal trotters and hooves or fish skins, they made savoury jellies, and sweet ones. They loved sweet and sour sauces, for in their theory of humours, vinegar was cold and dry while honey or sugar was hot and moist, and therefore if they were not to hurt the body they must be combined into one. Gelatin was dry and cool, therefore should be mixed with honey or sugar which was hot and moist. They also loved sausages, of all shapes, highly spiced and salted, offal sausages especially and all manner of pies in fantastic shapes and colours.

Later, the construction of edible entertainments out of spun sugar led to the invention of shaped tools capable of the most subtle modelling. Oil was extracted from flax, poppy, walnut, rape and mustard seeds. Poppy seed oil was used in cooking, hempseed oil for lighting and mustard seed oil for tawing (converting skins into white leather) and rope making. Both lard and butter were used in cooking. A thriving wool industry and the invention of the spinning wheel led to great wealth in England which soon in the plague years would be dissipated.

Food Trades

The guilds had the authority of holding their letters patent from the monarch; town authorities were represented on the guilds as their products exemplified the town's reputation. The guilds themselves levied fines on their members if there was any infringement of rules and standards from individuals. Chester laid down that 'no person of any art, science, occupation or craft could intermeddle or practice another trade'; in the fifteenth century the Innkeepers threatened to brew their own beer and the Brewer's took them to court. The guilds in any town effectively controlled the commercial value of that town and became its strength and character. No wonder the guilds built up such a strong reputation in London and that the Guildhall in all towns is one of the central buildings.

The idea that girls might be apprenticed to a trade would of course, never have occurred to anyone, so girls were simply household labour, fit for cleaning and given the worst possible jobs. But later in the Middle Ages when widows of trade and craftsmen were allowed to take over and run the business, there are countless examples of women being highly successful and turning a pedestrian business into a thriving one. (See later how the Black Death liberated them from traditional roles.)

The food and drink trades gave more employment in the towns than anything else, people in the towns could not produce food for themselves, it all came in from the surrounding countryside, nor did they cook for themselves, leading full and busy lives working their own trades that allowed little time to cook. Then in the towns there were the visitors that came thronging through the gates, the customers, the pilgrims, the travellers, the merchants with their goods. In Winchester in the thirteenth century, there were eight millers who ground grain and malt for consumption in the town, as well as twelve bakers, sixty brewers, eleven butchers and seven fishmongers; around five hundred people were gaining a living from preparing and selling food and drink, then there were the cooks and innkeepers, the dealers in fruit and vegetables, milk and cheese, honey and salt as well as those with both geese and poultry. Vintners sold wine, spicers and grocers sold the expensive items like spices, ginger, dried fruits and nuts while others went from door to door with eggs, bread, pies and vegetables; there were also garlic mongers and the stockfish monger who sold the dried cod from Norway.[49]

There was strict enforcement of the laws which covered the sale of foods. The purveyors of meat which were 'putrid and stinking, an abomination to mankind' and described also as 'unwholesome to the human race, putrid, rotten and stinking' were placed in the pillory and had the rotten meat burnt beneath them, where they had to gag and choke on the stench. The smell must have wafted over a greater area than the actual victim, one supposes, so others unfortunately suffered, but obviously better to smell it than to eat it. The waste from slaughter and butchery was also a great problem, as the animals were killed in the streets and back yards and the waste thrown into the streams and rivers, which polluted the water, which was also used to wash clothes, to take away sewage and to drink from. Numerous ordinances and indictments tried to combat the problem of butcher's waste in urban settlements; complaints were made frequently about the piles of dung, entrails and hair left open in the streets. As the problem grew the idea of dumping the waste further out in the mouth of the Thames at ebb tide became more attractive and was enforced. But the purity of the water used in cooking continued to be addressed, after all the staple food of the masses was soup and water was essential for the cereal, dried beans and peas to stew in for some hours; clean barrels to collect rainwater were essential for every household, parts of quick flowing streams were kept sacrosanct, but the best and most lauded were springs which flowed directly from out the rock. A Sienese physician Aldobrandino suggested: 'water which is good must be clear, tasteless, odourless and colourless, for it cannot have such qualities (of turbidity, taste, odour and colour) without having been contaminated with something...'[50]

The towns were full of convenience foods; the busy cook in a hospitable town house had a range of services in the streets around him to help him prepare a meal. Apart from the bakers for hot rolls and newly baked bread and the ale house for tubs and barrels of any ale or beer of any strength and flavour, there was the pie shop, which to order would do you a suckling pig well roasted, a goose and capons, while at the spice shop you could purchase them well grounded, to save you the hours of grinding which the kitchen lads would do. Now cook could put them to other tasks. The spice shop pounded the spices very fine, then put each one into sheepskin pouches to send to you. There were short cuts to sausage making, the carcass meat could be sent away to be pounded and chopped, minced and hashed, then packed into the intestines and sent back to you. Hulling wheat was another time-consuming tedious job to be farmed out to poor labourers, hulled wheat sold at the spicers for a silver penny per pound. Then there was the sauce maker who could make you a quart of cameline, or ginger, or mustard, or garlic or green sauce for your dinner. In fact to read the account books of prosperous merchant families from the big cities like London, it would seem that you could buy-in any food imaginable, much as you can today. What about sugar perfumed with rosewater or a marzipan tart, a pyramid of elderflower fritters, or what about the favourite dessert of all – wafers? Between two buttered heated iron moulds on long handles a thin flavoured batter would be poured then the irons would be thrust into a hot fire for a second. People so much loved them that they gave the wafers pet names – nebula, the cloud, angel's bread; they were sweetened with honey, rose or orange water, dipped in sugar and spices, smeared with pastes of quince, citrus and medlar. The wayfarer could go from door to door with her basket covered with a white napkin, offering customers a taste. Whole dinners for forty guests could be ordered from the shops, forty rabbits and another ten to make the jelly by which they would be served beneath. Then forty fowls to be roasted, the sauces made, the beans and lentils soaked and boiled, the almonds ground and made into milk, all the various aspects of a medieval meal made outside and brought together in the kitchen where final additions could be made before it was sent up to the table.

The kitchen on such an evening relied on casual labour for all those rough jobs which needed no skill, like drawing water, chopping wood, carrying heavy loads, scrubbing surfaces and floors, as well as washing dishes and carrying refuse and throwing it away. The greater houses had drains and chutes leading from the kitchens which took all the waste, though these had to be constantly watched and cleaned, or else they easily became blocked. They might even upon the evening have a laundress to wash the tablecloths and linen as well as musicians and minstrels. Some kitchen accounts show payment for making stockfish ready for cooking; when it was a great number in their hundreds, these dried fish stiff as planks had to be beaten with wooden hammers for an hour, then soaked in warm water for several hours, before being eaten with mustard and much butter. The casual labour, lads in their teens, would turn the spits, churn the butter, light the fires and oversee the flames, learning that each wood had its special quality whether it be oak, ash or beech. In fact, every market had its stall which just sold fire-making equipment, fire irons and flints, bellows, curfews[51] and needles, razors, whetstones and mirrors. (Every cook carried a small whetstone which hung on his belt.) A well managed kitchen never let the embers die out completely. Of course washing the dishes could be a huge undertaking, even cleaning the kitchen equipment, the cauldrons, brass pans, pots, basins, ewers, flasks, mortars, platters, sauceboats, spoons, bowls, gridirons, crumb graters and flesh hooks, was a formidable task.

Wastage was a continual worry. After the kitchen staff had eaten the choice bits most scraps were thrown out to the beggars, but in preparing food so much of it was inedible and this had to be thrown away, so vermin were a huge problem, rats and mice infested the building of every kitchen, and while cats were useful they too could be a difficulty and had to be watched else they steal food. Vermin were caught with baited traps, cheese was recommended, preferably roasted to entice the creatures with the smell. In 1313 at the Tower of London it took four men a week to clear and mend the drain from the great kitchen.[52] Some crafty cooks with an eye on making a penny or two would sell back the edible left-overs to the cook shop which would use them for their pies. Various bye-laws were passed to put a stop to this practice as too many bought foods were blamed for food poisoning outbreaks. There was one ingredient which was never wasted or thrown away but treasured and reused – the spices. Recipes pointed out that spices used in marinades, thus steeped in wine, verjuice and honey could be saved and used again in a stew.[53] Another advises the grinding of the spices in the mortar to be done before the bread, as the bread will be flavoured with the residue of the spice. This is a picture of the careful and economical kitchen, but it comes from the Goodman of Paris and his advice to his young wife. Did she feel like silencing this smug old man by stuffing him with a wet codfish? Alas no, as far as we know, but his universal knowledge of the food, its preparation and cooking, gives us an invaluable guide to what a bourgeois kitchen was like in the fourteenth century. Hospitality was an ideal, inherited from the ancient world; the tired traveller would be cared for, watered and fed, this was an essential part of being a host.

Fire was always a great problem, so many kitchens were burnt down, so many houses were set alight from sparks from the kitchen fires, that kitchens began to have a fire in the centre as far away as possible from the walls and a hole in the roof above to allow the smoke to exit; but fires needed draughts to burn well, so the hole in the roof would have louvres which could be opened and shut, the whole structure to be turned to catch or halt the wind, while one of the kitchen lads would keep an eye on the weather cock to see any change in the wind's direction. However, it was soon realised that more than one fire could be built if they used the walls and built of stone with chimneys above the fires, thus the design of all the great castle kitchens began. The abbot's kitchen at Glastonbury is an octagon with four fireplaces built in the fourteenth century; it even has a stone roof. Kitchens began to be built as separate buildings, but this was only possible if you had plenty of room, the drawback was that the food got cold after it was cooked when it had to travel from the kitchen and through a courtyard to the dining hall; it was not a design that was to be pursued. Yet the kitchen by the end of the medieval age was separated from the main hall either by a long corridor or by other rooms, or it was built at the end of the house so that it became convenient for deliveries and was part of a much larger complex of buildings, the scullery, bake house, brewery, store rooms and even pens for livestock, hen houses and fish tanks. So the kitchen was still a long way from the dining hall which still left the problem of rapidly cooling food; one small step to solve this problem was the invention of the serving hatch which could be made between the hall and the corridor. Bishop Swinfield in the midst of the thirteenth century had one, and they can still be seen at Durham Castle and at Hampton Court.

Manners

There is a poem 'Chastisement des Dames' by Robert de Blois, a thirteenth century trouveur who went on a crusade of 1239 , which gives a detailed account of feudal domestic manners which would have applied as strictly to Norman England as it did to Paris. I quote only those strictures which are connected with food and its consumption. 'A lady who is pale faced, or has not a good smell, ought to breakfast early in the morning; for good wine gives a very good colour; and she who eats and drinks well must heighten her colour.' One who has bad breath is recommended to eat aniseed, fennel and cumin at her breakfast and to avoid breathing in people's faces. 'In eating you must avoid much laughing or talking. If you eat with another, turn the nicest bits to him and do not go picking out the finest and largest for yourself, which is not courteous. Moreover no one should eat greedily, a choice bit which is too large or too hot, for fear of choking or burning herself. Each time you drink, wipe your mouth well, that no grease may go into the wine, which is very unpleasant for the person who drinks after you. But when you wipe your mouth for drinking, do not wipe eyes or nose with the tablecloth, and avoid spilling from your mouth, or greasing your hands too much.'[54]

The Goodman of Paris gives instructions to his young wife on her servants and how to treat them, he is particular that they should sit down to eat at midday for their first meal when they must be fed plentifully, but only of one meat and not of several or any delicacies. They should have only one kind of drink, nourishing but not heady and be admonished to eat heartily, to drink well and plentifully for it is right that they should eat all at once without sitting too long and at one breath without reposing on their meal or halting, or leaning with their elbows on the table and as soon as they begin to talk or to rest their elbows they should be made to rise and the table removed.[55]

Prosperity and Poverty

Prosperity began early in this new Norman kingdom for it had a continuously favourable trade balance from the late twelfth century, because it was the finest wool producer in Europe, as well as being the dominant producer of tin. While England then was self-sufficient in food, all that was imported were luxuries, primarily spices, but there were oranges and lemons from Castile, dried fruits and wine from Greece, sweet confections from Alexandria and the Levant. Trading ships, the carracks, had grown bigger and could carry food by sea across great distances. This trade was the most profitable because it was responding to the demands of the elite, both secular and ecclesiastical, for luxuries. Spices were of course in great demand, as they betokened in themselves both affluence and grandeur; pepper, all spice, grains of paradise, zedoary, cumin, cloves, nutmeg, cinnamon and ginger all came by sea, while saffron, because of its need for cheap labour, could still be harvested at home. But rice, dried grapes called raisons, dried figs, sultanas and currants came from Turkey and further into the Black Sea came more amazing foods like sturgeon, whether salted in barrels, or fresh kept alive in tanks while their eggs were put into casks and carried all over Europe into its ruling houses. Lemons, limes and the citrus fruit (even pomegranates) as well as Seville oranges all came from Castile or Cordoba in Andalusia, brought there and cultivated by the Arabs in gardens and orchards of great elegance.

Then there were the furnishings for the greater houses, tapestries from the Netherlands or Paris, from the workshop of Nicolas Bataille, as well as carpets from Persia or Turkey, and carpets sometimes referred to as 'saracen' to be used not only on floors but on walls and tables. But still the overall value of the imports did not exceed the value of the wool and tin. Also from the end of the twelfth century there was a large stock of silver, which however wasteful succeeding monarchs were, was constantly replenished from the mines.

A certain sign of the growing prosperity of Anglo–Norman England is the evidence of the growth of stone houses over lath and timber ones. In the port of Southampton as overseas trade boomed through the thirteenth century after the civil strife of the century before, encouraged by our extensive possessions in France, with much wine, silk and spices arriving on these shores, the houses of the merchants were built in stone and were spacious with huge cellars on the quayside. The lesser terraced houses of the craftsmen that once bordered the quay were banished to the north end of town. This trend continued; stone houses with slate tiles in prominent positions in the towns, which belong to merchants, were built in Norwich, Canterbury, King's Lynn and Shrewsbury. This evidence of wealth was accompanied by the buildings of thicker and taller walls and constant redefining of the borders, pushing the walls further out, digging the defence ditches deeper still, often, however this was too ambitious, a wall circuit taking too long to build and becoming too expensive, quite often the walls got thinner and sometimes, as in Coventry, were just left unfinished.

But far more noticeable than this was London and the example of the dignitaries of the Church. There in the course of the thirteenth century the archbishops and bishops, the greater abbots as well as the nobility began building themselves great houses along the Strand or the riverside road that joined London to Westminster. They were called 'inns', at least seven bishops built along the strand, the Duke of Lancaster built the Savoy palace in the strand next door to the 'inn' of the bishops of Worcester. As the lay elite as well as the church dignitaries concentrated their time and wealth in London around the royal court, they brought with them the produce of their country estates to be sold in London markets. In 1220-1 the Bishop of Winchester had 106,000 herrings delivered as well as 306 pigs to be fattened for Southwark market; here to were delivered amber and furs from the Baltic.[56]

On the four estates of the bishopric of Winchester after 1200 they farmed over 20 different species of animal; not unexpectedly the most common was the horse, over two hundred, most of them mares, plus a dozen stallions and over sixty foals. There were much fewer oxen – only eighty and about the same number of cows. The biggest number, over a thousand, was of the pig, which shows us how favoured pork meat was above all else. The flock of sheep numbered only six hundred, but there were over three hundred rams, for their wool was preferred as they had a thicker fleece. Only two of the estates kept chickens, under 200 and a different two kept ducks – just ten, while twenty peacocks were favoured by one estate and only eight were kept on another. Geese were the favoured fowl (a source of bedding, quills and meat); all the estates kept those, over a hundred altogether.

Generally only two oxen were needed to pull the plough, but sometimes on heavier clay soils eight oxen were necessary and on virgin land, ten or twelve oxen were used. The digging was done with spades, though mattocks were used for heavy work; the sickle was used for harvesting the corn cut just below the ear, which were then bound into sheaves and tossed with a two-pronged fork onto a two-wheeled wagon. The straw left behind in the field was for the use of the whole community (the right of gleaning), the corn was threshed with a stick and flails, and then it was winnowed and finally brought to the water mill to be ground.

Peasants still valued their woods highly, not only did they contain the wild food which augmented and varied a basic diet, food which the children were taught to gather while the parents laboured, but it was where, as in earlier times, they fattened their pigs; but it was not only the beech mast that they ate, as throughout the year they would take the young shoots and destroy the undergrowth which the game birds needed as their food and cover. But once the Normans had arrived great tracts of forest were taken for the monarch, while other woods were given away to various nobles. New laws came into existence that made the peasant a trespasser; unable to snare the wild life they once had relied on. The Anglo-Saxon Chronicle comments: 'He made many deer-parks, and he established laws therewith; so that whosoever slew a hart, or a hind, should be deprived of his eyesight. As he forbad men to kill the harts, so also the boars; and he loved the tall deer as if he were their father. Likewise he decreed respecting the hares that they should go free. His rich men bemoaned it, and the poor men shuddered at it.' Royal Forests quickly encompassed most of the vast wooded areas in Britain, but many of these were inhabited by peasants themselves, who lived in hamlets within the forest depths. In the New Forest the Normans merely dispossessed the peasants, so that they fled rather than be struck down, their houses and villages razed to the ground. But in many other forests the peasants hid and returned and somehow clung onto their shacks and their existence. However, they were subjected to draconian laws to preserve, increase and protect game – the four main beasts of the forest were red deer, fallow and roe and wild boar.

This had a profound effect on the population. It prohibited the peasants' pasturing rights and their gathering of food. The control of the under wood by the Crown limited the availability of fuel such as the cutting of peat. Any infringement of the law was punished by blinding. William justified the severity of his laws by producing a document Charter of Cnut that declared that the exclusive rights of the chase were vested in the King. This document has proved to be false, as there is no evidence that the kings before the Normans ever claimed the forest was theirs. William's son, when he came to the throne, increased the severity of the laws, adding fines, further mutilations and death to the punishments, so it is not surprising that he was found murdered in the New Forest itself. A crime that was never solved.

Though his successor, Henry I, at his coronation promised to change the stringency of the Forest Laws, he kept them and increased their severity making it a crime to hunt fox, wolf, cat, hare, rabbit, badger and squirrel. Henry II extended the forest area, while being slightly more lenient in that trespassers were committed to prison rather than being hung. All in all, the Forest Laws were thought to be tyrannical, for the peasants' whole quality of life suffered, plunging them into worse suffering than they had endured before.

But the tithe system was perhaps the greatest burden on the peasants and the production of food, a system which had begun with the introduction of Christianity and had strengthened and become more complicated over the centuries. The tithe was a tenth to a fifteenth part of the livestock and produce, there were small tithes of orchard fruits, of madder and hops, crying tithes of piglets, lambs and geese, while special tithes could be levied on land tilled for the first time. At harvest the tithe-collector had the right to select every tenth sheaf; there was a sack tithe when the corn was threshed. The Church collected all of this after the peasant had paid the manorial payments, rent and tithes to the landowner or the lord himself. No wonder the peasant survived only in the most wretched poverty, existing only to face unremitting hard labour in the fields to scratch out a living for his family, his wife working at his side, the children when they could walk, bidden to gather what food they could find growing in the few wild places they were allowed to wander in. It was a short life, dead in their thirties, worn out by it all, with the fear of eternal flames in hell their future if they had ever transgressed the strict Christian morality they were indoctrinated in.

Famine throughout the early medieval period was never far away and William the Conqueror early in his reign, when he put down a rising in the north, created one of the worst by his scorched earth policy where his soldiers destroyed crops, villages and towns, slaughtering the local population. It was effective; there was never an armed insurrection against the Normans again. In the mountainous regions of Wales and Scotland bands of rebels survived but they were never a threat to Norman rule. The historian Orderic Vitalis talks of 'men compelled to devour human flesh and that of horses, dogs and cats. Human corpses decayed in their houses, swarming with worms...' But the peasants were adapting to famine as an ever present threat and it would continue to dog them throughout the years until after the terrible century of the plagues.

Charter of the Forest

But in 1215 there was at last some respite, even promised justice, for the peasant, though not for a serf. In that year Magna Carta was signed. It is an astonishing document for a medieval king to be forced to sign by his nobility, for it aimed to protect all in the land whatever his station (except, as I said above – the serfs, who were still to exist for another one hundred and fifty years), for it is a humane document of sixty-three statutes that cover the laws of inheritance, rights of widows, debt, usury, freedom of cities, wills, land rights, property, forests and riverbanks, though the last two (most pertinent for the peasant) were not written out in necessary detail. Thus two years later after King John had died and his young son, Henry III was upon the throne, that particular clause was revised and became the Charter of the Forest. Thereby, one of the most important clauses which had been in Magna Carta, was revised to stipulate that all land which had been made into forest and all preserves of river banks under King John would now become free to peasant use. Thus, the Norman expropriation of common land, which the Conqueror had begun, was now halted; but so much else which affected the survival of the peasant and his daily food supply was also delineated. He could now collect fuel and graze his pigs (pannage); if he had some land within the forest he could have upon it a water mill, a marl pit (vital to the farmers as fertilisers) ditches for drainage or even arable cultivation in clearings; he was also allowed to keep eyries of hawks, falcons, eagles and herons. He could breed birds of prey in fact, a useful source for the nobility and also keep bees. He was still not allowed to kill deer and take venison, however if he did and was caught, he no longer suffered death or the loss of an arm or hand, but he was heavily fined. If he could not pay the fine or raise it in any way he went to prison for a year and a day – if he still could not raise the money then he had to 'abjure the realm'. He was exiled.

In the original Magna Carta there were two further clauses which helped the wretchedness of the peasant's existence. Clause 35 states that there must be one standard measure for wine, ale and corn and one width for cloths whether dyed or not, and clause 33 states that fish weirs must be cleaned in the Thames, Medway and throughout all England, except along the sea coast. I imagine that these alone might be encrusted with shellfish and would be regularly cleared of any obstruction by harvesting them. Lastly clause 41 allowed that merchants should be free to enter and leave England as they wished, and if the nation began a war with their country they would be given safe conduct back to their home.

This would encourage the trade in luxury goods which was so dear to the medieval world, not only the spices, the ginger, the citrus fruits but the precious silks, satins, damask and velvets. Several worlds away from the life of the peasant, there can be no doubt that his existence was now freer from the oppressive fears that must have accompanied him every time he entered the forest; it became once more his larder from which he could pluck a meal, snare small game birds, gather a honeycomb, pick damsons, and dig for truffles led to the spot by the squeal of his pigs and their snuffling pleasure.

Water Power, Gardens and Walks

It seems at first astonishing that the power of water had not been harnessed earlier than it was – the Romans used a mill driven by horses, mules or asses controlled by slaves. This is the key to why they looked no further, for slave and animal power was always at hand. Yet they knew of a machine driven by water, Vitruvius mentions it in 50 BC and latterly in the empire, when slaves had become scarce and expensive, the Romans began to use water power harnessed from the viaducts. In the fourth century after the adoption of Christianity water mills became the standard mill in the later years of the empire. When Rome was besieged by the Goths in AD 536 they attempted to starve the city by cutting off the water supplying the mills, whereupon the Romans moved the mills to boats moored on the Tiber. The Goths must have been impressed for they took the idea back home with them and built mills over German rivers, though the first one north of Italy had been built in Arles in AD 310. By the time of the Domesday Book in 1086 there were in Britain 5,624 water mills recorded there.[57] These were built wherever there was a fast running stream and sometimes the water was dammed, so that a pond for farmed fish could exist. Within the next two hundred years windmills also now came into existence; built on high ground they could only be vigorously active in strong winds, so were not as successful as the perpetual power that came from water.

Two other inventions occurred at the same time, the spur and the horse shoe; the first was invaluable in military strategy, it came from Islam and penetrated Europe by the seventh century, at the same time as improvements in the harness, the horse collar and the horse shoe which gave the animal necessary protection for gruelling treks over difficult terrain. But the last two were helpful in agriculture making the horse the prime labouring animal on the farm, as the horse collar took the weight of the new and heavier ploughs. You still see the horses in their heavy collars and harnessing clearing forests in places where no machine can go, a labour which has continued for over a thousand years.

Ever since the Norman occupation the water mill and its vital task of milling corn into flour had been taken away from the jurisdiction of the villagers and was now under the control of the squire who charged a tithe from everyone for milling their corn. As querns and the means of operating them were too heavy and huge for any individual to manage, the fact that this was forbidden seems erroneous, nevertheless the tolls paid to the miller were now part of the manorial revenue and the staple food, bread, became that much more costly.

So many accounts of early Medieval London evoke a crowded cesspit of overhanging wooden houses with piles of refuse and totally inadequate drainage, that it is a pleasant surprise to read of William FitzStephen's[58] account in his description of London of the gardens outside the walls, planted with trees, spacious and lovely, especially those at the north which had been planted around the wells, Holywell, Clerkenwell and St Clement's Well; these were frequented by students, lovers and anyone tired of the city who walked among the shade of the trees of a summer evening. The trees that were planted were elms, oaks, ashes and willows beside the streams. But we know from other sources that gardens had almond trees, black mulberry and walnut.

Gardens under Anglo-Norman rule thrived, every monastery and abbey had extensive grounds which grew vegetables and herbs – red, white and turnip rooted cabbages, chives, dittany, lavender, pot marigold and water lily, are all mentioned by the Abbess Hildegard of Bingen (1098-1179). Then, a hundred years later, Alexander Neckam's list gives over 140 species, only some of which are food plants, but some of these are surprising. Not only does he list both orange and lemon trees, but also date palm, and though at this time in Britain, it is warmer, these must have been pot plants which were brought inside in the winter months. Also he lists chickpeas, nutmeg, olive and a rarity, Terebinth (*Pistacia terrebinthus*) which is indigenous to the Mediterranean. We now call this the turpentine tree, it has a strong resinous smell, but while the fruits are used in Cyprus in baking, it also flavours brandy and its galls are used for tanning leather. This unusual plant seems to me obviously to have been brought back in the baggage of Crusaders as it would have been more common then than it is now.

Neckam wrote that a garden should be adorned with roses, lilies, the marigold and mandrakes, also with parsley, cost, fennel, southernwood, coriander, sage, savory, hyssop, mint, rue, dittany, smallage, pellitory, lettuce, cresses, oregano and the peony. He wanted beds of onions, leeks, garlic, melons and scallions. 'The garden is also ennobled by the cucumber which creeps on its belly and by the soporiferous poppy as well as by the daffodil and the acanthus. Nor let pot herbs be wanting, if you can help it, such as beets, herb mercury, orache, sorrel and the mallow. It is useful also to have anise, mustard, white pepper and wormwood.'[59] Neckam then goes on to talk of the fruit trees. 'A noble garden,' he says, 'will give you medlars, quinces, the pearmain, peaches, pears of St Regle, pomegranates, citrons, oranges, almonds, dates and figs. In his use of 'noble' he is thinking of a great magnate's garden, but even so, surely many of these trees would have to be under cover, well sheltered and warm in winter, and as this is long before glass houses or conservatories, his list seems fantasy. But we must take it as fact, for we do know that at this time it was rather warmer than today by as much as two degrees, the kind of warmth upon this island we shall soon be having again in the next decade and more. The pear of St Regle was one of several choice pears brought over from France, and is mentioned in the accounts of the Earl of Lincoln's garden in Holborn in 1296. In one corner of Neckam's garden he grew medicinal plants; this was usual and necessary as all the cures for various ailments stemmed from such a collection.

John de Garlande, who was a contemporary of Neckam's, also grew a garden in Paris as he taught at the University and he gives us a description in his 'Dictionarus', it is described as the garden of a respectable burgher. But what a garden this is, it is remarkable for its range and for the amount of medicinal healing plants. In Master John's garden there are plants such as sage, parsley, dittany, hyssop, celandine, fennel, pellitory, the rose, the lily and the violet; and at the side, in the hedge, the nettle, the thistle, and foxgloves. His garden also contains medicinal herbs, namely mercury and mallow, agrimony with nightshade, and marigold. Master John's gardener also grew pot herbs, borage, leeks, garlic, mustard, onions, cibols and scallions; and in his shrubbery grew pimpernel, mouseare, self-heal, buglos or borage, adder's tongue and other herbs good for men's bodies. Thomas Wright, writing in 1871, says of these lists: ' it may be well to remark, once for all, that it is almost impossible to identify some of these medieval names of plants.' Indeed, 'mouseare' still defeats us, though it calls up a pleasant image of a small cylindrical shaped leaf that uncurls to the touch. However, the list is there to remind us that the range of flavours for use in the kitchen is formidable. How can we ever reproduce the authentic tastes of the medieval dish when we lack so many of these herbs? It also vividly tells us how much the people relied upon plants, their oils, effusions and poultices for whatever ills and wounds they suffered from.

The cherry was one of the most popular of fruits throughout the medieval period; the King's gardener purchased cherry trees for the garden in Westminster twice in 1238 and again in 1277, first for the boy king, Henry III, then for his son Edward I. Cherries and cherry trees are enumerated in all the glossaries from Anglo-Saxon times to the sixteenth century, and cherries constantly are mentioned throughout the poetry of those times, there were cherry orchards in Worcestershire and Kent and cherry fairs every year, while cherry hawkers roamed the streets of London and every other large city throughout the month of June. They are a fruit which does not travel very well, they quickly get spoilt, so the reason for the fairs and markets was to celebrate, sell and eat the just picked cherry harvest, much as we do constantly today, stopping at the roadside to buy a bag to eat as we drive. William Langland in his poem *Piers Plowman* writes of the poorer classes who lived chiefly on vegetables and mentions that they mixed ripe cherries with the beans, peas and baking apples.

The Danger of Food

In an age when for the majority of people, the worst danger in food was not getting enough of it, they must also have found the many myths that circulated around food alarming to say the very least. Not only were there medics and quacks that were liable on market day to rise up and speak to the milling populace of these dangers, but they were backed by the voluble church fathers, themselves no innocent eaters, who would inveigh against the dangers. For example, the idea that white bread was most suitable for those people who did little physical labour and that coarse dark bread was best for labourers, had of course, not only a medical rationale but also a social distinction, see below.

One of the worst aspects of food, it was said, was to overheat the body; many foods could do this, wild game birds for example may be eaten, but to consume too many at one sitting could lead to excessive heating. This overheating could lead only to one sin, that of lust, so not only were you a glutton but now also you were guilty of lustful indulgence. Yet food for the elite was food on which you lavished pleasure in creating it, viewing it and eating it, such pleasure being part of the food's significance, which was lacking in social inferiors. Foods then had a distinct social relevance, people were taught that the best food went to the best people, that working people had rough food and what is more they were content with such food and demanded it as their right too. This has horrible relevance to our own age and time when this concept still exists (e.g. 'builders' tea'). However, then it had divine authority. God had ordained the world with the rich at the very top and the very poor at the bottom and there were corresponding foods for them. At the bottom were the roots, tubers and bulbs, the food the peasants relied on and this food might be dangerous for the elite to eat much of or very often, not that it is likely that they were tempted. Next came the herbaceous plants, the brassicas, leeks and the spinach, more food for the poor, and then came the fruit trees and all the berries, still suspect for they were very close to the ground. Next came all the water foods, starting with the molluscs, clustering on rocks and easily gathered, again food very much for the poor because they were often very tough, but they were food for free, therefore, God given for the poor.

Food in the public mind was (and still is) divided into good and bad, or the pure and impure; these black and white concepts were muddied in Christian thought by the Jewish concepts so fully expressed within the Old Testament. Foremost of these was perhaps the idea that blood represented the soul and must return to God, an exactly similar idea of the Greeks, for they in their sacrifices also drained the blood and allowed that and the smoke from the cooked meat to go to the gods. Early Christianity born in the eastern Mediterranean inherited the idea and went one better, claiming that not eating meat itself would please God, that meat must by its very nature being so much of the body, bred lust. From this suspicion Tertullian enthused upon the idea of fasting, which was taken up by other Christian thinkers, namely St Isadore of Seville (560-636). Their analysis of food and its effects upon the body was derived from Galen, the Greek physician, and his theory of the four humours. That these were the materials that made up the body itself, the flesh was earth, air was in the breath, the blood was moisture and fire was the heat of the body. What you ate must balance these vital components, to increase one while depriving another must induce illness and frailty. This led to the Church promulgating days of fasting which over the years grew in number, by the thirteenth century there were four periods of fasting for forty days: Advent, Lent, Epiphany and Pentecost. In theological terms fasting existed to purge within the body corrupt elements which had managed to accumulate there. It was not only meat that was to be denied, but its by-products, fat, milk, butter and cheese. Nuts, nut oils and their milk, as well as fish were all allowed. By the thirteenth century, meat was only eaten on three days in the week, for the rest of the time the Church fasted. That it had ingenious ways of getting around these commandments, if so wished, is well known but, of course, for the majority of people, their diet was so inadequate and restricted these church rules made no difference at all. If only the blessed were to be allowed in Heaven, the poor should all have been admitted, for they had little opportunity to break such culinary rules. Nevertheless, they were very well aware of the wickedness of meat eating and the moral danger of luxurious foods, and they must have watched as fat princes of the church consumed a dozen courses at feasts with envious and unbelieving eyes.

Yet hard working people have a marvellous ability to ignore the dictates from above if they contradict the practicalities of their own daily life, especially when food is essential to survival. For many thousands of years when a pig was slaughtered the blood was carefully drained, saved and mixed with flavourings, herbs, spices and cereals and turned into blood sausage – every country north of the Mediterranean which kept pigs rather than goats had their own blood sausage which was a treasured staple in the diet. The idea that the blood is divine and must be given to God, thrown away they would see it, would have been ridiculous, as would the thought that blood sausage on fast days had any relationship with a live animal. Part of our own survival seems to me to be a quality which is a sensible rationality, a sturdy awareness of vivid realities.

Saracen Flavours

The Normans had travelled, fought and often conquered in Sicily, southern Italy and further east, Cyprus, Crete, Rhodes and finally the mainland of Asia; they then brought back to this northern isle a taste of the sun, but what in particular were these flavours? On the long journey home across many countries one imagines that there are few foods that could remain edible. Yet there is evidence that for example exotic fowl were certainly caged – Greek pheasants – and brought home then kept to breed in England. Though citrus would dry and be unusable, they could have been pickled in salt, verjuice or vinegar. Dried spices were never a problem. But what, in particular, one wonders would intrigue and beguile the palate of a Crusader?

Arabs preserved food by pickling, or coating it with fat, honey or sugar, so there was a thriving industry of sugar refining. The Crusaders would have discovered sugar cane and be informed that this plant would not grow further north than the coast of Africa, but they would have discovered too that the product travelled easily. Here was the great alternative to honey, sugar was so delicious and so addictive it immediately had the cache of medicinal necessity to one's health and candied fruit, marzipan and sugared spices to suck became a daily addition to the diet among the ruling classes. The Normans loved bright colours in their food, so when they came across golden rice, coloured by saffron, the spice became a firm favourite, so much so that they began to grow it in northern Europe. It was the most expensive spice then and still is now, as harvesting it is labour intensive; this was not a great problem in the early medieval period as labour was plentiful and very cheap. (Some time after the Black Death, though it was the change in labour practices which began the decline, our own saffron fields failed to be economic and left nothing but their name, i.e. Saffron Waldron in Essex.) But the saffron-coloured pilafs and the golden sauces (foods were also sometimes gilded) must have especially impressed the Crusaders. The Arabs also had a favourite vegetable, spinach, which grew well in northern Europe, but the Arabs used spinach to colour the food as well as eating it. The colour was a dark and lustrous green, certainly one the Normans grew to love and used frequently.

I am certain that one of the most seductive aspects of Arabic food now and then were the perfumes and aromas of the street cooking in braziers over charcoal burners, which must have assailed the Crusaders constantly. The curious would have discovered that one of the most powerful scents was rosewater and it was this and its companion, orange water, that they brought back into Europe and which became hugely popular added to salads and many dishes; another ingredient, which must have puzzled and beguiled them, was mastic[60] which can turn the plainest of foods into something miraculous. Mastic though is difficult to export far, as the air has to be excluded, so there is no evidence that it reached Britain that early. In the food itself they would have tasted ginger, nutmeg, cardamom and mace, they would have seen dried fruit and nuts mixed in with the rice dishes, in the markets there would have been piles of dates, raisons, almonds, walnuts, hazelnuts, pine nuts and pistachios.

Did the Crusaders notice the fat that Arabic food was cooked in? Did they remark on the fat tailed sheep or watch as the olive harvest was milled for oil, did they see sesame seeds crushed for their oil or taste the paste? There was oil from walnuts and almonds too, butter was clarified, rice was cooked in milk, while sour milk was used on dishes after they were cooked. But it was not only the sugar that appealed to them, but the wide use of vinegar, citrus juice and sour fruits to balance out the sweetness, which they must have particularly liked; for certainly sweet and sour dishes and that combination appeared early in Anglo-Norman cooking, as did sweet and sour marinades for meat and fish. There seemed to be no shortage of these marvellously aromatic sour flavours from whey, bitter orange, pomegranate, apricot or sumac berry mixed with meats like mutton, goat, even camel (for the Prophet himself was partial to this animal) or the favourite game – gazelle. Small birds were spit roasted, as at home, but often they were stuffed with meat and fruit mixtures; one of the most favoured dishes which stemmed from Persian court cooking as most of the Arab dishes did, was stuffed vegetables, meat or poultry, the stuffings being full of many spices and fruits though chicken was the most favoured of all the fowl, chicken simmered with plums or blackberries, or roasted with pistachios and poppy seeds. Meat and poultry were often marinated in yoghurt or vinegar filled with herbs and spices which both coloured as well as flavoured it. Almonds were used whole or crushed and made into a milk or a buttery spread, while hazelnuts and walnuts were also crushed to thicken sauces.

Fish was thought to be not always the most healthy food, as it was too cold and moist, so was grilled, baked or fried to dry it out. The fatty fish was preferred and there were tuna factories (sited next to the culls as in Favignana off the west coast of Sicily) to process, pack and preserve the fish in salt as were sardines and anchovies which were then sent to Spain. These must have delighted the Crusaders and the most knowledgeable of them would have realised that we had a thriving fishing industry for herrings, sprats and sardines around the south and east coast that produced a food that might be used in the kitchen of the nobles in a more sophisticated manner. Did they return home and while entertaining the local bishop serve him a dish of salted herring which had been marinated in white wine, onion and rosewater, then served with chopped dates and walnuts? For fish dishes on those interminable fast days began to get more and more adventurous as the medieval period advanced.

As to vegetables, the Normans would have been struck by the strangeness of the aubergine, its beauty and its size as well as its variety, though they might have been put off by its initial bitterness, simultaneously being pleased by how palatable it was once cooked. The aubergine was brought to Spain and became an integral part of the cuisine there, but it never travelled further north until recent times. Beans and lentils the Normans would have recognised and perhaps noticed that their earthy tastes were complemented by sweet and sour sauces, but the chickpea would have been new to them, for they would have long forgotten that their forefathers had eaten it under Roman occupation. Doubtless now they first met it in stews, but would they have recognised it when ground into a paste and mixed with oil as hummus? There were plenty of familiar vegetables they would have recognised in the markets; onions, white, yellow and purple carrots, leeks and garlic. The Arabs used cucumbers in many dishes loving its cool taste, as well as asparagus, artichokes and cardoons. These last were known in England but eaten rarely, so perhaps tasting them in the Mediterranean countries would encourage the Crusaders to tell their gardeners to cultivate them at home. Indeed, there must have been enthusiasts who collected seeds and made notes of all these new experiences they were discovering. Both fennel and celeriac would have been new vegetables, beloved of the Romans, but long forgotten in Britain.

Crusaders must have come across the noodle also for the first time and possibly been mystified as to what it was; Arabs favoured a long thin noodle like spaghetti and a small one like vermicelli, and they were served with meat and lentils and cooked in meat stock. They would also have first eaten rice and sorghum, both of which they could not have grown at home. But rice was to become a firm culinary favourite at the medieval court, so it would have been imported from North Africa soon after the Normans returned. Sorghum only grows in tropical and sub-tropical climes and though now the fifth most important cereal crop in the world, it has never been eaten in Europe. There were many types of bread from the very coarse, flat kind, eaten by the poor and baked in the ashes of the fire to raised loaves made from fine white, wheat flour which the rich insisted only on eating. Crusaders were well versed in the social nuances of bread consumption back home where exactly the same standards existed. To end a meal there was always an abundance of fruit: Damascus grapes, figs, plums, apricots and peaches and above all the sweet melon. Arab princes ordered fruit to be packed in ice and shipped in lead containers, the watermelon had come from India, but now was grown in Baghdad.

Obligingly the confectioner also acted as apothecary and possibly the most appreciated food that the Crusaders would have found in the baking heat of the Holy Land was that which they named syrups and sorbets. Refined white sugar was a Persian invention in the seventh century and they used it liberally in pastries and confections. Drinks were made from sugar, quince and apple, and shaved ice brought from the mountains, then kept in cellars were spun into peach and apricot sorbets. Then there were the pastries made with huge amounts of almonds (surely this was where they found their love of ground almond mixtures to become *de rigeur* on fast days), semolina, eggs, pistachios, walnuts, dates, cinnamon, saffron and spikenard – an aromatic root from India. Pastry batters poured into shaped moulds, then filled with crushed pistachio and honey, batters deep fried in oil then dipped into honey and sprinkled with rosewater, marzipan coloured and shaped into roses, all of this would have delighted the Normans, made them feel that such culinary wonders if brought back to court could only add renown and elegance to their huge, stone fortified palaces. Surely here was the origin of the banquet course to appear several hundred years later in all its extraordinary variety. But the Normans were to make sugary spiced sweets or comfits as they called them, almost immediately and as sugar had a reputation for being medicinally beneficial, the sweet had a golden future ahead of it in Western Europe.

There was one last aspect of Arabic food the Crusaders embraced totally and with fervour that would be constant once they returned home. Colour. If the natural colour of food faded in its cooking then it could be strengthened, deepened and generally enhanced – in Arabic literature the radiance of colour is exalted as a prime gift from the divine. Yellow, the colour of sunlight, was the most sought after, and saffron was the major source of it, egg yolks were used to colour too, but as a glaze, if cooked they also thickened which might not be desired. A variety of herbs was used for green: parsley, herb bennet, sage, onion tops and chives, and vine sprouts. If mixed with yellow it gave a vivid green, called gawdy grene in English and vert gay in French. Browns came from sandalwood, cinnamon or ground charred toast; for a pinkish hue they used Red Sanders (*Pterocarpus santalina*), further pink colouring came from rose petals or a plant, alkanet (*Anchusa officinalis*) the henna plant, and even animal blood, though once cooked it became black. Medieval cooks back home searched for every possible ingredient which would bequeath colour to the dish, such was the craze. Of course, the highest accolade for a dish was to be endored, glazed with gold – for mere gentry egg yolks would serve, but for the nobility and royalty the glazing would be done with gold leaf.

Scholars do not believe the Crusaders brought back to northern Europe new foods, ideas or flavours about their new culinary experiences, simply because there appears so far to be no proof. Yet in my last book I cited a ravioli recipe, which could have been scribbled down as early as 1100. There is 'general agreement that the Arabs introduced into Europe rice, spinach, eggplant, watermelon, citron and bitter orange. There is doubt about the artichoke and the shallot, despite their names.'[61] Later from the same essay Rosenberger says: 'Scholars often cite the case of a Frankish knight in Syria who ate as the Muslims ate and employed Egyptian cooks. Yet even if some individuals appreciated Arab cooking, few managed to bring it with them upon returning from the Crusades, which in any event did not detain them long.' Well, only a few years and when we remember that even a trip that we take now of two weeks can lead us to returning with foods and recipes, it seems astonishing to dismiss such a possibility. Rosenberger believes that all the major Arabic influences came via Spain and certainly later in the thirteenth century when Plantagenet kings took queens from Castile it gave a great boost to trade between the two countries. But when close relations of Norman barons in England were also ruling Sicily there was a flow of ideas which inevitably must have included food. Sweet and sour sauces came to be a favourite of the medieval court, and this cannot be explained by citing that the sauce was known to Rome, for Roman cooking traditions must have faded away many hundreds of years before. The use of flowers and fruits in savoury dishes is also another significant clue, what is a puzzle is that these Arabic influences were unknown in Paris and the royal court there, so maybe the Frankish knight above was a Norman after all?

Yet what was it that the Normans were saying through their food? What was the message, brilliantly hued, subtly seasoned with the richest of spices, the delight in the strange, the exotic, the jokes like the dish called the Saracen's head. It was highly theatrical; food was certainly an entertainment, possibly the most significant entertainment of their social life. But surely, their main message was that this was the food of the conqueror. As the Romans had insisted on using every ingredient and spice from the farthest reaches of their empire so did the Normans from as far east as they travelled. As that was the Holy Land itself, and as their society was permeated with church ritual and the most sublime expression of their art, the cathedral, one can see that their food combined both sacred and profane. But this, unmistakably, was the food of the conqueror, the ruler, who amassed the riches of others and celebrated them with gusto. It was also at times gastronomy of the highest order for it had a secure structure within the meal, based on ideological ideas of health and wellbeing of body and soul, but directed wholly towards the centre of the court, the monarch himself, praising him. Throughout the medieval court, the meals were ostentatious in the extreme, executed with a huge labour force, designed as spectacle which must be seen as acts of worship.

By 1300 the population of England was around five and a half million; ten million sheep produced 40,000 sacks of wool, our most important export, but average life expectancy was for men only thirty, while for women just a few years more. The most populous city was London with one hundred thousand citizens, York, Norwich and Coventry were far behind with ten to thirteen thousand inhabitants. This whole period from the Norman Conquest to early in the fourteenth century was blessed with fine weather and was slightly warmer than it is today. Vineyards proliferated and bad harvests were a rarity. Yet it was only the Norman elite that enjoyed the fruits of it all. But in 1315 things changed violently.

CHAPTER SIX

The Plague Years and After

There are throughout history seismic events, a culmination of many complex and conflicting stresses, which force the volcanic eruption, oddly in sociological terms not recognized at the time itself as being such a world shattering change, for people are so thoroughly committed to surviving the disasters that it is impossible to rationalize them. But such a century was the fourteenth, and as the working masses toiled on through famine, plague and civil war, did they ever realize, I wonder, throughout their short and harrowing lives, whether the future for people like them would become more bearable? Possibly not. For the future, of course, for them lay in another world, the divine hereafter promised to them through holy ritual and tracts. They endured a life of unremitting hard labour with little reward in return, but they knew that if free from sin they would live in paradise in eternity. Such is faith; it allows inhuman systems of exploitation not only to exist but to flourish. There is little doubt that throughout history widespread religious belief has allowed systems of social tyranny.

The Great Famine

It is commonly accepted now that in 1348 when the Black Death ravaged Europe, the population dropped by almost two thirds, which caused huge social changes in the manner by which the community was fed. What seems to be little known is that the decline in population started soon after the century began and that the Black Death was not quite the thunderbolt from a clear blue sky that earlier historians had imagined. Severe climate changes started soon after 1300 which placed the food supply in jeopardy. A series of storms which led to flooding followed by severe winters where the harbours could freeze over and halt imports began in 1315. The torrential summer rains of 1315 destroyed the harvests from Ireland to Poland causing famine across northern Europe. In those two years it is thought that a tenth of the population died. The price of grain rose to heights so absurd that it became necessary to import grain from the Mediterranean and the Black Sea. In March 1317 a Genovese galley, usually a carrier of luxury goods and not a bulk carrier, was chartered in Seville to row across to North Africa and collect wheat to take onto England.

A bad harvest can be disastrous, but icy cold winters can harm the growing grain with frost or the stock may be infected with cattle sickness. These famines and others which happened in the next few hundred years killed off thousands of the impoverished and were solely due to the vulnerability of the staple food that had been chosen twelve thousand years earlier – cereals. Grain is so highly vulnerable to climate changes, that to have a secure food supply based upon grain products you need to have a settled climate which will give five months of sun and rain in the right proportion at the right time for growth and ripening; any even slight variation from the normal weather pattern disrupts the quality of the harvest and can easily destroy it altogether. To have avoided the famines which blighted human life throughout these many thousands of years a choice of different staples (for there is safety in variety), not vulnerable to swings in weather patterns might have been chosen. (See Afterword)

There were many factors in what we would now call a recession that began in the new century. Civil war being perhaps the first hazard to the life of the agricultural worker, not only could he be taken from the land, armed and made to fight, but armoured cavalry could decimate a field of corn or the peasants might have to leave the land and take refuge in the towns. In the first three decades of the century there was much fighting between the King and the barons and they constantly took any provisions that existed, small farms were impoverished and agricultural produce was decimated.

From Somerset to Surrey wheat yields fell to 60 per cent of the normal rate, while rye fell by 30 per cent in the north, the heavy downfalls spoilt the supplies of peat and reduced salt production while those high salt prices affected the butter, cheese and preserved meat industries. Then from 1319-20 cattle disease was rife, servants were dismissed from estates and priories, for they could not be paid in corn and the need for their labour was no longer pressing. Peasants who had struggled to buy land and small homestead farms in the last century now sold them to buy bread, if they could, to their richer neighbours, but there were far more sellers than buyers. The crime rate rose; moreover, small thefts of food stuffs, even fathers accusing sons of thieving from their stores, poverty and most of all hunger sometimes broke the closest of ties. But not only did bad blood within the family develop in this struggle for survival, it affected the whole class structure, so that throughout every village and town there was great bitterness growing between those that had and those that had not. Gleaning was an example, traditionally the village allowed the genuine poor to collect the ears of corn left in the fields after the sheaves had been carried. Various bye-laws laid down that the healthy and strong were not permitted to glean, only those in dire need. But now there were many complaints that the poor did not observe the rules, that they took and more often stole whatever they could and the that ranks of the destitute had swollen to permit many others.

Some effort was made to carry grain from the less affected areas in the far west of the country, but there was not enough. The royal court imported grain from southern Europe and they were making some small profits from all the land exchanges, while also trying to regulate the price of livestock, but deaths rose inexorably across the land – from 10 to 18 per cent of males died between 1315-1322. If not from malnutrition they died from outbreaks of typhus which now spread among them and, all in all, about half a million died. No wonder that the area of land under cultivation began to fall. (Actually there is evidence that this had trend started earlier, at the end of the thirteenth century when there were outbreaks of sheep scab and the large scale reclamation of fens and marshes stopped.)

In the first forty years of the new century thousands of acres of good land was lost through flooding. Additionally, the civil war killed off some of the great barons, and their estates were allowed to decline into ruin. For example Earl Thomas was executed for treason in 1322 and six thousand acres of land and one hundred and sixty-seven cottages were abandoned. Yet the new young King, Edward III, passed more fiscal laws upon the peasantry in an attempt to claw back some of the funds lost through natural disasters. Many of these laws were flouted and bands of thugs set up local protection rackets and terrorized their neighbours.

The other great drain upon the land and the nation's coffers was the pursuit of the French Wars by Edward III, convinced that he must regain the empire which the first Plantagenet king, Henry II, had once possessed, while also furious at the humiliation insisted upon by the French monarchy that he made obeisance in person for the right to possess Gascony. (The fiction was that it was a fief of the French crown.)

Nor was the King's popularity helped by the way he began to pardon criminals if they agreed to serve in his armies, for there was a widespread belief that soldiers returning from the wars were responsible for the rising levels of crime and violence. The King ignored new statutes that had been passed in 1328–36 which limited the crimes for which pardons were granted. Though the Church took, as it always had, a tenth of the agricultural production of each peasant, because of the war, parliament in 1340 passed a law to take a ninth of every lamb, fleece and sheaf of corn. This met with angry opposition and many refused to pay, giving various excuses – coastal parishes in Sussex for example blaming flooding for destroying their fertile land – but all over the country peasants claimed that land was lost, whether the sandy soils of Bedfordshire or the clays of Buckinghamshire, because of disease, death or flooding.[62]

There also seemed to have been a growing but general concern over soil fertility. One of the greatest pressures the peasant and small farmer had to endure in these years was purveyance, the compulsory purchase of food stores for the soldiers which was often never paid for and if it was, the sum was well under the market price. Another burden was that there were custom duties placed upon the export of wool that hit the greater merchants and magnates, so they had to raise the price which made it uncompetitively expensive where it had sold readily before in Flanders and Tuscany. Though the King was unpopular in the first eighteen years of his reign, the peasants in turmoil often at the point of starvation, he managed to divert the latent hostilities within the realm and unite the country in its hatred of the enemy – the French and the Scots. What clinched the matter was, of course, the fact that he began to have a series of military successes, through the mastery of the longbow by his archers and the way he used them against the cavalry in battle.

In the twelfth and thirteenth centuries money began to have a vital role as, the bulk of the agricultural produce was taken to market. For as urban settlements grew the itinerant pedlar could not barter with town dwellers, for the latter had nothing to barter with, it was coins or nothing. For him it was easier to sell straight to the market stall which then would re-sell to the buyer after a surcharge. Thus, simple capitalism is born. Other factors in the decline of barter were the impossibility of fixing absolute standards for weights and measures, for consumers who were basically illiterate and could be easily conned by the rascals in the markets, of which there were legion. Then there was the depreciation of coinage which was a repeated occurrence in the Middle Ages.

The period from 1150 to 1300 was one of rising prices and wages; the price of cereals rose as the population also rose and the demand for more food meant the need to expand farmland. The mining of silver for coinage also grew; this silver fuelled the Crusades with plenty over to go into the Royal Mint. Gold coins began to be minted in Genoa in 1252 and Florence soon followed. Gold appeared to be a fundamental part of the expansion of the western European economy, as real wages also rose the demand for labour grew. But once the population declined because of the endless series of epidemics, for now there was too much land under cultivation, as there was a paucity of labour available. The silver mines closed throughout the fourteenth century. The recession was further prolonged by the devastation caused by France and England in the Hundred Years War, for the long lived Edward III was determined to add most of France to his kingdom.

By the end of the thirteenth century great changes had already taken place, the Manorial system had proved to be an unsatisfactory one, for people produced no more than was needed for their consumption and to pay the tithes, nothing was exported and no capital was accumulated. There was full employment certainly, but only continuous hard work and a very low standard of living. However, as the money economy grew during the thirteenth century feudalism rapidly declined. The acquisition of fresh supplies of money together with loans, credits and bills of exchange and the use of mercenary soldiers to fight wars instead of untrustworthy vassals were examples of a radical shift in social mores. It is interesting to note that the earliest goods to be sold for money instead of being used as barter were those that did not keep well or were only produced in small quantities, such as fish, butter, eggs. It was grain that was used longest for payment in kind, as it stored well. But in other matters there were signs of progress, the design of small boats and ships improved greatly, sea and river journeys were quicker, so there was increased use of waterways to convey food stuffs, salt and fresh fish in tanks; windmills became almost as common as water mills for milling corn, and fish farming grew with the number of fast days throughout the year.

Trade was the key to the middle-classes that now grew rich in this inventive society. As urban centres grew large and cut people further off from the countryside the middle man needed to exist, the one that bought food from the farmer and carried it to the city consumer, selling at a higher figure than its true price and thereby beginning to make a decent living. The realization that trade was one of the great keys to wealth had been known for many hundreds of years, but the fact that trade in foodstuffs was central to making a fortune was an idea that now became widespread.

In 1438 the Spanish traveller Pedro Tafur wrote of Bruges, 'anyone who has the money and wishes to spend it will find in this town everything that the whole world produces. I saw there oranges and lemons from Castile, which seemed only just to have been gathered from the trees, fruits and wines from Greece, as abundant as in that country. I saw also confections and spices from Alexandria and all the Levant, just as if one were there...' He goes on to mention furs from the Black Sea and brocades and silks from Italy; London, no less a port than Bruges would have had a similar, impressive array of luxury goods.

London was a city now of eighty thousand people and they relied on foods from all over south eastern England, much of which came by river. All the towns along the Thames sent wheat, vegetables, barley and malt; Henley grew rich from the demands of London. But other rivers were in constant service, the Medway brought goods from Maidstone, grain came down the Nene from Wisbech. But also much food came by sea from the ports of Suffolk and Norfolk as well as Faversham in Kent. Cattle were driven across the country to be fattened up in the Fens of the Essex marshes and then along with pigs, geese and sheep, driven into the London markets.

But by the beginning of the fourteenth century the recession had begun, it is clearly seen on the estate of the Bishop of Winchester during the years from 1300 where there is a fall in the price of wheat from 100 grams of silver to only 47 grams in 1479 but where the wages had risen throughout the same time span from 100 grams to 217 grams of silver – the great jump in the wages had happened after the Black Death where they had more than doubled. Moreover, at the beginning of the century throughout the famine years the price of wheat had doubled so the later drop was catastrophic. As in all recessions, everything is affected, so the price of iron fell because iron farm implements became too dear for the few peasants that could work at all. The price of building materials, meat, butter and livestock all went down.

Plague and War

The name Black Death was applied only several centuries after it happened. One theory is that it was a mistranslation of the Latin word 'atra' meaning both 'terrible' and 'black'. It was carried by sea and only Finland and Iceland remained untouched. It began in the spring of 1346 in the steppe region of southern Russia on the north western shore of the Caspian Sea. The Mongols were besieging the Italian merchants' last trading station, Kaffa in the Crimea and plague broke out among them which penetrated the town, so when the Italians fled on their ship to Constantinople arriving in May 1347, the epidemic began in early July.

The great irony is that it only spread, and only spread quickly because of the economic tentacles of the market community that Europe had become in the previous half century, through efficient trade routes with the larger ships carrying the luxury foods and goods, the wines, the spices, all packed into the large, broad-bellied along ships with the black rats and its toxic fleas. From Constantinople to Genoa and Venice, then by land across to Florence and its seaport, Pisa, from there to Marseille and northwards up the Rhone valley to Lyons, then southwest along the Mediterranean coast towards Spain. From Narbonne across the edge of the Pyrenees towards Bordeaux, a fatal port for us, for Gascony was English and its wine was sent every week to our south coast ports. On May 8th 1348 the consignment docked at Melcombe Regis (part of present-day Weymouth) in Dorset and the epidemic broke out five weeks later. The plague travelled by land certainly, but by ship it was quicker, Bristol was also contaminated in June and Dublin soon after, then in the autumn of the same year Grimsby was contaminated and they in turn sent the plague onto Oslo, Norway. Europe's population at the time was around 80 million; it is now estimated that about 50 million died, 60 per cent of the total.[63]

This was a devastating drop in population levels; it is twice the number murdered by Stalin's regime and overshadows any other great catastrophe that we are aware of. The radical change that must have hit the whole of Europe in a couple of years can hardly be grasped. Yet, astonishingly, much of the policies that flourished before the plague continued, and those that were the main drain on manpower and economy went on as if seemingly nothing had happened.

Consider the war in France, in 1356 just six years after the Black Death, the Black Prince (called thus because of the colour of his armour) was leading a small English army of seven thousand men in western France near the abbey at Nouaille. They had ravaged the countryside, had taken the few eggs, had slaughtered a few sheep, had killed anyone who had tried to stop them, had taken all the flour and bread they could lay their hands on and the wine they had found in the cellars and then they eked out and shared a meal which they had done every day these past months in the countryside they had been taught was rightfully theirs. They were tired, they had marched 260 miles from Bergerac in Gascony, they were ready to fight, but whatever French forces existed were refusing to engage in battle. The Prince was twenty-six and though his father had promised to send another English army, in fact to lead one himself, it had not even crossed the channel. To the north all the bridges across the Loire were broken and the main French army of fourteen thousand men blocked his way south near the town of Poitiers. He knew that the country was destitute; both armies had lived off it and there was little left to steal or scavenge. The Prince refused to negotiate and turned to face an army twice as large as his.

This was the battle of Poitiers where he captured the French king, bringing him back in triumph to England where he was imprisoned in the tower. This was the second monarch which Edward III had captured and imprisoned, for he already had the Scottish king, David II, incarcerated. This feat was previously unheard of and it was to the medieval mind hugely impressive. Monarchy was near to godliness, in fact Edward had already been compared to Jesus and Edward in conquering two kings at once seemed to have consumed their power and majesty also. In old age, for he did not die until 1377 aged 63, he grew a long beard which was white and resembled images of God the father, surely a self-conscious decision, because he could have easily trimmed and groomed his beard.

He was immensely popular with the people, they loved and admired the military victories in Scotland and France, and they considered Edward to be a great king and was a striking example of the monarch as sacred and touching the divine. This king would surely cure by touch and he performed this ceremony (whereby through the royal touch he cured the sick of scrofula) throughout his life with the same devotion that he paid to all his other religious observances. (In the year from November 1340 when his popularity was on the wane he performed 355 laying on of hands, some 257 of them at Westminster.) He showed devotion to the Virgin, he visited shrines and patronized cathedrals and abbeys, he was, in fact, a natural showman and proved remarkably successful at manipulating public opinion through displays of majesty – the long white beard was his last great role. So the food that sustained this living god must be touched also with the divine, and it is interesting to note that the first collection of recipes stem from just after this reign, from the kitchens of Edward's grandson, Richard II.[64]

Feeding a Depleted Community

With two thirds of the labour gone from the land after 1350 and the plague revisiting the land once in every decade until the end of the century, though nothing like the virulence of 1348, the character and purpose of the land changed. The proportion of peasants that died was above 40 per cent and in some places could reach 70 per cent, the villages and hamlets were the most vulnerable, as travellers bringing cartloads of hay or goods could not help but also bring through the infected fleas. Mortality among the privileged was much lower, 27 per cent, for they lived in stone houses and at a distance from the rats.

But one of the king's daughters died from the plague, Princess Joan, vulnerable because she was on a journey on her way to Spain to be married. Among the parish clergy 42 per cent died, but then in some areas they were under attack, as people thought God was angry with them and the dissolute clergy and was punishing mankind for their sins. Most peasant families lost at least one member if not several. There was no one to plough, sow or harvest, so much land remained untilled and was liable to return to the wild; much of it then, which was the easiest option, went to pasture, and more sheep were reared. Wool was still the major export, though wool from Castile was the main rival in sales, and now with more ewe's milk more sheep's cheese could be made and eaten.

Inevitably there was a rise in the quality of living for the peasant, and for the first time in history he was in a bargaining position. Never before had the peasant flexed his muscles and got somewhere; now, unless he got the labour organized the land went unploughed, so he bargained with the landowner for more wages, a larger tithe house complete with baker's oven so that he need not rely on the one oven in the village which belonged to the squire and have to pay a further tithe for its use. But at first the king and the government were deaf to his demands; they passed a Statute of Labourers Act in 1351 which was to keep wages at pre-plague levels. The act was written… "against the malice of employees who were idle and were not willing to take employment after the pestilence unless for outrageous wages, that such employees, both men and women, should be obliged to take employment for the salary and wages…that were paid in 1346…" But it made little difference for when the landowners saw the countryside going to waste they too ignored the new act and began to pay what the peasants demanded. This was the real beginning of the rise of the middle class. The Rochester Chronicler noted the change and wrote dryly that those formerly at the top now ate bread and pottage, while the labourers whose wages had risen could buy expensive food. 'Those who were accustomed to plenty fell into need and those accustomed to want now experienced abundance.'[65]

The landowners resented this state of affairs deeply, bemoaning the fact that the wage earners would not accept a contract to work for a year, preferring to ask for a short term of three months, or even insisting on working just for three days or even by the day or just the job in hand. By moving on and taking what was on offer they earned far more and were always in a good bargaining position. They also made it clear they wanted a better quality of food; the grain allowance must be all wheat with plenty of meat and ale.

A Dominican friar, Nicholas Bromyard, disturbed by 'merchants and moneymen' who thought they were the equal of noblemen, delivered a sermon, likening society to a harpist playing, the music being only sweet when each string kept its place, the rulers being the harpist who was in control.[66] There were endless legal wrangles where a whole family had been wiped out and there were no heirs to take over the property. The mines were empty of workers, the lead, tin, silver mines remained open, unlocked, unguarded and unworked; buildings were half finished, great holes in the thatch and only a wooden framework below, the vegetables lay unpicked with a few thin animals nibbling at them. But it was, after all, only temporary, as in the first few years of the 1350's production began nervously again. People had to eat; besides in such a situation, where all the normal rules have stopped applying, people are totally confused, there are plenty of opportunities for crooks and con men and through theft and fraud some of the survivors benefited. It meant that one of the great changes to come about was the end of serfdom, as in such a maelstrom no one much noticed if the serfs just vanished turning up later in the towns or somewhere else in the land; there was too much going on to even think of pursuing serfs, so many just slipped away, while others were given their freedom.

Many other factors came into play in the years that followed. The plague never quite left the land, Scotland noted eight plague years from 1361-1415, Wales suffered nine from 1361-1415. Life expectation began to fall, and as these plagues tended to kill the children and young, this affected the birth rate later in the century. There was a general migration towards towns, women especially left the country for the towns for there was a greater chance of both jobs and marriage, which was the goal, for it meant the main chance of gaining property as well as children. Traditionally women worked in the clothing and wool business, combing and spinning, but they also always helped in the harvest, weeded and hoed – for all these they demanded higher pay, but though they improved their rates they never reached pay equal to the men. In the towns they moved into the traditional roles of preparing food and drink, being pedlars selling from door to door and from market stalls. Where they did well was as widows in taking over their husband's trade where they showed their grasp of credit negotiations, purchase of goods and the training of apprentices. Land did not automatically go to the heirs anymore, for kinship links were no longer close, so land was sold and because there was so much of it for sale the price was low. But the towns were crowded and insanitary, disease was rife, another reason which shortened life expectancy. The privileged monks at Westminster with good diets living like gentlemen in some comfort did no better than the citizens living their overcrowded lives outside their walls.

Class and Manners

The poet, William Langland, hated the changes that he saw and in his long poem *Piers Plowman*, exposed what he felt were the amoral tendencies of the age. Langland makes clear that Piers has no money for food, he cannot buy pullets or suckling pigs, but that he lives off green cheese, curds, oat cakes and a bread made from beans, chickpeas and bran, nor has he any salt bacon, cabbage or ale, wheat bread and meat after the harvest. Langland, a cleric, enjoys his prejudices which chime with the feelings of the time, he comments on envious peasants and greedy labourers who insist on the best food and drink, and waste their newly discovered wealth in excessive consumption and never contributed enough in taxes. The poem was widely read and hugely popular and obviously reflected the views of the 'haves', the *nouveau riche* were on the march. The Sumptuary Law of 1363 complained of excessive apparel and set maximum levels of expenditure on cloth and accessories – ploughmen and shepherds, for example, were not allowed to wear cloth that cost more than 12 pennies per yard (a carpenter could earn 4d per day) but it was quickly realized that the law was unenforceable and never passed. The fact that the visual signs of being a gentleman and knight were being misused, that silver buckles, fur linings, silk and embroidered borders could be worn by lowly workmen, was distinctly unsettling. Food was another example, if peasants were taking to eating their meat with elegant sauces they should be stopped, it was felt, aping their betters was unnerving.

There is no more striking example of social mobility rising ever upwards than the poet Geoffrey Chaucer; his father, John Chaucer, was a London vintner, a step upwards from his family of vintners who were all in Ipswich, he managed to get a post as deputy to the king's butler and in 1338 was a member of the young king's expedition to Antwerp. He died in 1366 aged 53, but he had managed to find for his son Geoffrey a post in the household of Elizabeth, the Countess of Ulster. She was married to Lionel, the third son of the king, so Chaucer gained a courtly education, one of the most valuable of all gifts, for he learnt there all the etiquette needed to move in society. For a time he was part of the king's army, was even captured at the siege of Rheims, and obviously having put no foot wrong was chosen for various diplomatic missions in Spain and France. He married Phillipa Pan who was also in the service of the countess, but who soon joined the household of the queen. As luck would have it though Phillipa had a sister who became John of Gaunt's mistress and then his third wife, Froissart has passages depicting the court's shock and horror that this elder statesman, who was so highly honoured and distinguished, could lower himself by marrying a commoner. This connection with the powerful Duke and Duchess of Lancaster must have served the Chaucers well. Geoffrey and Phillipa had one son, Thomas who was five times Speaker of the Commons and between 1424 to 1427 was part of the regency Council to Henry VI, but it was his daughter Alice, who though thrice widowed, married the first Duke of Suffolk and it was their son, John, the second duke who was heir apparent to the English throne. So within six generations we travel from wine seller to monarch, not forgetting that one of our very greatest poets was at the centre of this lineage.

No wonder then that around 1430, a servant, John Russell in the employ of Humphrey, Duke of Gloucester (1391-1447) wrote a book of etiquette which could be used to train the noble sons of the aristocracy when they acted as grooms and henchmen in their father's household or, as often happened, in the households of other great magnates where they would absorb courtly life and its strict rules. A later version was called the *Booke of Nurture* and another *The Boke of Keruynge* which specified the art of carving. 'Manners maketh man', as was said by Alexander Barclay in 1509 when the book had another lease of life, so necessary was it to carefully delineate the upper class from anything below it. Certainly these manners and rules of etiquette were so detailed and precise that no one who had not been schooled in them for a couple of years had much hope of ever learning them, so impregnable do the top people ensure their position. (It reminds me of the great debate in my youth over U and Non U and the barely suppressed hilarity that was caused by a clumsy mistake). It was discovered that etiquette rules are far more effective at weeding out the *nouveau riche* and social climber than any sumptuary laws.[67]

Another use for the land, which earlier had grown cereals, was to make deer parks and to enclose it, and eleven new ones were created between 1350-1370, so the elite could tuck into more venison. Then there was rabbit, the nobility loved this meat and it was quite the fashion to both eat it and wear it, as a trim on hats, cloaks and garments. The rabbit, which they called cony (as it appears in the recipes), came from warrens which were as fiercely guarded by warrenders as deer parks. The conies were the kind of rabbits we now make pets of and keep in hutches, but the conies would inevitably escape, mate with the wild rabbits and within a few years lose their distinctiveness. So now with land to spare more rabbit or cony warrens could be established, and by the following century their meat was not as expensive and could be enjoyed by people outside the nobility.

Slowly the privileges of the nobility were being eroded; the next to go were the dovecotes, the right to breed pigeons for the table which once only belonged to the manor. But after the Black Death with too much land still producing corn there was enough to feed the birds. Whole villages began to build dovecotes and to sell the doves, alive or dead, squab or adult, at the markets. Diversification was the guiding principle, and any new agricultural idea was pursued by both gentleman farmer and peasant entrepreneur,[68] even those which demanded large tracts of land were eagerly sought when before they had been rejected, so herds of livestock grew, even changed to those once thought too damaging to pasture land like goats. Both lard and butter were used in cooking, pork fat was used extensively as well as goose, oil was extracted from flax, poppy, walnut, rape and mustard seeds, poppy seed oil was used in cooking, hempseed oil for lighting and mustard seed oil for tawing (converting skins into white leather) and rope making. Large orchards were planted and more variety of foods were now taken to market, scallions, chervil, chives and rosemary are referred to, while root crops like skirrets, carrots, parsnips and turnips begin to be eaten by the nobility for themselves and not mixed together in a stew. Farmers noticed too that when arable land went to pasture and remained so for many years it was enriched, which became a valuable lesson acknowledged at last by legislation in 1597, the idea becoming accepted as an integral part of farming practice.

Late Medieval Food

Kingship explained the nature of the food for the cream of society, that 2 per cent which still ruled Britain. Food was there as a potent force to embellish the grandeur, wealth and authority of the monarch. As wealth became the new key to nobility, ostentation in clothes, abode and food served was the way by which you were recognized. It was back to Ancient Rome where money was king. You rose in society because of the wealth you had amassed (not because of who you were, a salient difference from other Catholic countries) and then used it to serve your monarch in whatever way kingship desired, though also hopefully keeping the great power of the Church well satisfied too. Food in this age in the second half of the reign of Edward III, after the Black Death, in the midst of the great military triumphs in France and Scotland to the Reformation, just under two hundred years later, reached towards sublime heights of gastronomy. An earlier food historian says of the cook at this time, 'His aim was to send to table a dish transformed by taste, texture and appearance, into a work of art. If he had ever stopped to consider the matter, he might well have taken as his example and inspiration the Eucharistic wafer, whose fragile perfection is an exquisite refinement of the humble, homely bread broke at the Last Supper.'[69]

My contention is that the driving force into turning a monarch's feast into sacred art was merged into the inspiration behind the rituals and consumption at the Eucharist. That the food of this time was a combination of the sensual and the divine, an edible equivalent of the great gothic cathedrals which dominated every city and town. In indeed the architectural aspect of it was striking in the *sotelty* (delightfully termed in Italy the *intermezzo*) which were inventive dishes, sometimes life size in what they depicted, which were brought on at the end of a course, as edible entertainment.

The meal began with dishes that were designed to titillate and stimulate, to awaken the digestive tract so that it would perform perfectly – for example seasonal fruits and salads of vegetables sharpened with salt, pepper, verjuice and oil. The second course was all thick stews and soups, the potage, vegetable purees, pastas stewed in stock, or on fast days in almond milk or fish stock with added vegetables and spices. The latter were there to fuse with the main ingredient, to sharpen and add to its flavour by giving contrast, so that the palate was always intrigued as well as excited. It was considered that these were all easier to digest being basically liquid than the third course – a series of roasts. Undoubtedly this was the centre of the meal and so the boar or haunch of ox, the roasted swan or peacock, perhaps gilded and bedecked with fantastic decorations would arrive at table surrounded by smaller roasted fowls, game birds, saddles of mutton and rabbits and an array of sauces, maybe twenty-five different sauces, each one dedicated to a particular meat. These sauces were the most essential part of the cook's artistry, traditional though many of them were; he was also encouraged to create new ones. But the medieval court had firm favourites, ginger or garlic or sorrel were a few, there was an onion sauce and a sweet and sour sauce too, but each sauce had ten or so different spices as well as the main one. Flavours were complicated, perhaps even as complicated as the spice mixtures in a good curry today, but like those, where one can disentangle four or five different spices in the general mélange so could one do the same, I suspect, in medieval times. Though such an effect depends entirely upon the cunning, expertise and experience of the cook.

We should remember that because Catholic Europe was a Christian entity there was much travelling from court to abbey, from castle to monastery and in that there was a constant interchange of ideas which included the exchange of plants, of ingredients, of recipes and it did not take long for a culinary experiment which was successful in Rome to reach London or Paris. After the roasts were cleared the next foods were designed to close the stomach down, to quieten it, to let it rest, so the entremets could comprise egg dishes, foods in aspic, fritters, pies and tarts, dishes which mixed savoury and sweet, then came the dessert (the word was not used until the seventeenth century) – fresh fruits and cheese and lastly sweetmeats and light pastries.

Preceding the main course, or after it, would come the *sotelty* or *intermezzo*; castles under siege rose up with marzipan soldiers and pieces of camphor were lit to produce flames, blackbirds flew out of pies, fully rigged ships floated among clouds, saints prayed on meadows alive with fantastic creatures, unicorns fought with lions, fountains were filled with wine. At Philip the Good's Feast of the Pheasant in 1454, twenty-eight live musicians emerged from a pie all playing while a choir sang. In England we were more modest, but the *sotelty* became an established part of the feast though in time the word got changed to 'pageaunt' the precursor of masques. But still silver swans could hatch golden eggs, trees with glittering emerald fruits would droop from gold-petalled flowers, and the fruits that hung from other trees were already candied in glorious colours of green, red, purple and gold. Eating had become theatre and tumblers, acrobats and fools quickly became part of this entertainment.

In French it was called *entremets* and can be traced back to the end of the twelfth century when it appears to be a highly coloured dish. By the middle of the next century we are in the throes of a love affair with shaping foods as if they are wax and making effigies out of them, the first most notorious one that we know being the one called the Saracen's Head where the decapitated head of the enemy is carried around on a platter. The rice, vegetables and stuffed meat mixtures are dyed black and brown and everything is modelled with great care. This gives so much delight that cooks and their large kitchen staff and many minions are hard at it to create life-size figures, all edible, in robes that look like silk and velvet, ermine trimmed. Just as their figures carved out of stone on the tombs in their churches and cathedrals become more lifelike so do these creatures made from capons and pheasant flesh, reduced to a flavoured paste with flour, gingery spices and honey, but these are all demolished and eaten and only the remains are taken back to the kitchens. One of the great puzzles is why they were eaten at all, for they appear after two huge courses and before the desserts.

Perhaps the most significant aspect of the medieval feast, because it is characteristic of its age and time, is the use of the almond in celebrating fish or fast days. The import of almonds rose steadily throughout the period, for this was one crop that though it could be grown here (indeed, we have all seen and admired almond blossom today, the nuts do not ripen and there is no possible harvest this far north), the summers were neither long nor hot enough for the desired nuts to ripen though they formed. Almonds make a marvellously tasty cream, butter or milk, and their use as an ingredient can turn a meal into an exquisite gourmet experience. The fast day when strictly enforced had to omit all meats, eggs and dairy, yet here was the perfect substitute – an almond sauce only needed the barest extra flavouring, a touch of vanilla, citrus or cinnamon to sharpen the creamy taste and texture. Besides, crushed and ground, bound with a little rice flour then flavoured more robustly with garlic, asafoetida, ginger and fenugreek, a cook could shape it into cutlets and anything else he wished. Almonds effaced the whole experience of any sensual hardship that fast days might have induced, for fast days after all occupied two thirds of the year and world diplomacy and feasts which honoured important guests from other countries often had to be celebrated on such days. Royal cooks on these occasions were enthusiastic to show their skills, to vie with each other in concocting more and more fantastic dishes and the almond was the most obliging ingredient in their repertoire. Almonds were much in demand, of course, as part of the dessert, turning up in numerous recipes; for example, a Lech Lumbard has many variations in ingredients, but is a pressed cake roll served when cut in slices with dates, honey, quinces, bound together with breadcrumbs and ground almonds.[70]

But let us now turn away from the elite and look at what this newly born middle class were eating, for it is they who will fashion the future of our national cuisine, and not the fantastic excesses of the royal feasts. Almost at once we immediately recognize how familiar this food is, in its choice of ingredients and how it was prepared and cooked. Take eggs, we rely on hens' eggs and today a huge and horrifying industry has grown up around this daily ingredient, indeed, in the rationing caused by the Second World War. The loss of the fresh egg was perhaps the one food that we all mourned and the few we had to eat were enjoyed with a fervour that no other foods gave. In the medieval world all types of eggs were used and enjoyed though again only the elite would dine from a peacock's egg. But hen, goose and pheasant eggs were all eaten, though like us most reliance in cooking and eating was placed on the hen and all families kept a few hens even in the midst of towns. They ate eggs hard boiled and runny, they believed that scrambled eggs, just mixed with butter was good for the invalid, they used the raw egg to bind mixtures, to thicken sauces, while the whites they whipped into a froth and the yolks they used to brush the surface of food before baking to give it a golden sheen. Eggs were used in all their most favourite recipes, for wafers, pancakes and omelettes, and perhaps one of the most ubiquitous dishes in all its variations was the custard, served as a soup, where the eggs were raw and just beaten into the milk with flavourings; for a tart, both sweet and savoury, they had an ingenious method of filling a pastry shell while it was still baking in the oven with the custard by using a long stick called a peel which was attached to a pouring dish. One hoped that no one jogged his elbow. A simple but favourite dish was beaten egg and breadcrumbs flavoured with herbs and spices and then poached in chicken broth. Sometimes ground meat was added when it had to be cooked in a cloth, and after it had been boiled, it was taken from the cloth and with a gridiron grilled to give a crust.

The other main ingredient in a custard was, of course, milk, but this had to be used straight from the cow, ewe or goat, or else it began to turn, mind you, they enjoyed the curds and also drank the whey, so it was not wasted, but they could not use it to create a smooth, velvety custard. They quite happily turned fresh milk into curds by adding a drop of verjuice, wine or ale, depending on what flavour they wanted the whey to have. The curds were eaten with either salt or sugar. They made savoury custards flavoured with herbs and onions, sometimes even cheese, while the sweet ones would have fruits and honey, both dusted with sugar before serving and sometimes in the last few minutes of baking to give a light crust. They were especially fond of textures and combined smooth sauces beneath a crusty joint or pie, as they were passionate in their love of colour.

By far their most favourite colour was yellow and it was this shade they longed for all food to be, to shimmer and glow like gold, the more gold leaf, the more endoring, the better. Gold is infinitely malleable and unlike other minerals it can be spread thin. Why, one wonders, was yellow so liked? It was obviously the nearest colour to gold and therefore desirable and linked with riches and infinite wealth, the colour of the most valuable of coins. Medieval scholars were familiar with classic mythology, they knew how Zeus disguised himself in a shower of gold to visit the virgin, Princess Danae, and there was conceived Perseus, so gold was potent too, the semen from which heroes sprang. But it was also the colour of praise and worship, of religious votive offerings, of intricate chalices, of the bindings of devotional works, the crown of Our Lady; yet not only religion but monarchy too was suffused with the same radiance which dazzled both the mind and the eye, this was the cloth of gold, the royal garments, the colour of the queen's slippers, the inlay on the throne. Yet surely too, psychologically within the collective medieval mind, it must also have been the colour of the ripe harvest, the fields of corn that meant survival and strength, the source of a nation's power. Yellow was the colour of the divine then, the food fit for gods and kings.

For this glorious colour they relied on gold leaf itself, but more commonly for everyday use upon saffron and egg yolk. So the fields of saffron in north Essex which showed regally purple when in flower and about to be harvested, were laid out over the fields around the village of Walden, also in Cambridgeshire and East Anglia, but the industry spread over many counties in the south for it needed only small amounts of land. By its nature, a small area relying on female labour only at one particular time of year, it was a perfect crop for cultivation after the plague. There was always a good market for the product and the price was always high. If the saffron field was sited near to some rich estates all the better, there was one for example at Bethnal Green which must have sold to the magnates of church and state at Westminster on the banks of the Thames. We could never produce enough saffron for our needs, so much was imported, some came from the Levant, but supplies there were erratic because of the Crusades, but both Spain and Italy began growing the plant and exporting it to northern Europe.

The second favourite colour was red, in all its shades from scarlet and vermilion to the darkest crimson. This they achieved from Red Sanders (*Pterocarpus santalina*) imported from India, or henna (*Alkanat tinctoria*) from Spain. Red was the colour of violence, aggression and passion, red was blood, the colour of the wounds of Christ and the robes of a king, red was the colour of overlords and of triumph, it was a distinctly Anglo-Norman colour.[71]

Eggs, which they used so extensively, could very obligingly be coloured in all the shades of the rainbow. Dishes which were multicoloured, a custard or a tart say made to look like a heraldic shield, were particularly enjoyed. One of the most attractive imports which the Crusaders brought back from the Levant was the use of flowers in dishes. They might be carefully cooked and pulped for their colour and made into a sauce, roses, violets, hawthorn blossoms and primroses were all used, or their petals just sprinkled over dishes whether salads or meat balls. Flowers and herbs were valued as medicinal, the Anglo-Saxons were great herbalists and their traditional knowledge was stored by the monks in the monastery gardens.

Though cereals continued to be the main carbohydrate factor in their diet, peas, lentils and beans were also a staple, most often being cooked slowly to become a puree which they flavoured and coloured, also quite often then shaped, floured and fried in lard. Their stock was made from plentiful meat bones and foods were poached in beef or chicken stock, both the meat and the vegetables, so the stew was almost a daily dish and a stew which sounds perhaps to our contemporary tastes almost too rich. For it would have in it what was at hand, the beef bones which gave the stock its main flavour, then a rabbit, some woodcock, a pheasant or two, a haunch of veal, some purple carrots, a chopped cabbage and a handful of dried peas, some rosemary and marjoram, a few cloves and cumin, the whole cauldron cooked in the embers of a fire for a day and a half.

Beef stock was prominent to begin dinner for it would have been a potage thickened with beans, vegetables or oatmeal – a plain, hearty soup. The elite version would be either Brewes, where small pieces of meat are stewed with spices and croutons and thickened with egg yolks. Frumenty was a staple which seemed to have crossed the class barrier, hulled wheat poached in milk and meat broth flavoured with saffron and thickened with egg. Pease was a soup of thick pureed pea flavoured with mint or sage or saffron.

But of course the main part of dinner, the essential part for all those that had their monetary position established, so profoundly true for the *nouveau riche* in their hectic ascent – was meat. That roasted carcass that spelt your place in society as a worthy and valued member, no more general dogsbody, no more to be shouted at and scorned, the cooked carcass on the turning spit was a badge of honour. Not one carcass but possibly several, a row of three geese, or five pheasants, or four suckling pigs; so roasts were king, perhaps stuffed with suet and herbs, or a capon stuffed with mince meat, pork and bread crumbs, bound together with egg, served maybe with tarts of quince and medlar, mixed with more mince meat. Pigeons could be poached in a beef broth, filled with a peppery stuffing, then a sauce made finally from the stock with added citrus and ginger. Then there might be hare, rabbit or goose with marrow bones, the rabbit could first have been poached in chicken broth, then boned while a sauce was made with chopped raisins and dates which is added to a sweet wine which has been flavoured with cinnamon, cardamom, ginger, vinegar and sugar, which is cooked then mixed with a thick almond milk which is poured over the rabbit pieces and served. There could be Charlet, chopped boiled pork in a saffron custard, or Mortrus where the pork is minced with chicken to be cooked in a spiced broth, thickened with egg yolks. To our own eyes it seems like a plethora of foods without any guiding principle, but perhaps this is the point, the variegated foods appear like a cornucopia of plenty and the message is that affluence is power, we are judged by our waste and the servants in the kitchen, hungry to eat some of the leftovers are only the first to enjoy our charity, for the beggars in the street are next surrounded by the hungry curs waiting for their turn also. One tends, however, to agree with Philip Stubbes when he complained of Elizabethan nobles and the way they dined.

'Nowadays, if the table be not covered from one end to the other, as thick as one dish can stand by another, with delicate meats of sundry sorts, one clean different from another, and to every dish a several sauce appropriate to his kinde, it is thought there unworthy the name of a dinner. Yea, so many dishes shall you have pestering the table at once, as the insatiable…the devouringest glutton, or the greediest cormorant that is, can scarce eat at every one a little. And these many shall you have at the first course, as many at the second; and peradventure, more at the third; besides other sweet condiments, and delicate confection of spiceries, and I cannot tell what.'[72] From this description you would think nothing has changed in two hundred years, yet as we shall see in the next chapter a radical alteration was made, a major change in religious sensibility, which affected how people ate and specifically the sacred ritual of fast days.

Fast days when no meat or dairy foods were eaten showed how the rich could be humbled, in other countries the nobility sometimes went through an elaborate ritual of feasting the poor and washing their feet; the English did not appear to go to such lengths, our charity was less theatrical. But the fast dishes are most interesting for their gastronomic splendour and their use of almonds, as a paste, a sauce, a butter and a milk. (In our contemporary obsession with dietary inadequacies the gluten allergy has found a solution in using ground almonds instead of flour for cakes and biscuits, in my view a huge improvement both in nutrition and taste, there is much for us still to learn from the best of medieval cooking.) On such days, perch might be poached in ale and salt water, and then served with a herb sauce. Sturgeon was poached, but always served cold, garnished with parsley and chopped onions. A green sauce for fish, always the most favoured one, was made from parsley and mint, thyme, savory, grated horseradish, fish broth and white wine. Porpoise was enormously popular to eat on fast days because it was bloody enough to resemble meat. Cooks cut it into steaks, then added chopped onions with whole cloves, mace and pepper and poached the steak in a fish broth and wine, and finally they grilled it with salt and ginger. People were also fond of porpoise pie, cutting it into steaks, sprinkling these with salt, pepper and cinnamon, adding wine, then covering it with pastry and baking.[73] There was squid with a sweet and sour sauce, the squid pieces dipped in flour, egg and crumbs, the sauce made from citrus, verjuice, honey, dried fruits and wine. A large fish stuffed with a nut and herb mixture, then baked, might have a chestnut and currant sauce. Stuffings which used nuts, dried fruit, herbs and minced meat were almost commonplace and suited fish, meat and fowl, and were useful both in flavouring food and in making it go further, while also adding a complementary flavour to the main dish or one which emphasized it. The medieval cook was a master of this partnership between sauce, stuffing and the food they served.

The desserts might be a host of different fritters, waffles, wafers and tarts with fruit pastes, fruit candied, marchpanes, fruits in syrups. Both quinces and medlars were much loved and the pear, a warden, was a ubiquitous feature, for it stored well throughout the winter. Chardwardon was a popular recipe, where the pears are quartered then simmered in ale, then once soft they are put through a sieve, the pulp is mixed with honey, pepper, ginger, galingale and cinnamon and left to cool. There was much use of rosewater in many dishes and every possible fruit in the summer was put down and preserved for the winter. Part of the instructions in the *Boke of Keruynge* reads, 'Also see that you always have butter, cheese, apples, pears, nuts, plums, grapes, dates, figs and raisins, preserved green ginger and quince marmelade.' There can be no doubt that the medieval palate adored sweetness as much as it did a peppery, spicy, gingery heat, an addiction I would contend which has never left us. We like our food strong and hearty in its flavours, subtlety and discretion in the realm of taste we are slow to appreciate.

The Economics of the Elite

A medieval king was at the centre of a huge household, in which the retainers had to be paid a sum which reflected their august position. For example in the time of King Edward III there were listed two knights and ninety-one squires, eleven men of arms and one hundred and fifty-four archers on horseback; there were also forty-one clerks, including a clerk of the pantry and another of the spicery, there was a physician and two clerks of the wardrobe, all of whom were paid two shillings per day. (A skilled craftsman, a carpenter perhaps – King Edward had one hundred and thirty-eight on his pay roll – then earned 4d per day, a thatcher earned 3d.) There were other clerks below these that earned less, three at the spicery, another who worked in the kitchen and eleven others all were half the top rate – 12d per day. There was more kitchen staff, of course, one Sergeant of the Pantry, three of the Buttery, while another looked after ewers, another the sale and yet another the larder. There were three Herbergers nothing to do with herbs, but their job was to be sent on ahead of a group of knights or the royal party to find lodgings. Akin to this role were horsemen who would take messages, the only means of communication between towns, cities and countries. These were vital for a medieval king, as he relied on these in order to rule at all.

Music was important, there were five trumpeters, one citoler, akin to a Cithara, a stringed instrument of the thirteenth–fifteenth century, five pipers, one taberett, two clarions, one playing a makerer and one fideler.

There were strict rules on the costings of meals for each category of person in the royal household who lived and ate there and, of course, for the guests. A duke of the blood royal was allowed £15, 13 shillings and 4d for his daily food, but a duke not of the blood royal was only allowed £10, 13 shillings and 4d, same as an earl of the blood royal, while another earl was only allowed half that and each of his hundred horsemen were allowed 12d a day. The account books of the day list each person, their position in court and their daily allowance of food. So a duke might eat sturgeon, partridge and peacock, have his pies endored, eat only the finest white flour rolls, sip claret and have grapes and cherries. While a duke not of the blood royal might have to do without the endored pies and the peacock, an earl would merely have roasted pigeon, rabbit, and a slice of mutton, brown bread and lentils. And the horsemen, they would have a hearty soup made from scraps and meat bones with the roughest bread, washed down with ale and count themselves lucky that their bellies were full and they had employment.[74]

The picture we have of feasting by the nobility from Alexander Barclay (1476-1552) is hardly very decorous, because as the servers left the dishes upon the table for the diners to help themselves, there could be with favourite dishes an ill-mannered scramble to help yourself. 'If the dish be pleasant, either flesh or fish/ ten hands at once swarm in the dish/ and if it be flesh, ten knives shalt thou see/ mangling the flesh and in the platter flee/ to put there thy hands is peril without fail/ without a gauntlet or else a glove of mail.'[75]

In the Earl of Northumberland's household book of 1512, the only published version of 1770 has a preface that speaks of 'the great magnificence of our old nobility who feasted in their castles, lived in state and splendour very much resembling and scarce inferior to that of the Royal Court, their household was established on the same plan, their officers bore the same titles…'

The book itself is meticulous and extraordinarily detailed in its list of expenses, the household of an earl is so vast and complicated that administrating it was like a military campaign, or indeed, like the governance of a separate, small state, which is precisely what it was. The preface comments on the surprising lack of glass, both on the tables and in the windows, as it seemed that the earl and his family ate from wooden trenchers, for sometimes they hired pewter vessels, another surprise is that when they travelled to stay elsewhere in another of their estates, they took with them all the hangings, the tapestries, the bedding, rugs and carpets, denuding the castle completely.

Henry Algernon Percy the 5th Earl of Northumberland was descended from Edward III via John of Gaunt, the king's fourth son. He was born in 1477 and before he was twenty he had fought in the battle of Blackheath, against the Cornish Rebellion which, incited by Perkin Warbeck's pretence to the throne, was a revolt by Cornish miners against taxation for King Henry's Scottish wars. Six years later Henry Percy then achieved renown for escorting Princess Margaret to the borders of Scotland for her marriage to James IV, a time-honoured alternative to going to war. The earl's retinue was of such magnificence and splendour, 'his dress, feasts, furniture equipage and attendance' that all thought him a prince, reported the Chronicle. So this is the great earl's household book and one surely should catch a glimpse of the source of all this splendour.

Wheat and malt are the first ingredients to appear followed by mutton and beef, Gascon wine, pork, veal, lamb, stockfish, salt fish, white and red herring, sprats, salmon, salt sturgeon, figs, great raisins, hops for brewing, honey, oil, wax, bay salt, white salt, vinegar, verjuice, linen cloth, brass pots and mustard. 'All manner of spices' lists all the favourites but the colouring ones are prominent, there is turnsole, so named because the plant turns towards the sun (*Croton tinctoria*), its flowers give a purple dye, with saffron and sanders for the red dye. The food for the servants as well as for the earl's family is listed together, stockfish, the filleted dried cod from Newfoundland, stiff as a board and quite as tasteless is the cheapest fish available fit only for servants, while Gascon wine and salted sturgeon are preserved foods suitable for the elite, hops for flavouring ale are used some years before they were supposed to have entered the country in 1530, (there was a saying that hops, beer and reformation all entered the country in one bad year) but the emphasis on colouring herbs shows that the earl was concerned with putting on a show, the kind of show which he had exhibited escorting Princess Margaret to Scotland.

The horses demand shoeing and their pasture and the making and carriage of the hay, all is recorded, and so is the amount of money given to each servant, officer, yeoman, secretary and clerk for feeding their horse through the winter and the summer. The wages of all that live on the estate is recorded. The rules affecting food are stated. There must be no bread brought into the house, 'only that bread that is baked in my lord's ovens shall be eaten', the same is true of beer, only the beer brewed in the castle could be drunk. Throughout Lent no red, white herring or sprats may be purchased for serving at breakfast. (It seems that they relied on their stores in this time.) The vinegar must be made from the wines of the house, the trencher bread be made from the corn that is freshly milled. (The custom was to leave the bread for three days before slicing for trenchers.) There are nice touches like 'whereas mustard has been bought from the sauce-maker, now it be made within my lord's house and that it be ground in the skullery.'[76] The seeds were ground once a week. The clerk of each department was asked to observe all these rules strictly, one imagines that such detailed instructions must have been read out to them for literacy had not yet become common, though throughout the sixteenth century it rose rapidly as printing in the vernacular became available.

The breakfasts throughout Lent are described for each person of whatever station, from the lord to the clerk. There seems only to be a difference in quantity, for example the lord and his lady are given a quart of beer and the same of wine, they have manchet trenchers (that is fine white bread), pieces of salt fish, herrings and sprats, while the stable lads get a loaf and beer, similar to most of the other servants. Breakfast after Lent for the earl and his lady are the manchet trenchers with a dish of butter and a dish of buttered eggs washed down with the same amount of beer and wine. While the retainers and servants now get a piece of salted fish with their bread and beer. But on flesh days the lord and lady went to town; as well as the bread, beer and wine, they had a chine of mutton and that of beef both boiled as well as a chicken and three mutton bones boiled (for the marrow). For their children, Lady Margaret and Mr Ingram Percy, they had a quart of beer and the three mutton bones with their bread, but the older children, my lord Percy and Mr Thomas Percy, a quart of beer and that of wine and half a chine of mutton and beef boiled. They dined always in medieval fashion, two portions of food upon one plate, or mess, as it was termed.

Articles of food for the earl and his wife are given, dictating those that he must be served weekly and those only monthly, for example he should eat capons, chickens, pigeons and rabbit weekly but pigs and geese only once a month. Plovers may only be eaten at Christmas and at principal feasts, where cranes, redshanks, peacocks, curlews, bustards, dotterells and herons may also be eaten; mallards, woodcock, quails, snipe and partridges should only be eaten monthly. There is a note at the end of this section to the effect that no herbs may be bought, so that the herbs in the earl's gardens may be constantly renewed.

There is, as we read the household book, a growing impression that the earl is a mixture of parsimony and extravagance, but are we really to believe that the earl and his wife dine off trenchers? Well, they state these thickly cut slices of three-day-old bread are of the finest flour, but surely if not gold plate, they might have used plates of pewter, wood or terracotta? Or was this just for the Lenten fare? The other impression is how stuck they still appear to be in the medieval age, when one thinks that for at least the last seventy years Italy has been in the throes of the Renaissance, revelling in the freedom, sensuality of a new humanitarianism. The idea of cold mutton or salted fish for a child's breakfast when their parents have a dish of buttered eggs, calls up a disciplined world where obedience and duty are more important than pleasure.

Alas, with all these details, how useful it might be to have had some recipes, but though the ingredients are listed with their prices, the manner of how they were put together and cooked is not mentioned. In this respect there is no pursuit of the royal example as in Richard II's *Forme of Curye*. Yet the Household book is a monument to medieval bureaucracy, to its thoroughness and efficiency, it is an example of the Teutonic pedantry that was within the Norman knight still alive and well in 1512, when the young King Henry VIII had been upon the throne for a mere three years. While the new queen the young Spanish princess from Aragon, who had been for a few months the wife of the king's older brother sat quietly upon the throne beside him, no one suspected that this arrangement would detonate a violent change in the country which would affect the world and the fabric of all their lives seventeen years later. But for the moment the stronghold that was Anglo-Norman England with its strict hierarchy denoting class by half pennies and teaspoons, which for a hundred years or so had also ruled two thirds of France, seemed as impregnable reflected within the pages of countless household books across the land as Catholicism itself.

As I have suggested gastronomy began in prehistory as a manifestation of the divine, the food that was presented to the gods, which then widened to embrace the divinity of kingship, an aspect of the priest-king, one of the emoluments of monarchy, to flatter king and court circles and in that the concept itself of gastronomy was also born. But now in England we reach a time when the nature of monarchy changes, when the food will begin to lose its sacerdotal image, while the rise of the middle classes modifies the change into something more robust and of the people, but the sacerdotal manifestation has one last glorious fling before it dies.

CHAPTER SEVEN

The Gastronomic Peak

There has existed until now, the late fifteenth century, what could almost be described as an 'international cuisine of Europe' except the latter title was only just to come into usage, while there was no recognisable idea of distinctive nationality, for the most defining differences in the known world was the division between Catholic Christendom and Islam. In the Catholic kingdoms ruled from Rome there existed styles of cooking which were similar and dishes which could be instantly recognisable from Stockholm to Naples. Now, with the Reformation Catholic Europe would be divided itself and this would prompt the emergence of nations with a sense of their own identity in themselves and their food.

Finding Nationality

Because the cuisines were held together by a common faith and the strong grip on policy and manners which the Catholic Church exerted, the highly different character of each country was slow to imprint itself upon the food. Of course, within this system national cuisines did manifest themselves, but they did so discreetly, yet the fifteenth century was a time when social orders broke down, countries were still recovering from the plague century before and population growth was still slow. As the cracks within the social fabric began to show the power of the Catholic Church was questioned even more stringently, and as the Bible was translated into the vernacular so now the people could read the word of God for themselves and they were freed from the priest's interpretation. So what was merely whispered before, the suppressed *vox populi*, could in the sixteenth century be shouted in the market place; the dissenting religious voice was heard more clearly all over northern Europe and the people's food began to come into its own. It was a struggle, a Latin song hymned, 'The whole world is topsy-turvy! The blind lead the blind and hurl them into the abyss, birds fly before they are fledged… what was once outlawed is now praised. Everything is out of joint.'[77] The people found their voice in the most graphic manner, by being able at long last to read in their own language; Latin, the international tongue, had flattened out this individuality, rendered it uniform, digestible to all and allowed them to be more easily governed.

The concept of 'Europe' did not form until the sixteenth century, though the word stemmed from classical geographers to distinguish the land mass from Africa and Asia. Throughout the middle ages there had been a constant cultural flow of architects, designers and artists, invited by monarchs for specific tasks, who if the commissions continued lived on in a country into which they were not born. This was commonplace, they were all citizens under Christendom and all celebrated it with similar foods and dishes, like the ones in the last chapter.

But the birth of Protestantism split this unified network into zones that were still Catholic or newly Protestant and these new regions hectored its believers into re-examining their life and acts. People had rebelled against the idea of accepting that the word of God was the pronouncements of their priest, they could now start by questioning Catholic behaviour and the choice of food to be eaten on particular days was one of the most basic aspects of human life. It was a time of violent schism and though saints' days were to be questioned, there were enough new martyrs to fill the year and though the very act of fasting was to be questioned there was a constant psychological need in the faithful to purge and penance.

But let us first glance at the character of our food before the Reformation and we find that by the early part of the sixteenth century English food had gained a certain notoriety. We ate a lot, we were unmannerly, we had a reputation for greed, and our way of dining was chaotic. The unruly behaviour at the table noticed by Barclay at this time (see the last chapter) was no doubt encouraged by the stories travellers told of riotous behaviour among the unruly serving men and retainers of the new nobility. For the old landed gentry had been decimated in the Wars of the Roses and Henry Tudor had rewarded his followers with what they noticeably lacked, land and titles. There was a new wildness and impudence shown in young men which is reproved by the older writers, they appear in plays. The Wakefield or Towneley Mysteries[78] of 32 plays based upon the Bible has a character called Jack Garcio from a play The Shepherds based upon such types. Barclay's description of meals at the houses of the nobility show a scene of confusion with dirty tablecloths and inedible food, with the worst dishes being served first so that people might sate their appetite upon them before the scramble over favourite items, leading people to eat far more than they needed or even wanted. There is a story of an English merchant dining abroad with a foreign noble who is amazed that the merchant eats modestly. The noble asks why he does not consume as much as other Englishmen. The merchant answers that there are three reasons why so much food is served on the table in England. We are accustomed he says to have 'divers meats because some love one manner of meat and some another'. Then because of 'divers maladies' some prefer one meat and some another. But the third cause is dread, there is so much abundance in the land, so many beasts and fowls, 'that is should we not kill and destroy them, they would destroy and devour us.'[79] This whole farrago sounds like nonsense, like one of those fantasies one nation has about another to downgrade them in the public mind, but the fact that the story exists at all is at least an example that eating in England was a different and sometimes dangerous experience.

There were taverns and cook shops at Westminster Gate which were celebrated, they flourished there as most of the travellers from the south and west would have entered London by this gate and rested for a while. Women went there, we are told, to gossip which was a subject of many songs of this time in both England and France. One song begins with a woman asking another where the best wine could be had and she is led to a tavern in secret, explaining that her husband must not know, the women bring food and picnic there, in the song she brings goose, pork and pigeon pie, 'Each of them brought forth a dish/some brought flesh and some fish.' They talk of the goodness of the wine and the badness of their husbands, they return home by separate routes and tell their husbands they have been to church.

Literacy spreads and with it an increasing intellectual agitation. It is pertinent to note that both spectacles and writing materials are now part of the inheritance in wills. John Baret of Bury St. Edmunds in 1463 left to the monks of Bury his silver gilt spectacles and his ivory tables.[80] Not that the monks had many years to enjoy such gifts, for the Reformation of 1538 was to destroy the familiar world as they knew it. For the people of England were now told that the rituals by which they may intercede to God, purge their soul and earn their place in paradise were all a profound error and they had to learn new ways to worship. The monasteries were emptied of monks, their treasures vanished, their lands taken, their stained glass broken, their statues of Our Lady smashed, their gold and silver collected by the King's ministers and what the

King did not personally amass he gave away to favourites. The Church's great wealth enriched the new nobility that the King 's father had created, and this century was a time of newly built private houses of great size which had the first enormous kitchens not owned by a monarch.

The Vanishing Almond

There were two great changes which took place in the food of the elite after the Reformation. Those skilful and adroit dishes resembling meat, fowl, eggs and fish, all made out of crushed almonds were not necessary anymore and a culinary art was lost. Moreover, the art, craft and secrets of the still room were now dispersed from the monastery to the farmhouse and great estate.

Many of the monks fled from England altogether taking their rare and precious knowledge with them, many others dispersed across the country searching for refuge, on the run, hidden by faithful Catholic families, others changed over to Protestantism and whatever they privately thought they kept it to themselves. However, in terms of the food that people ate, several changes took place, but not suddenly, for such world shattering change often takes time to absorb. Those medicinal herbal concoctions, brewed and distilled, the eau de vies made from flowers, which the monks were so skilled in making and had done so since Albertus Magnus (1193-1280) had described the process, the housewife who ran the farming estate now had to discover and did so, learning also the extra plants and herbs she now had to sow and cultivate, harvest and dry. But how did she learn so much so quickly? There can be little doubt that many of the monks were glad to accept work or a position in a private house, and no doubt there were monks who now became gardeners in those estates who were glad to continue distilling and communicate their knowledge. But the still room now became a valuable part of every farmhouse as well as an integral part of the buildings that surrounded the kitchens in every great magnate's estate.

The early Church had embraced distillation as a God-given blessing and monks created new flavours, extolling them as medicinal cures, if taken in tiny doses. The Italian monks had a special talent for creating liqueurs, adding sugar to the wine distillation; while alchemists further north were making an aqua vitae from grain, and called it burnt wine, hence brandy. All this knowledge and the recipes themselves were kept secret and heavily guarded, but in the destruction of the monasteries such information was there for the taking. Some of the most famous liqueurs from Italy were *Populo*, a herbal liqueur with musk, aniseed and cinnamon; *Rossoglio de Rossolis*, a rose-scented liqueur; *Vespetro*, a blend of coriander, angelica and aniseed, the Maraschino made from a small sour cherry from Dalmatia, while others were called *Eau d'or, Eau de cedrat,* and *Eau eternelle.* Imagine the excitement when such exotic sounding names were first heard for an alcoholic drink that was supposed to give you long life and good health, no wonder still rooms were built with such enthusiasm.

Every printed recipe book that was now published ((the first *Book of Cookery* especially compiled for princes was published in 1533 or 1540) had sections on the making of lotions, ointments, powders and drinks, for all the ailments and injuries that might afflict people. There is rosemary water, a syrup of quinces, an imperial water made from toadflax, scabious, endive, pimpernel, wormwood, rue and a dozen other herbs. There are remedies for shingles, scabs, shrunken sinews, for wounds, cankers and being struck dumb.[81] This particular book has two hundred and eighty recipes, but only two of which use almonds and the second one is an old medieval favourite *blancmangle,* literally white food which here in late Elizabethan England has the usual capon flesh minced and mixed with the ground almonds, flavoured very simply with cinnamon and ginger. The other recipe, a white broth, is a spicy meat soup, buttery and creamy with the almonds, which, of course, effaces entirely the raison d'être of the original recipe which was a meatless soup for a fast day. But then that is the difference between food before the Reformation and afterwards.

Days of fasting, long hours of abstinence were not regulated by the church on all the catholic saints' days and the devout felt lost without them. But those dishes on such days, when both kingship and the divine were lauded for great royal feasts, when elaborate sauces were contrived with ground almonds, rissoles and cakes, cleverly spice, were not made anymore. What was the point? Here, for example, is a recipe for a porpoise poached in a white broth that instead of being thickened and made creamy with almonds is thickened with white dried peas. A far more down to earth flavour, pleasant enough, but this is a sauce for a peasant not a prince, though the fish marks it as a dish for the elite, yet this cookery book is for the middle classes.

The vanishing almond and the particular style of skilled cooking that went with it, is most vividly illustrated by the culinary collection that was used in the home and kitchens of the very first Archbishop of Canterbury. This is Matthew Parker who had been Master of Corpus Christi College, Cambridge, before he had been chaplain to Anne Boleyn. In Edward VI's reign, with the continuing rise in Protestantism, when laws governing the marriage of priests were repealed, Matthew Parker married a childhood sweetheart and she became his wife when he was Master of the College, but when Mary I came to the throne in 1553 she enforced the annulment of the Edwardian act of permission for priests to marry. Parker resigned the mastership and lived quietly in the country with his wife, then in 1558 Elizabeth became Queen and she asked him to be her first archbishop and he and his wife, Margaret, moved to live at Lambeth Palace. Matthew Parker was a writer and a scholar and while there he amended the Thirty Nine Articles which govern the Anglican Church, so he was very much the architect of the Protestant faith in England. His friends and colleagues in that schism, Latimer, Ridley and Cranmer, were all burnt at the stake in Mary's reign. It is then particularly interesting to be able to have some insight into the food that he served and ate throughout the time he was Master at Corpus Christi and Archbishop.

The recipes are contained in a book[82] and we can turn to the service for fyshe dayes which were now on Fridays and every Wednesday. The Wednesday was now included because fish eating had declined so steeply that government had to pass legislation to help the fishing industry. The menu for the Parkers' fish day began with a broth of sand eels and river lampreys, and then smoked herring with fried parsley, there was also fresh herring with mustard and a choice of ling and spotted cod, also with mustard. There was minced salmon with mustard and green sauce and a choice of other fish, in fact fourteen other fish, and this was only the first course. There are seventeen different fish in the second course, from turbot to sturgeon, some served with a vinegar sauce; the meal ends with a tart, cheese, figs, apples and pears, and at last the ingredient appears – blanched almonds. The once great sauce, cream and butter has vanished and only the shelled nut now appears much as it does in our own diet as an adjunct with fresh fruit at the end of the meal. Such food that once crowned the medieval feast upon fast days was known to be Popish and was eschewed as a signal that the diners were thoroughly Protestant, their devotion to the Anglican Church unquestioned. As this was the food that stemmed from the Archbishop of Canterbury's kitchens we can take it that the character of such food was an ideal guide to all Protestants and that the word 'proper' in the title may well have had more than one meaning.

So what of the rest of the book, in the midst of the English renaissance, does the food set new styles, have new ingredients, reflect the richly exuberant creativity of the Elizabethan age? The shadow of the medieval age is still very much present, the meal times are the same though edging towards being a little later; the main meal, dinner, is still between noon and one however. As we see from Margaret Parker's book there are still a host of different foods to choose from and the first and second courses are difficult to tell apart. For the first course there is soup, then boiled or stewed meat, chickens and bacon, salted beef, pies, goose, pig, roast beef, roast veal and a custard either with a crust or without. In the second course there is served roast lamb, roast capons, roast conies, chickens, peahens, baked venison and a tart.

Now we know that each person ate according to his or her appetite and that many might only have had a portion of one or two dishes from each course. I also suspect that when a cookery book lists the dishes for these courses they mention all the possible ones knowing that the cook will choose depending on how many he has to feed and the tastes of the diners whom he would have been familiar with, so that such a record is not illustrative of day to day cooking. Such a record too would be useful on feast days when the Archbishop entertained fifty or so distinguished guests or when the Queen herself came to dine. Matthew would have known well that the Queen was modest at the table (unlike her father) and found a show of indulgence distasteful.

The food that is presented in the book seems no different from that which was eaten a hundred years before, except for the one striking fact that there are no almond sauces, butters or creams, for there was now no need for them. Though the *Book of Martyrs* gave Protestants new saints to show their devotions to if they wished, few people went on any great spartan fast, nor were there now a multitude of monks who pretended to do such fasts but actually consumed gourmet dishes with adroit sauces made from almonds. In Catholic Europe these dishes continued for a time. In France 'over the course of the seventeenth century sugar, almond milk and fruits were rooted out of all but the dessert dishes, not only because they were part of the Arabic style of cooking but simply because they were sweet.'[83] The French got over their liking for sweet and sour sauce, the British never; the vinegar sauces served from the Parker kitchens with the fish were all sweet and sour.

Yet almonds continued to be imported, though nothing like the amount of tonnage before Henry's split with Rome. It was almost as if the English could not quite wean themselves away from this subtly flavoured nut, nor need they, it was merely the sauces and butter they stopped making. Almonds now reappeared in the new course called the Banquet and the charming and decorative new architecture which housed it – the Banqueting House. Almonds were prominent as part of the sweetmeats in what was known as 'banquetting stuffe'. Henry Machin wrote down in his diary what they would eat for this course of the Skinners' Company in June 1560: 'first spiced bread, cherries, strawberries, pippins, and marmelade and sucket, comfits and portyngalles (semi-sweet oranges which took their name from Portugal) and divers other dishes, hippocras, Rhenish, claret wine and beer…'[84] No almonds mentioned there, but we can be sure they appeared, ground, chopped or crushed in cakes biscuits and fillings. Here is Lady Desmond's Recipe for Almond Butter: take a quart of cream and a quarter of pound of almonds blanched, beat them fine with a little of the cream to stop them from oiling, then strain them into the cream and let it boil, then put in the yolks of ten eggs well beaten and let it boil till it curdles, then put into a cloth and let the whey run from it, then take it out of the cloth and season it with rose or orange flower water and sugar to your taste, bruise it with a spoon that it may look smooth.[85]

This little recipe intrigues me for it seems to me to be mis-titled; it is nothing at all like a medieval almond butter that does not include dairy cream, because its very existence is to be a substitute for it. No this almond butter (for a start compare the amounts of cream to almonds – a quart of cream to a quarter of a pound of nuts) would not have any flavour of almond at all, swamped by cream, egg yolks and rosewater, nor could the almonds be there to thicken the cream, for the ten egg yolks would do this, besides they don't thicken so much as curdle, so one ends up with a sweet scrambled egg. You might just as well not have any almonds at all, which after all, is the zeitgeist of the age.

The question whether all the community even kept those two fast days when once freed from the strictures of the Catholic Church is an interesting one. For fasting had imposed a strict routine upon the kitchens of the land; to change that in a radical way would have needed a new direction in the policy of an establishment, however large or modest, where for example, the amounts of fish and almonds to order and buy would have been laid down for decades. In the Catholic regime there were the weekly days of abstinence, Fridays and Saturdays, the whole of Lent, the period of forty weekdays from Ash Wednesday to Holy Saturday, then there were the fast days held before the saints' days which were feast days, the apostles and All Saints, and the four Ember days. Through the hundreds of years of church law the days of fasting and feasting changed, but sometimes fast days took up almost two thirds of the year.

Under Protestant rule it was obligatory still to have two meat-free days of the week when only fish was to be eaten in support of the fishing fleet so vital as a navy for sea defences, but the new church was relaxed about observations of other fasts, which was sensibly left to people's private conscience. Supposedly, you could be fined for breaking the fast, and though these fines were drastically reduced in 1593, the head of the household was liable to be fined for every one of his servants who broke the fast, which is why we discover the ridiculous situation of the servants in the Willoughby household observing the fast while the family broke it. A too rigorous timetable of fasting, of course, risked those partaking being mistaken for papists, a highly dangerous position to be in, yet complete non-observance would exhibit an ungodly stance that was also not desired. For standards had to be kept if you were part of the nobility and we see a confusion in the Willoughby family over the matter.

Their household accounts show a decline after the Reformation in purchasing almonds, herring and salt, while throughout Lent there was a reduction in fresh meat purchased, special foods were bought in for the servants for the Ember days – butter and eggs. Yet it took them time to change, for in 1548 no fresh meat was consumed throughout the whole of Lent, though they had plenty of butter and eggs. Throughout the year they kept the fast on 152 days out of the year. Ten years later they are still observing Lent by not eating meat, but their consumption of butter, eggs, dried fruit, almonds and figs is well up. It is not until later in the century that they become more relaxed; by 1587 they ate small amounts of meat throughout Lent, mutton, chicken, ducks and woodcock. It would seem that these were the tastes of the new head of the household, Sir Francis Willoughby, for when he went away, no meat was eaten, but when he returns two capons and a veal pie appear. We find this throughout the year, as on Ember and on the eve of saints' days meat and game are enjoyed.[86] It is all a matter of personal preference, as well as the fact that the Reformation was such a huge and violent change in society (the Willoughby family refused to buy any of the church land on sale cheap, though they were loyal to the Tudor dynasty and had been from the beginning) that it took decades to sink into the actions of daily life. Even when there were decrees calling for more observance of fasting at the end of the century when there was more famine years connected with high prices and greater pressure of population, it had little effect on people's habits. Such fasting was a Catholic mode of living and the English population had grown beyond it, proud of their independence from Rome, proud that they had created a new church and a different hierarchy of clergy, not aware in the least though, that they had lost a fascinating repertoire of gastronomic dishes which stopped being cooked except in secret for Catholic nobles.

The New World of Reading
It was not only the Bible that now became available for reading and perusal, but also works from the classical world, and contemporary writers on a variety of

subjects were quick to climb onto the bandwagon. The first recipe books had as many directions for making medicinal mixtures, salves, potions and ointments as they did for making a tart or potage. Books from other countries were eagerly translated, books on gardening, agriculture and travel as well as cooking, but the classical world, newly rediscovered, was the most revered of subjects and it was their authors who were studied with attention. Writers who had written upon the cultivation of plants and agriculture were read and considered – Pliny, father and son, Aristotle, Columella, Cato, Varro and Xenophon were read eagerly and many of their beliefs followed, 'they challenged their readers to experiment, observe and innovate.'[87] Varro had written 'that we should imitate others and attempt by experiment to do some things in a different way.' This, after all, was an age of discovery, a fleet of ships was crossing and re-crossing the Atlantic, the lands on the other side of the great sea were being explored, a feeling of progress was in the air and the brave were the victors. The New World was a source not only of strange new foods, but also of many plants. Gerard grew maize successfully, both sweet and white potatoes and even a tomato plant, all four of which they treated cautiously and with great suspicion, possibly because they might have tried eating the leaves of both the potato and tomato and found them toxic. It took another few hundred years before either was accepted as part of the diet.

The garden itself, as opposed to agriculture outside the walled enclosures, had started to change radically in the time of Henry VIII. His new palace at Nonesuch at Cheam in Surrey had extensive garden walls with espaliered fruit trees, all new varieties, for it had been deemed that the old ones brought over by the Normans had lost their vigour. In 1533 Richard Harris, the fruiterer to the king brought over grafts of new fruits from France and the Low Countries; later, William Lambard in his book *A Perambulation of Kent* in 1576 wrote: 'Our honest patriot, Richard Harris planted – the sweet Cherry, the temperate Pipyn and the golden Renate.'

Another writer wrote a glowing account of the landscape at that time, William Camden in *Britannia* in 1586: 'Almost the whole county abounds with meadows, pastures and cornfields, is wonderfully fruitful in apples, as also cherries, which were brought from Pontus into Italy in the year of Rome 680 and about 120 years after into Britain. They thrive here exceedingly, and cover large tracts of ground, and the trees being planted in the quincunx, exhibit an agreeable view.' The quincunx arrangement of the planting was the one used by the original Roman growers when they invaded Britain, the pattern being that four trees are planted at each corner of a rectangle, while the fifth is placed in the centre.

The new varieties were planted in an orchard at Tenham in Kent of 'seven score acres' as a later writer, calling himself N.F. in *The Fruiterer's Secrets* (1604) explained: 'which orchard is, and has been the chief mother of all other orchards for those kinds of fruit in Kent and divers other places...' Orchards filled with the new varieties were planted all over the land, in Derbyshire, Lancashire, Suffolk and Gloucestershire; Justice Shallow in Shakespeare's Henry IV, Part II talks of eating in his orchard, 'last year's pippin of my own grafting'. Once the immigration of Walloon refugees began between 1560 and 1570 our dependence on foreign imports of fruit declined rapidly, for the Walloons settled in Sandwich in Kent and began their market gardens, then to be nearer the London markets, a few years later they moved to north Kent and Surrey, where they planted their orchards.

The refugees came from Wallonia, a narrow strip of land between Germany and France, now Belgium, they were famed for weaving and tapestries, as well as for fruit growing. Their country had been taken over by Spain (as part of a marriage contract) and the Catholic church deemed them as heretical. There were Walloon settlements in Yarmouth, Norwich, Colchester and Canterbury.

The medieval world had been suspicious of fresh fruit, but loved it dried or cooked, but now under the Tudors a new appraisal of its possible virtues occurred. The first was in *The Grete Herball* by Peter Treueris in 1526 and he tended towards the vague, on the strawberry he remarked, 'is principally good against all evils of the mouth'. William Turner was another writer with influence, possibly as he was also the Dean of Wells, though he tended to copy much of what he thought straight from Pliny, yet Turner loved plants and encouraged people to create gardens. Sir Anthony Fitzherbert in his book on husbandry dealt with the propagation of fruit trees using crab apple seedlings as rootstocks. Yet they were still equivocal upon the subject, when epidemics raged the sale of fresh fruit was banned and instructions for cooking fruit for pies gave long times for stewing fruit in red wine. With all the new influences from so many sources, new crazes and fashions came, for those modish enough; the passion was for Italian gardens.[88]

In the last quarter of the fifteenth century Italy had discovered the ancient world and Rome's love of the garden. Inspired by Ovid's description in *Metamorphoses* and by Pliny the younger's letters, Italians wanted order and symmetry, wished to break down the walls of the medieval mind which had encased fruit, vegetables and pasture into separate rooms, to open out the garden and show the space, so that nothing interrupted the views from the house through to the gardens and landscape beyond. The gardens themselves they filled with fountains, cascades and running brooks, with statues and grottoes. Such gardens moved on to France and thence to England. They were, of course, highly labour intensive and could only exist in their breathtaking beauty with the sweat of a large gang of underpaid minions.

The Tudor world was one of violent change and it was, not unexpectedly, a century where women came to the fore in a new and vivid way. In the medieval world it was generally only when women were widowed that they were allowed to take over a business and run it themselves. They seized the opportunity and this was still the case. But with the church's strictures upon women's activities fading, though new Protestant ones were soon to take their place, women could move into the empty spaces and start to fill them. Obviously, there were the demands of the still room, as I have mentioned above, after the monasteries were dispossessed; the science of distillery was often taken over by women in the manor house. Sometimes instantly, as when the Earl of Rutland at Belvoir in 1540 ordered distillery glasses and further items, while paying for his herbs to be gathered at the height of summer in July of that year. In the following year he received a gift of distilled waters from Lady Markham, perhaps she wished to show him the excellence of her own distillery. It was not until later that a book was published to help these new distillers – John Partridge's *The Treasurie of Hidden Secrets* in 1600. This was not a new fad, as some historians have thought, but a necessity. How else could they make the herbal medicines they had relied on for centuries to cure the many ailments that afflicted them; but freed from the rules, restrictions and mysteries that the monks had used to bound these products down by keeping them exclusive, the Tudor housewife found she was confronted with a whole array of pungent aromas and distilled essences which were too exciting in their possibilities to ignore. Hence they often added them to food.

At the same time of course apothecaries also began to flourish as more and more apprentices studied the art, so that adding a flavoured herbal oil or violet water to a dish was not completely the domain of the landed gentry but could also be experimented with by the bourgeoisie. Orange water was still imported and a favourite addition in the kitchen, but now the housewife or a trained assistant could make rose and lavender water, and *eau de vies* from elder blossom, rose hips, angelica and bilberries. Then there were the oils, from Italy came the idea of adding olive oil to salads and from Holland the concept of winter fodder for cattle being made from rape after the oil had been crushed, such oil being used for lighting. The oil from walnuts and almonds as well as rape now crept into use in the kitchen and a new purpose found in the walnut harvest. Though the method of making liqueurs had been brought to Paris from Italy in the early fourteenth century and then to England soon after, this was yet another skill the monks kept a secret until Catherine de Medici in 1533 had made the drinking of them fashionable. So liqueurs now were also made using a whole range of herbs and spices for flavouring; favourites were firstly ginger root, then anise (*Pimpinella anisum*), the seeds are used, bay, the leaves and berries, caraway, celery and dill, to name only a few.

The Elizabethan housewife was responsible for a whole range of other activities, which placed a frightening work load upon her: all the laundry, the dairy and milking parlour, the dovecote, henhouse and flock of geese, she brewed ale and commanded the kitchen, she clipped the sheep, she wove and spun, then well nigh exhausted, one thinks, went into her garden and chose the leaves for the pot pourri, the flowers for the eau de vie, the herbs for the stew or stuffing for the roast. The garden with its neat rows of vegetables and its fruit trees, the latter being in the charge of the husband, was inspired by Thomas Hill's book *The Gardener's Labyrinth* (1577). Its geometric designs sheltered from wind by high hedges, gives one immediate pleasure even before an examination of each bed and its plants. Another hugely popular book was Thomas Tusser's *Five Hundred Points of Good Husbandrie* (1580), which was his augmented volume as the original only had one hundred points but which had been published fifteen years before and been such a success that Tusser easily thought up another four hundred points. It was written in simple verses, so simple and banal the book is almost impossible to read, 'good tilth brings seeds/evil tilture, weedes.' Nevertheless, he mentions 27 different fruits, both tree and soft, including barberries and bullace, damsons and myrtle, medlars and mulberries.

I have said above that throughout the medieval world there was a form of international cuisine but that before the Reformation national tastes began to obtrude, or perhaps it was that people valued them more, and so praised and used them more often . Certainly it was true that the English travellers (only the nobility were rich enough to do so, unless it was the craftsmen and artists who were highly skilled enough to be given work abroad) noticed national differences in culinary taste and began to enthuse about them back home. The copious amounts of fresh fruit eaten by both Italians and Spaniards without any ill effects, the Italians' addiction to calf meat and asparagus, the frequent use of cooked cheese as an ingredient as well as the olive oil we have already mentioned, but of all these, it was perhaps the reappearance of pasta which was the most notable.

What is most striking in this age of ferment, when all the ideas seemed to be on the boil, is to discern that much of the cooking is still in the medieval mode and that those influences and the particular ingredients brought back from the Crusades five hundred years earlier are now an integral part of English cuisine. The taste for sugar has grown steadily, the discovery of the sugar cane by the Crusaders has made the sugar loaf, a tall cone of hard sugar which had to be scraped away, a part of every kitchen. Sugar like the spices[89], like rose and orange water, were expensive but were used extensively, especially now in the new fashionable banquet course. Sugar also now had such a healthy reputation (so unlike its present one)that Andrew Borde considered it to be especially nutritive making all foods that were sweet especially good for you. Sugar came from imports from Morocco and the Barbary Coast, but much of it was stolen from Spanish ships bringing it back from the West Indies. Although the taste for saffron had begun to wane, nevertheless, Sir Francis Drake thought that it made the English people sprightly, for it had gained a new reputation for its restorative properties, for so the herbalist, Gerard, had claimed. Spinach was now grown all over the land and used often with pastry, spices and cheese, artichokes and salads were grown in gardens, favourite stuffings tended to use chopped dates, pistachios, or other nuts like pine nuts and walnuts, and rice and rice flour was a standby thickener. As to pasta, so popular at the medieval court, now there is a revival of interest in it because Sir Hugh Platt is fascinated by the Italians' consumption of it in London. *Epulario* or *The Italian Banquet* by an Italian author was translated into English in 1598, though an early Venetian edition had reached England in 1549 which this gave a recipe for making pasta; a flour and water paste to be dried in the sun and boiled in broth. Another method said that the paste had to be broken into pieces, and then dried in the sun so it could be kept for two or three years.[90] One wonders whether the English climate was hot or dry enough to preserve such a food, one cannot help fearing that many an English pantry after six months had a terracotta container filled with little pieces of green mould. The fascination with Italy filled as it was with the ruins of ancient Rome, is reflected in the plays of Shakespeare and was a stimulus to rediscover some of the foods and flavours from the past.

The Rector of Radwinter
Food historians place great faith in William Harrison (1534-1593) who was the Rector of Radwinter, a small village near Saffron Walden, and who toured the British Isles and wrote a report upon his findings. He is widely quoted,

especially one section upon the food of the nobility reproduced below. Certainly, there are examples which give us useful information, but it is all highly opinionated, all eighteen chapters which range across the clothing of the poor, sundry minerals and metals, punishment, dogs and degrees of people. On that subject he divides society up into gentlemen which covers all the nobility and the professions, therefore himself (however one doubts whether the nobility would have considered a Rector of Radwinter to be quite in their class) secondly the free citizens of the cities, thirdly yeomen of the countryside and fourthly, labourers, servants and vagrants who have 'neither voice or authority'.

There is a chapter on 'Cattle kept for Profit' which is a hymn of praise to domesticated livestock, believing English cattle to be by far the best in the world. 'Kine more commodious for the pail, sheep more profitable for wool, swine more wholesome of flesh' you will not find, he declares, anywhere else. He tells us that the brawn made out of tame boars is quite unknown to the French, for when finding some in the houses of Calais, after it fell to the French at the time of Mary Tudor, they attempted to 'roast, bake, broil and fry the same'. He goes on to tell us that an English noble sent a present of brawn to a Catholic gentleman of France who thought it was fish and kept it for Lent, loved it so, and asked for more the following year. He dismisses all cooks as 'musical-headed Frenchmen and strangers', so there is little hiding of his dislike for foreigners, especially Catholics, who must perforce be all stupid.

However, within such confused observations we come across others which are interesting. Such as this one on the making of brawn which begins a year, sometimes two, before the killing of the pig: 'a whole year or two, especially in gentlemen's houses in which time he is dieted with oats and peason, and lodged on the bare planks till his fat be hardened sufficiently for their purpose: afterward he is killed, scalded, and cut out, and then of his former parts is our brawn made. The rest is nothing so fat, and therefore it beareth the name of sowse only, and is commonly reserved for the serving-man and hind, except it please the owner to have any part thereof baked, which are then handled of custom after this manner: the hinder parts being cut off, they are first drawn with lard, and then sodden; being sodden, they are soused in claret wine and vinegar a certain space, and afterward baked in pasties, and eaten of many instead of the wild boar, and truly it is very good meat: the pestles may be hanged up a while to dry before they be drawn with lard, if you will, and thereby prove the better. But hereof enough, and therefore to come again unto our brawn. The neck pieces, being cut off round, are called collars of brawn, the shoulders are named shilds, only the ribs retain the former denomination, so that these aforesaid pieces deserve the name of brawn: the bowels of the beast are commonly cast away because of their rankness, and so were likewise his stones, till a foolish fantasy got hold of late amongst some delicate dames, who have now found the means to dress them also with great cost for a dainty dish, and bring them to the board as a service among other of like sort, though not without note of their desire to the provocation of fleshly lust which by this their fond curiosity is not a little revealed. When the boar is thus cut out each piece is wrapped up, either with bulrushes, ozier, peels, tape inkle, or such like, and then sodden in a lead or caldron together, till they be so tender that a man may thrust a bruised rush or straw clean through the fat: which being done, they take it up and lay it abroad to cool. Afterward, putting it into close vessels, they pour either good small ale or beer mingled with verjuice and salt thereto till it be covered, and so let it lie (now and then altering and changing the sousing drink lest it should wax sour) till occasion serve to spend it out of way. Some use to make brawn of great barrow hogs, and seethe them, and souse the whole as they do that of the boar; and in my judgment it is the better of both, and more easy of digestion. But of brawn thus much, and so much may seem sufficient.'

Another chapter deals with Wild and Tame Fowls and again we read 'no nation under the sun hath more plenty of wild fowl than we' and he lists them: 'we have the crane, the bittern, the wild and tame swan, the bustard, the heron, curlew, snipe, wild goose, wind or doterell, brant, lark, plover (of both sorts), lapwing, teal, widgeon, mallard, sheldrake, shoveller, peewitt, seamew, barnacle, quail (who, only with man, are subject to the falling sickness), the knot, the oliet or olive, the dunbird, woodcock, partridge, and pheasant, besides divers others, whose names to me are utterly unknown, and much more the taste of their flesh, wherewith I was never acquainted.'

He tells us how seasonal game birds are; partridges and plovers are eaten in August followed by snipes and teals from September then larks, woodcocks and pheasants in October. Later he admits to loving the barnacle more than any other game bird and later still ruminates on why we do not geld other fowl like a gander, a turkey or an Indian peacock; he concludes that we do not because their flesh would grow rank. But it is the much quoted section on the food of the nobility which, I believe has given us a skewed view of Elizabethan food.

'In number of dishes and change of meat the nobility of England (whose cooks are for the most part musical-headed Frenchmen and strangers) do most exceed, sith there is no day in manner that passeth over their heads wherein they have not only beef, mutton, veal, lamb, kid, pork, cony, capon, pig, or so many of these as the season yieldeth, but also some portion of the red or fallow deer, beside great variety of fish and wild fowl, and thereto sundry other delicates wherein the sweet hand of the seafaring Portugal is not wanting: so that for a man to dine with one of them, and to taste of every dish that standeth before him (which few used to do, but each one feedeth upon that meat him best liketh for the time, the beginning of every dish notwithstanding being reserved unto the greatest personage that sitteth at the table, to whom it is drawn up still by the waiters as order requireth, and from whom it descendeth again even to the lower end, whereby each one may taste thereof), is rather to yield unto a conspiracy with a great deal of meat for the speedy suppression of natural health than the use of a necessary mean to satisfy himself with a competent repast to sustain his body withal. But, as this large feeding is not seen in their guests, no more is it in their own persons; for, sith they have daily much resort unto their tables (and many times unlooked for), and thereto retain great numbers of servants, it is very requisite and expedient for them to be somewhat plentiful in this behalf.

'The chief part likewise of their daily provision is brought in before them (commonly in silver vessels, if they be of the degree of barons, bishops, and upwards) and placed on their tables, whereof, when they have taken what it pleaseth them, the rest is reserved, and afterwards sent down to their serving men and waiters, who feed thereon in like sort with convenient moderation, their reversion also being bestowed upon the poor which lie ready at their gates in great numbers to receive the same. This is spoken of the principal tables whereat the nobleman, his lady, and guests are accustomed to sit; besides which they have a certain ordinary allowance daily appointed for their halls, where the chief officers and household servants (for all are not permitted by custom to wait upon their master), and with them such inferior guests do feed as are not of calling to associate the nobleman himself; so that, besides those afore-mentioned, which are called to the principal table, there are commonly forty or three score persons fed in those halls, to the great relief of such poor suitors and strangers also as oft be partakers thereof and otherwise like to dine hardly.'[91]

Oh really Mr Harrison what are you complaining of, you go on about this huge spread, moan you can't taste everything, but then tell us that the custom is that everyone eats the dish they like. So what is wrong with choice? What is more he speaks of the spread at the tables of the nobility, where there were often many guests and a large staff which had to be fed from the left-overs.

As William Harrison ended up as Canon of St Georges Chapel, Windsor, this may at the end of his life have softened the envy and general asperity which colour his observations on food, and he does go onto mention that the class below eat much the same, but have fewer dishes upon their tables. His description of the course after the meats again strikes me as condemnatory, 'jellies of all colours mixed with a variety in the representation of sundry flowers, herbs, trees, forms of beasts, fish, fowls and fruits, tarts of divers hues, conserves of fruits, foreign and homebred, suckets, marmelades, marchpane, sugar bread, gingerbread, Florentines...'[92] The representations he mentions he could have added were made from marchpane or marzipan, but perhaps he didn't know. He seems to enjoy listing the food without describing it, certainly never mentioning what it tastes like. Because, of course, he was not invited to eat at the tables of the nobility, so he could only stare as he surveyed the scene as an onlooker, when on some great feast, it was open to the public to congregate in a designated area and be allowed to watch the great magnates being served the food.

Harrison also never mentions the salad, and yet they grew copiously in every vegetable garden and the ingredients for it appeared to have come out of the flower garden as well, another Persian influence that the Crusaders returned with. An early sixteenth century list of herbs for the garden *The Fromond List* of 1525 gives over a hundred, but they are also divided into those for a soup, or sauce , or a drink or for distilling, or just for savour and beauty. There are twenty listed for a salad: Alexanders, Borage, Catmint, Chickweed, Chives, French cress, Daisies, Dandelion, Fennel, Heartsease, Mints, Nettle, Red Dead, Parsley, Primrose buds, Purslane, Rampion, Ramsoms, Rocket, Violets salad Burnet and other cresses.[93] The earliest salad recipe dates from 1393. 'Take parsley, sage, garlic, chibols, (now referred to as Welsh onion) onions, leek, borage, mints, porray, fennel and garden cresses, rue, rosemary, purslain; wash them clean, pluck them small with thine hand and mingle them well with raw oil. Lay on vinegar and salt and serve them forth.' One could hardly think of a more delicious salad today. Porray was a name for leek or the green leaves of any allium or for a soup based on green leaves. As the Elizabethan age loved Italy and gardens, they also loved garden produce and salads, herbs and spices were very much in this category, one imagines a salad would have been part of the daily diet, but perhaps there was no liking for it, similar to the dismissal today in the majority of the population for a five fruits and vegetables per day regime. There was a case of a wealthy woman curing herself of ailments through, the physician tells us, 'her own wit'. She took a salad ten times a day that she had concocted from watercress, sowthistles, wild sage, parsley, betony, millefoile followed by a drink made from barley, wormwood, marigolds, sage, sowthistle, Alexander roots, parsley, aniseed, fennel, chicory boiled in three gallons of clear water till half boiled away.[94]

Harrison does not describe the way a dish has been cooked or flavoured, so we get the impression of plain cooking, meats just roasted not even stuffed; the manner of flavouring pies and tarts does not seem to interest him, as if he never tastes this food. He leaves us with an impression of too much food cooked without skill or pleasure, bland and ultimately uninteresting, which is an appalling portrait of our food at this time and, I believe, has been responsible for much of the bad press our national food has garnered. A glance at contemporary recipes tells us a different story: A capon cooked with oranges (they were the sharp variety) its peel, mace, cinnamon, rosemary, ginger, butter, prunes and currants being added to a stuffing. Artichoke Pie, where the bottoms and hearts are poached in white wine with added sugar, ginger, orange peel and mace until just tender; stir in minced dates and raisins, arrange in pastry shell, cover with a little butter and bake in oven. (*The Good Housewife's Handmaid for Cookery in her Kitchen*, 1597.) Fillets of Beef, seasoned with pepper, salt, cinnamon, ginger, butter cooked inside pastry. Baking a Gammon, par-boil it first, then take the rind off and stuff the ham with cloves, then season with pepper and saffron and bake it inside pastry. To stew oysters, take out of their shells, place in a skillet with their liquor, add butter, verjuice, pepper and tops of thyme, let them boil a little then serve on sops. (These three recipes from *The Good Housewife's Jewel* by Thomas Dawson). All of these recipes and many more are very much to our own taste, there is nothing bland or plain about this style of cooking, they reflect an age of aesthetics and adventure.

Let us imagine a dinner, which the good rector would never have seen, for the Queen given by her favourite in his extensive Italian gardens one summer evening. A table has been arranged for a small gathering of perhaps twenty courtiers, on a piazza with two side tables at each side, one laden with the food, the other with wine, the whole is alive with flickering torchlight, though there is no need for the sun has not set. There has been dancing, but there are musicians hidden in the garden still playing, above the table for the occasion there are branches festooned with garlands of flowers and fruit. The tables are draped with heavy linen cloths, napkins are folded like flowers, the glass is Venetian, and sugar sculptures of Venus, Cupid and Bacchus are at the centre of each table. The diners wash their hands in perfumed water, on the table already there are the finest manchet rolls and several small cold dishes to merely whet the appetite, oysters chopped and tossed in verjuice, honey and ginger, sturgeon roe, sautéed quail breasts, fish livers fried with orange, cinnamon and sugar, scallops roasted on picks, tiny pastries stuffed with truffles, lobsters fried in butter .... a girl sings a madrigal, while the table is cleared and the next course arrives, a roasted boar stuffed with fruits and truffles, a great game pie, filleted breams in a white wine and garlic sauce ... courtier plays a lute solo, there are salads of minced carrots and shrimps, others of chives, scallions, purslane and radish, yet others of asparagus and cucumbers, marigolds, spinach, lettuce and violets, dressed with oil and rosewater. A courtier dressed as Orpheus sings to a lyre and then led by dancers bearing torches they stroll to the banqueting house, newly built with views across the parkland and there is another astonishing array of sweet foods piled high around sugar sculptures.

In the Italian renaissance they brought the art of dining to a fine peak and their style soon influenced the whole of courtly Europe. The Elizabethan court danced, sang and ate in the Italian manner, but as they always had and always will, somehow adjusted it all with their own national idiosyncrasies.

The Seeds of Empire

Unlike the beginnings of the Spanish Empire our own did not start with a search for pepper and the Spice Islands, which ended with the discovery of gold and silver mines. As our own empire is such a vital part of our own gastronomic story, how it began should be briefly told. In one word – piracy. Our navy as William Harrison tells us was divided into three, ships for war, ships for trading and the rest were used for fishing, which was why the cinque ports on the south coast were still important, and why at least three Acts of Parliament had to ensure that fish days, on Wednesday and Friday, were kept by the public to ensure that fishermen had enough income to spend on keeping their vessels seaworthy for the defence of the realm when necessary; eating fish was part of the war effort.

The last course of the meal for the nobility was the banqueting course with a fantastic array of sweetmeats. As sugar was a luxury item a course built solely upon it reflected the great wealth of the host, especially as you also had a new room or building created especially for it. 'The combination of elaborate sculptural creations in sugar, with sweetmeats, fruit and nuts, all highly finished in naturalistic colours or gilded with gold leaf were the most magnificent assemblies of dishes ever to have been presented on English tables.'[95] There would be dried sweetmeats and suckets of oranges, lemons, citron, conserves and candies, rock candies of cherries, apricots, damsons, pippins, angelica, marigold flowers, raspberries, jellies and creams, made from quince, plums, gooseberries, almonds, clotted cream, snow cream, fresh cheese, syllabubs, egg pies, custards, white pots, fools, tarts and marchpane.

The popularity of these meant a huge demand for sugar, which in the past had been grown in the Levant and on Cyprus controlled by the Venetian empire and then also in North Africa and Sicily in Muslim-controlled lands. In the sixteenth century most of the sugar producing areas were controlled by Catholic Spain and their navy was constantly vigilant in policing the seas. The first sugar plantation that was reliant on black slaves was developed by a Genoese, Antonio da Noli on the Cape Verde Islands in the 1460s, so successful was this experiment that others sprang up the following century in the New World. But what drove the voyages of English sailors like Sir Richard Greville and Francis Drake to cross the Atlantic was the search for gold. The Virgin Queen had a notorious love of gold, silver and precious stones, and the fact that sometimes they boarded a Spanish ship and found it stuffed only with sugar must have been disappointing, yet as it was now the most expensive item in the kitchen, it was a cargo worth stealing. An English ship returning to Bristol or Plymouth with a cargo of sugar was still a great prize.

In world exploration food was secondary then to the search for gold, but it still meant that roots were put down on the coast of Virginia, West Africa and India which, though fighting with both the Portuguese and the French over such settlements was inevitable within the next two hundred years, concluded in territorial possessions which would become part of the British Empire. These added new ingredients and dishes to the British food repertoire for both good and ill. But it was in the Queen's tacit acknowledgment of the most blatant piracy on the high seas that it all began, if *she* had not taken such an amoral stance the empire may well have gone to another nation altogether.[96]

Take for example, curries. We were because of British India the first country outside the sub-continent to be so heavily influenced by those spice mixtures, by hot ketchups, and rice as an alternative to bread, such influences appearing at the end of the seventeenth century and being welcomed because of our early addiction to spices brought back by the Crusaders. It is one of the mysteries of the English character, that we seem to be so easily seduced by quite alien tastes and embrace them very readily, bringing them home and Anglicising them. But without the empire none of it could have happened. However, I think one has to go back a little further.

I believe that as we are mostly Norman in our genetic inheritance we have a natural adventurous spirit in matters of travel and taste. As they did for those few hundred years at the midst of the medieval age, we explore and take what we like, a somewhat piratical approach to other cultures.

The Queen

She, of course, is the essence of the zeitgeist of this age, which drove the latter part of the sixteenth century, for though the Queen was modest in her personal dining habits, she was excessively flattered (which she knew to be her right) by the culinary celebrations, the pomp, masques and happenings of her entertainments which were *de rigeur* in her processions around her realm. 'Where the Queen paraded through a country town, almost every Pageant was a Pantheon; even the pastrycooks were expert mythologists: at dinner select transformations of Ovid's *Metamorphoses* were exhibited in confectionery and the splendid icing of an immense plumb cake was embossed with a delicious *basso-rilievo* of the destruction of Troy.'[97]

The art of the cook is hymned by Ben Johnson in a Masque, *Neptune's Triumph* written for the court for twelfth night in 1594.

'A master cook! why, he is the man of men,
He's a professor; he designs, he draws,
He paints, he carves, he builds, he fortifies,
Makes citadels of curious fowls and fish.
Some he dry-ditches, some moats round with broth/
    Mounts marrow-bones, cuts fifty-angled custards,
Rears bulwark pies; and, for his outer works,
He raiseth ramparts of immortal crust...'

Such astonishing skill and imagination employed for the royal presence – one wonders with so much emphasis put upon the visual aesthetics that flavour might be sacrificed. But as we have seen there was, because of the still room, a new emphasis upon flavour too.

As the royal progress always included much feasting ending with the multiplicity of desserts in the banqueting houses, there can be little doubt that at this time the divine-regal fusion that is the driving force in gourmet food reached its apogee. The Virgin Queen herself was surely the main stimulus to this movement, for she was the most educated, cultured and intelligent of all our monarchs, but the general creativity of the age could not help but respond, and they did so in astonishing ways.

Take the Earl of Leicester's entertainments when Elizabeth visited him in July 1575, eighteen years after she became queen and Robert Leicester still being her main favourite; while walking through the grounds she came upon a large pool where a mermaid swam with a tail so long she was all of eighteen feet. Another masked figure, Triton, who called himself a servant of Neptune was restraining the mermaid and allowed her to be misused by a cruel knight, Sir Bruse Sauns Pitee. The Triton spoke and asked, would the Queen deign to cast her reflection upon the waters, then and only then, could she effect the deliverance of the mermaid out of her thralldom. The second the Queen leant over the lake, the bands around the mermaid dissolved and she floated towards the Queen and declared that her Majesty's presence had so graciously wrought her deliverance.[98] The Queen did not even have to walk across the water, she merely had to lean over it to prove her divinity and hence to create the miracle. Food for such a goddess must indeed be made up of nectar and ambrosia, and later in her stroll around Kenilworth Park she was offered it. A temporary bridge had been built over the main court with seven pairs of pillars bearing offerings to the Queen, and guarded by gods and goddesses. Crowning the first pair of pillars were large cages containing live bitterns, curlews, hernshaws, godwits, and such dainty birds, offered her by Sylvanus, god of woodfowl. The next pair bore two huge silver bowls with pears, apples, cherries, filberts, walnuts, all fresh on the branches, the gift of Pomona, and on the pair following, wheat in ears, oats and barley, waved from the bowls. After these, two pillars bore a huge silver bowl, filled with purple and white grapes, and, opposite, huge pots of silver filled with claret and white wine.[99] A scene fit for a goddess, yet I can't help feeling that this intelligent woman must have found many elements of it all rather tiresome.

But perhaps not, for Lord Leicester writing to the Earl of Sussex in 1574 expressed with resigned distaste: 'we all do what we can to persuade Her Majesty from any progress at all.' No wonder when you read of the food that had to be collected from the surrounding countryside, seas and rivers for a short stay, for example when the Queen honoured Lord North with a visit from Monday the 1st of September arriving for supper to the Wednesday following, leaving after dinner. The cooks had prepared: '1,200 manchets, 3,600 cheatbreads, 74 hogsheads of beer, 2 tons of ale, 20 gallons of sack, 1 hogshead of vinegar, 11 steers and oxen, 66 muttons, 17 veals, 7 lambs, 34 pigs, 32 geese, 30 dozen capons, 6 turkeys, 32 swans, 9 mallards, 1 crane, 12 shovellers, 125 pigeons, 68 godwyts, 17 gulls, 8 dozen dotterels, 8 snipes, 28 plovers, 18 redshanks, 12 partridges, 1 pheasant, 27 dozen quails, 8 dozen conies, 4 stags made into 48 pasties, 16 bucks, made into 128 pasties, 8 gammons of bacon, 24 pounds of lard, 21 neat tongues, feet and udders, 430 pounds of butter, 2 thousand five hundred eggs, 4 dozen crayfishes, 8 turbots, a cartload and 2 horseloads of oysters, 1 barrel of anchovies, 2 pikes, 2 carps, 4 tenches, 12 perches, 4 hundred red herring, 6 holland cheeses, 10 marchpanes, 6 gallons of hippocras.' [100] The last two items would be for the banquet course, but little else is there for this which is puzzling. Also I wonder who ate the one pheasant. And in all this plethora of game there is no bustard or peacock. But the Queen at the centre of this huge gathering must have loved the devotion and the attention of the assembled multitude for, if not, she would have taken her favourite's advice and stopped the progresses altogether. After all, here she was seen by her subjects to eat, she was almost in that sense one of them, and I think, knowing Elizabeth's character in all its complications, she liked, even needed this intimacy and togetherness.

It could be said that for Elizabeth the ritual was perhaps more divine than the food. Indeed, if her daily food was modest, the ritual which accompanied it was of such august splendour it seems to us quite astonishing. Visitors could watch this event even though it began with an empty space – the dining hall, which now, when trumpets sounded and kettle drums rolled, turned into a theatre or a church as a noble retainer entered carrying a gilded rod followed by another with a tablecloth. Towards the dining table they knelt three times with the utmost veneration, the tablecloth was spread, the rod passed over it smoothing any invisible wrinkles, then they knelt again and retired. Now two other retainers entered, one carrying another rod, while the second had a salt cellar, gilded plates and bread; they also knelt before placing the objects upon the table, they retired after obeisance. Now a countess entered, followed by another, one was unmarried the other married carrying a tasting knife, the first was dressed in white silk; they prostrated themselves three times, then they approached the table and rubbed the plates with bread and salt 'with as much awe as if the Queen was present'. They then waited, still as statues; the audience waited, still as statues, perhaps now the Queen would enter, everyone waited. But no, the yeomen of the guards now entered, bare headed, clothed in scarlet, with the Tudor heraldic golden rose upon his back, leading other guards who each brought in a dish, placed it upon the table and uncovered it. Now the lady taster gave to each of the guards a mouthful to eat, so that all the dishes were checked for poison. This was not done in silence, throughout twelve trumpets and two kettle drums continued to play making the hall resound with triumphant fanfares for half an hour altogether. After the tasting, two maids of honour appeared and carried the dishes away into the privy chamber where the Queen chose one or two, the rest of the food went to the ladies of the court. [101]

'This extraordinary display has to be considered in the context of a country where there were no longer altars nor Christ's presence in the bread and wine.

The altar in a sense had become the royal table and the mass the royal dinner,' wrote Sir Roy Strong in *Feast*.[102] He is right of course, but I see it also as the culmination of the divine food for a monarch which we noted at the beginning of the worship of the gods in the refined flour used for cakes thousands of years before. In the Renaissance this reached its zenith, the meal becomes a vehicle to celebrate the divinity of monarchs, though in public they are rarely seen to eat. At a state banquet at the papal court, the pope eats alone on a dais which is a little higher than anyone else, if another monarch is present, then he too eats alone on another dais to one side. Strong goes on to point out that the connection between royal eating in public when it does happen and significantly, on days of holy feasting, is the action of the mass which began at the Burgundian court, was carried on by the Habsburg descendants and from there spread over Europe.

When Philip II of Spain married Mary Tudor in 1554 and came to England, the dining ritual had to be learnt, for it occurred four times a year in public, but if some small mistake was made, the Spanish were mortally offended. Elizabeth changed all this by her progresses, making herself visible to her subjects. The great irony is that both the Stuart monarchs that were to follow Elizabeth, James and Charles, proclaimed the divinity of kings, and it destroyed them and finally their dynasty.

The use of bread and salt which we now consider as being specifically Jewish is interesting at this time, showing how an English monarch's rituals are so deeply rooted in the Old Testament. This is an imitation, of course, of Temple ritual, where offerings are prepared with salt. But it alludes to Genesis 3: 19. 'By the sweat of your brow, shall you get bread to eat…' salt represents the sweat. Also, bread and salt are regarded as a pair because the Hebrew words 'lechem' & 'malach' are both spelled from the same three letters.

In this ritual, copied in almost all ways from her father, the Queen makes one significant change, the greatest change of all, certainly the most dramatic. The Queen is invisible. While Henry ate in public beneath a canopy surrounded by a hundred retainers eager to fulfil every desire, watched by an adoring public, the Queen ate in private, hidden from public gaze. Like God she was invisible and mysterious; no monarch before or afterwards, had such mystique.

CHAPTER EIGHT

Comfort, Pleasure and Security

It is this comfort, pleasure and security, that the middle classes desire from their food. All the working classes want is to stop feeling hungry. While all the upper classes desire from food is that it is seen to be wasted. A great boost to the power and influence of the middle classes and the rise of women's domination of food styles was given by those Cromwellian years when Britain became a republic. The term 'middle classes' had not yet been coined then, it first appeared in the early part of the nineteenth century when there was huge ferment and threatened rebellion over the Reform Bill.

The Interregnum

This was a pre-industrial society which was quickly moving towards one, for it was on the move, indeed over half the population died in a different parish from the one that they were born in, and in one Worcestershire village 80 per cent of the 75 surnames disappeared from the parish records between 1666 and 1750.[103] Forget the myth of a rural society with villages where families have lived for centuries, this was a society where people left home for work yes, but also to improve their lot, they were searching for the good life, which is yet another reason for demanding from their food qualities of reassurance.

But under Stuart rule in the seventeenth century there is also revolt as the middle classes are gaining ground – literally. As we have seen they first gain notoriety after the Black Death, such a fracture within society allowed social mobility and the entrepreneurs took their chance and with it aped the food tastes, as much as their income allowed, of the elite. Now several hundred years later and with the advent of books and their continuing publication, they are strengthened by education and knowledge, but their real advantage, as the governing elite always knows, is wealth. It is that factor which keeps the social order and the elite in their place – at the top. That is until the excesses of the Stuarts which toppled the elite and for a short time led to the middle classes governing society.

The monarchy and the social structure which supported it had engendered hostile criticism for some time; a Scottish observer had commented in 1614 on the 'bitter and distrustful' attitude of English people towards the gentry and nobility.' By 1600 food cost five times as much as it had in 1500, due primarily to the monopoly system which had been allowed to grow unchecked, as it enriched the monarchy and nobility. A series of Tudor Poor Laws were enacted between 1531 and 1601 to try and deal with the growing number of beggars and paupers. In the sixteenth century as population rapidly expanded in England (from 2.6 million in 1500 to 5.6 million in 1650), 'London became the refuge of masterless men – the victims of enclosures, vagabonds, criminals – to an extent that alarmed contemporaries.'[104] Between 1500 and 1650 London's population had increased from fifty-five thousand to two hundred thousand and London quickly became a hotbed of crime and dissolution, as for the scroundrel it now was what the greenwood had been for the medieval outlaw. It was obvious that government led by the monarchy could not restrain this criminal underclass which stemmed after all from gross poverty, starvation and oppression, there had to be answers and surely one of the answers lay in a consistent and adequate food supply for all people and not just a few.

There were some remarkable men and women who led the thinking at this time in the second quarter of the century, and their anxieties have echoes for our own problems today. Much of the new thinking was led by Samuel Hartlib (c.1600–62) who was a Prussian who came to England in the mid-1620s, to the University of Cambridge, having been exiled from Germany because of the Thirty Years War. He believed that the reform of education and philosophy might lead to universal improvement and peace. He was part of a much wider movement towards fundamental enquiries, new thinkers who speculated about the end of the world, about the justice of God in condemning men to eternal torment, some becoming sceptical about the existence of hell. Some even considered that there might be no creator at all. They attacked the monopolisation of knowledge within the privileged professions, divinity, law and medicine. They criticised the existing educational structure especially the universities and proposed education for all. These were the intellectual quests that partly fuelled the Civil War. But the passion which provoked and sustained the war between parliamentarians and the monarchy was the monopoly system.

In 1621 there was alleged to be seven hundred of them. The social mobility in the Tudor age, which could lead to fortunes being made by entrepreneurs, induced unease within the nobility, who sought to create methods by which this free market could be controlled and exploited. Monopolies were available to those with court influence and patronage, the producers of rock salt for example had to bribe courtiers to get a charter of incorporation and thus courtiers gained control of a new company.

Food was completely controlled by separate monopolies, companies which owned salmon or lobster or red herrings, butter, currants, the wine and spirit trade, for example, were controlled by them. The bricks and glass in a man's house was owned by them, the coal in his fire, the tapestries on his wall, the soap, lace, linen, leather and gold thread. In 1612 the Earl of Salisbury was receiving £7,000 a year from the silk monopoly, the Earl of Suffolk £5,000 from currants, the Earl of Northampton £4,500 from starch. But it was the Exchequer that was principally enriched – by 1630 monopolies brought in a hundred thousand each year. As prices inevitably rose public fury was incensed to learn that not only was the monarch taking a hefty percentage but in the case of the soap monopoly so were foreign papists. It is interesting to note how this subject divided the warring parties in the Civil War. The affluent bourgeoisie who held court-granted monopolies in shoes, cloth and gloves were all Royalists, while the nobility who had been refused a monopoly by the court system joined the Parliamentarians. The manner in which a man worshipped his God hardly seemed to enter this decision.

For men like Samuel Hartlib there was no question about which side could further his educational plans. He had a wide circle of friends and acquaintances, landowners, farmers and food producers whom he wrote to asking for their advice and experiences; he remained committed throughout his career to the extension of empirical knowledge, and the application of practical solutions to problems of the day. They worked on ideas to improve the food supply, meat, fruit and fuel, working on new breeds of livestock and plants, and he urged his friends to write books, to disseminate the information they were gathering. They did so, Walter Blith wrote on arable farming in 1653, *The English Improver Improved*, or *The Survey of Husbandry Surveyed* – an endearing title that makes one long for a Restoration Comedy. Then there was Ralph Austin who believed in the compulsory planting of orchards and wrote a treatise upon it which was also published in 1653 and which ran into several editions. He thought that if peasants were compelled to plant their own trees they would be less likely to steal the trees or fruits from others; he also thought that the prunings would provide valuable fuel. 'Fuel is grown exceeding scarce and dear and will certainly be much more scarce hereafter if men be not more diligent in planting.' Undoubtedly, Austen made a difference, as there is a letter to the secretary of the Royal Society from Anthony Lawrence in 1677 which praises Austen for the planting of orchards around Oxford and suggests that the same might be done for Cambridge.

Finally there was John Beale, a vegetarian (but only in the summer) and enthusiast for salads, pulses and herbs, who wrote extensively on cider production. 'The lower and broad spreading tree is the greater bearer, by reason the blossoms in the Spring are not so obvious to the bitter blasts, nor the fruit in the autumn to the fierce and destructive winds.' *Aphorisms concerning Cider*, 1664.

These years of the interregnum, of Britain as a republic spurred individual thinkers to consider in depth the problems that beset society. They aimed for more variety of food, suggested the domestic rearing of rabbits in hutches, farming pheasants and partridges, keeping bees and growing more interesting vegetables like artichoke and asparagus beds, for they maintained that vegetables and fruits were just as life sustaining as meat and fish, so the very poor should never go hungry. Adam Speed in 'Adam out of Eden' suggested growing pumpkins, musk melons and roots, herbs, pulses and the new kidney beans. Hartlib believed that education and the reform of knowledge provided the means to purge minds of stubbornness and conceit, he was convinced of the special nature of the times through which they were living, and worked arduously towards a positive future.[105]

There was in the thought of the time a new emphasis upon the people, with the groups that sprang up, the Levellers, Diggers, the Quakers, even the Ranters. There was a revaluation of the individual as a person worthy of respect, as needing a piece of God's earth to grow food and with it, a respect for the plants, the animals and the food itself. The books on food that were published were as full of recipes for curing ailments as for dishes to consume, but the former relied on the herbs and plants that the experience of the still room had taught them two generations before. Thomas Hobbes was to stress that change was important in stimulating mental activity and this world with its violent Civil War, the execution of a king, the wars in Ireland and Scotland, the spell of bad weather from 1646-51 which destroyed harvests and livestock year after year, where cattle disease spread, the rye was killed by April frosts and the fruit rotted on the trees, was one where change was both rapid, radical and painful.

The effect on the quality of food production was frustrated by the restoration of the monarchy, but their ideas lived on and were employed in future decades. Too often their remarkable work on our food and diet in this too short an era is entirely forgotten and the Puritans are traduced in popular myth as mammoth spoilsports who attempted to get rid of Christmas pudding and were the first to start a decline in British food. It is nonsense. The idea that they banned festivities including the making of Christmas pudding and mince pies is particularly silly. It stems from before the Protectorate in the midst of the Civil War when a Puritan junta was in charge, which was nervous of public festivals as they allowed great crowds to meet and they feared such events hid dissident rebellion. When Cromwell became Lord Protector such attitudes were relaxed, but even then in May 1655 a garlanded maypole in Bethnal Green aroused such a pitch of excitement that it attracted a great crowd, which the troops had to disperse. Christmas continued to be celebrated throughout the Interregnum. Both bear baiting and cock fighting were banned outright, it is true, but bear baiting was dangerous causing human injury and the gambling that inevitably occurred caused much mayhem and disorder, but naturally they continued secretly and then once the Restoration happened they flourished again. Another related myth is the banning of theatre performances, indeed there was an attempt to do so, for reasons which contemporary views would tend to agree with. Boys played the women still and such boys were notorious catamites, selling their favours for a high price; indeed because the King's father, James I was an enthusiastic client of such boys, the theatre got a name for unspeakable debauchery tinged with Cavalier connections. However, the ban was ignored, private performances continued in all the great houses, notably Holland House in Kensington. But once Cromwell came to power, society became far more tolerant reflecting his own personality. Music, dancing, food, were all unchanged from the Stuart days, in fact Cromwell drew around him a flourishing culture including writers of genius, not only Milton, but John Aubrey, Dryden and John Locke, while in his years the first English opera was composed and performed – *The Siege of Rhodes*. The music was composed by five different composers, the performances were held at Rutland House and appearing was the first professional actress, a Mrs Coleman.

Antonia Fraser in her biography of Cromwell comments that he brought to the role... 'a grandeur both of condition and of attitude which was not unacceptable to the country as a whole. Some of this must be attributable to his own personal character, and the fact that he was in no sense a killjoy, nor indeed in any way "Puritanical"in the modern, pejorative sense of the word. Here was a man who not only demonstrably enjoyed the English gentleman's pleasures of hawking and hunting, but also saw nothing wrong in pleasure as such.' After all, he introduced into England the habit of drinking port at the end of dinner, while he encouraged dancing, music and poetry.

It is not then too surprising that out of this maelstrom should come the desire to eat food which comforted body and soul, which was nourishing, which was solid, which came from the land around Britain and seemed to promise stability. This is the food we exported both in the memory of the new settlers in Virginia and in their scraps of written recipes. For the first settlements that clung precariously in the New World, underscored by a fierce and passionate faith, celebrated their new life with dishes to remind them of their roots. This was food for the majority, not the elite, for they ate much the same, in times of war and campaigning in rough countryside food is what you can pillage and combine together quickly. So though the administrative force which garnered and provided the food is solidly middle class and their taste permeates the character of it, this is food for all classes for that short time of the Interregnum. However, afterwards, as more great afflictions came, including the great fire in London, but also the affluence from a growing industrial society, though still in its infancy, the middle classes because of their huge buying power, then as now, became the main consumer, their influence was all pervasive down to the last crumb they ate.

How to be a Lady

Gustatory ambitions were no longer dedicated to succouring the divine within the monarch and had certainly vanished within religious ritual, now the subtext was concern with the niceties of food and dining, how to prepare and cook dishes, which were the correct ones in society, so that the middle classes who had the money to buy the books could know how to behave at table. What is more they would be told how to behave at home in front of their servants so that they could appear as refined as the nobility. No one ever asks whether the nobility were refined or not, but appearances were all.

Until the end of the century books of etiquette were repeating the same message, fingers should not be wiped on tablecloths, food once bitten should not be dipped into the salt cellar, soup must not be audibly eaten nor blown upon to cool it, bones should not be tossed to the dogs, forks, introduced at the beginning of the century, should not be used as toothpicks and above all diners must not belch, hawk, spit or scratch their heads at table.

Underlying this drive for social improvement was also the desire for comfort food and in a simple way pleasuring the body in all its many and complicated needs; this was never stated, but nevertheless it is the underlying character of the food that the middle class provides for itself. They had certainly become aware of one of the most comforting of all foods by Cromwell's army, who campaigning in Ireland had come across fields of potatoes, which were unharmed even when they marched across them or battled over them – the tubers could still be dug up, boiled and eaten.[106] Some now grew in Lancashire and by the turn of the century they had spread around London in Hackney.

But there was a third factor present within these books and in fact it is the most obvious one – Protestant morality, the urge towards self-improvement in the woman's godly character, which we find strongly presented in Gervase Markham's *English Hus-wife* (1615). In this book he delineates 'the inward and outward virtues that ought to be in a compleat woman'. She must be skilful in physic, cookery, banqueting stuff, distillation, wool, hemp, flax, diaries, brewing, baking and all things that belonged to the household. She must also be of great modesty and temperance, she must shun all violence of rage towards her husband 'coveting less to direct than be directed'. She must be pleasant, amiable and delightful. Markham goes onto to remark upon the woman's clothing, her garments 'should be comely, clean and strong, made as well to preserve the health as adorn the person altogether without toyish garnishes or the gloss of light colours and as far from the variety of new and fantastic fashions as near to the comely imitations of modest matrons.' Markham was a farmer and a writer, a poet and dramatist. Likened to Shakespeare in his lifetime, he wrote books on horse management and farming, in his recipes in the medicinal section he in fact adds horse dung and urine to the list of ingredients, but then his popularity was partly accounted for because he stressed the economies in housekeeping, believing there was a use for everything that was at hand.

The idea of 'the Good Wife' commanded a lot of attention in this century. It was, I believe, because the concept of the male and female gender was beginning to shift, and men sensing this had to define ' the wife' anew. Thomas Fuller in *The Holy and the Profane State* (1642) defines her as obedient to her husband, keeps home, the clothes are comely rather than costly, she will not divulge her husband's secrets or infirmities, her children are quiet. Biblical authority is cited that men are superior to women. Anything less than this one suspects and the woman becomes a shrew. Does one glimpse a happy marriage or a smug husband when the poet Richard Braithwaite (1588 -1673) hymns his wife's virtues. 'Oft have I seen her from the Dairy come/attended by her maids, and hasting home/to entertain some guests of quality/she would assume a state so modestly/sance affection, as she struck the eye/with admiration of the stander by.'

Another glimpse of hospitality in the country is given to us when the unexpected guest protested against giving trouble by his arrival. He did not want the lady of the house to take too much trouble with his dinner. She replied. 'Not a whit, sir, you must be contented with country fare. You shall have neither red deer, marchpane nor sturgeon, nor any courtier's fare, but an egg, a sallet, a Pullet or a piece of lamb washed down with our country wine.'[107] Here obviously was a countrywoman who brewed her own wine from their few vines, who knew exactly the quality of her mind and life and obviously despised those fashionable foods which others affect.

The urge to improve the mind and body resonates in the books published in this century, as if the nobility were well known for their energy and health. In 1615 *A New Book of Cookery* was republished which is a new edition of a favourite Elizabethan book filled with medicinal recipes as well as some distinctly odd dishes like a tart of borage flowers, followed two years later in 1617 by a *Daily Exercise for Ladies and Gentlemen*. The exercise seems to be in the art of making pastes, preserves, marmelades, conserves, tartstuffes, jellies, breads, sucket candies, cordial waters, among much else. Health was a great concern, the relationship between food and well being was recognised and it engendered much thought, physicians wrote books on the subject; one, John Hart, was angered by quack doctors, women healers and parsons who thought they knew about medicine, as well as over feeding and piling too many clothes on patients in bed. It was an age when there was much anxiety about food, for the food supply could never be secured when bad weather destroyed harvests so completely – the year 1630 was a year of famine in the Midlands.

The new cookery books and the books that follow them are all socially aspirational, they teach the middle class housewife how to be a noblewoman. But then all cookery books, which one can class as self-improvement manuals, come down to this. Present ones teach the reader how to be a celebrity, or to pretend to be one for an evening, but then and now, I am sure, the books were also a stimulus to dreams and fantasy, 'how life might be if only...'

Eight cookery books appeared in the 1650s and five were by members of the nobility or servants in their households. One of the most popular purported to be the recipes used by Queen Henrietta Maria, the widow of Charles I, *The*

Queen's Closet Opened compiled by one W.M. It was first published during the Interregnum which possibly helped its popularity, and consisted of three books: *The Pearl of Practice* which was solely medical, *A Queen's Delight*, concerned only with the banquet course and the *Compleat Cook*, compiled of culinary recipes. W.M. claims to have transcribed the recipes for the Queen into a book and these papers were preserved by him throughout the many difficulties of the time. There is an element of truth in all this as some of the recipes are so obviously ones which need several kitchen servants to cook it at all.

Take for example the instructions for a pie. 'Take four tame pigeons trussed and four ox palates well boiled, blanched and cut into small pieces; also six lamb stones, as many good sweet-breads, cut in halves and parboiled, twenty cockscombs boiled and blanched, the bottoms of four artichokes, a pint of oysters parboiled and bearded, and the marrow of three bones, seasoning all with mace, nutmeg and salt. Afterward lay your meat in a coffin of fine paste proportional to the quantity thereof; put half a pound of butter upon it and a little water into the pie before it be set in the oven. Let it stand in the oven an hour and a half, then having drawn it, pour out the butter at the top of the pie and put into it gravy, butter and lemons and serve it up.'

One of the most vivid impressions one gains in flicking through these pages is that the food derives from a country rich in dairy produce. The amount of cream, cheese, milk and eggs which is added to recipes is certainly excessive. To make fine pancakes without butter or lard you simply add pints of cream to the beaten eggs. To finish cooking boiled artichokes, you add a pint of cream to the sauce. The other impression is that recipes like for example a Bisque of Carp rely on a huge amount of other ingredients other than the carp farmed from your own pond – on oysters, anchovies, the carp offal, 12 egg yolks, cloves, mace, white wine, pepper, nutmeg, salt, sweet onion, lemon, oranges and pickled barberries. This indeed, is court cooking, and I imagine the Jacobean housewife read it with pleasure, then made a mental note that she might cook it for next Christmas Eve, then perhaps wondered whether that poor queen ever could sit at a dinner table when it was served with a calves head (after the king had been executed that is) and then she ordered the cook to serve a plain pea soup. It is likely that the book though authentic in reproducing many recipes had others added by the author; garlic is quite commonly used as a flavouring, which the ladies of the court would have avoided, for example. It was the most popular book of the time, for by 1680 it had gone into nine editions, and with Sir Kenelm Digby's book upon the same subject, it crystallised court Jacobean cooking forever. That both books were also compiled and written by devoted Roman Catholics would not have been obvious to the general reader, yet such cooking as excessive as the new baroque churches kept medieval traditions alive.

This was an age when gender was being re-examined, when the role of women was being re-assessed and new ideas about it were being expressed. Mary Evelyn, the daughter of the diarist gave her opinion that women were not born to read or censure the learned, their job was to care for children's education, observe their husband's commands, assist the sick and relieve the poor. She was up at six in the morning for prayers then she breakfasted off a pint of cold ale or a cup of sack, a homemade syrup and a mouthful of bread, then she was off on her duties. She first of all inspected the dairy, viewed the milk, butter and cheese, tasted it all, talked over any problems, checked that everything was spotless and clean. It was realised by then that dairies had to be constantly washed down or else there was trouble, moulds you never wanted and everything had to be thrown away. Then onto the fish ponds to see that the water was running, that the weeds were kept in check, that the supply of perch and carp were as it should be and to give any orders for the coming week on the supplies needed. Then to the dovecote to talk about feed, how the birds were fattening up and again what was needed for the coming week. We can tell how popular, perhaps even commonplace, pigeon was in the diet because so many elegant dovecotes were built at this time – both Wren and Wycherley designed them – both round and octagonal with glazed lanterns and cupolas. Their size varied, a small one had 200 nest holes while the most common were ones which had 365 nest holes, one for each day of the year. Then we must not forget the poultry yard and the girl that looked after the eggs, chickens, ducks and geese. Mary still had time for music and embroidery and an inspection of the still-room.

Sadly Mary died young from the smallpox, and her father wrote to her sister warning her of 'trash and sweetmeats which have chiefly been the cause of Mary's death. She ate those filthy things so constantly at My Lady Falkland's that it was impossible to overcome the tough phlegm they had bred in her.' Evelyn was obviously not a fan of the banquet course, but it was then in decline. In a book *Mundus Muliebris* Evelyn praised the virtues of Mary, her modesty, frugality, her good housekeeping, all the qualities, he claimed, that men looked for in a woman.[108]

It was rightly said that until Queen Anne's reign (1702-14), a wife had been little more than the best of servants, for upon marriage she lost the power over her own person, her will and her goods, depending on her husband for her happiness and all the necessities of life. Queen Anne died in 1714 and the Hanoverian dynasty began when change in a woman's status would then occur. But first let us look at the food of the seventeenth century.

The Food Itself

After the Restoration of 1660, when one examines household books of the time and looks at what people actually ate, it is surprising how little the style of food has changed from the medieval meal. There are still two courses with many dishes of meat and fish which in their character are difficult to distinguish between, followed by a sweet course which at the beginning of the century attempts to follow exactly the sumptuousness of the banquet, but only the very rich and noble can do this.

Thick, nourishing soups and broths were a daily staple for the working and the middle classes, broths made out of meat bones and poultry carcasses with root vegetables, carrots, turnips, onions and leeks, favourite herbs being sage, thyme, marjoram, rosemary and mint, which were in constant use in the kitchen. Farm workers with their own cottage had a plot of land to grow their vegetables and herbs and they kept a cow and some hens to supply milk and eggs, some also kept bees and a pig. They could also snare wild game, birds, rabbits and hares, and fish until the Game Act of 1671 which brought punishments for infringing the new laws. Then too, the Enclosures Acts began to take away the common land, a process which slowly impoverished the agricultural worker. These were acts of Parliament (four thousand acts covered 7,000,000 acres from 1660 to 1845) which took common land away from the people and into private ownership to be farmed by large estates; no longer could a farm worker use this common pasture for his one cow, pig and few hens, use it to gather kindling, to snare wild birds in the woods, and gather the beechmast for the pig. But until then the rural worker had enough food, even if it was only subsistence level. 'They lay out seldom any money for any provision' wrote William Webb of the Cheshire farmers in 1656, speaking of the small landowner, 'but have it of their own, as Beef, Mutton, Veal, Pork, Capons, Hens, Wild Fowl or Fish.'[109] But half of the population scraped a living, indeed Gregory King in 1696 estimated that the number of cottagers and paupers amounted to one quarter of the population while another quarter were labouring people and servants. Both groups, he thought, had to spend more than they earned. These men worked thirteen and a half hours per day, six days a week.

When a minor nobleman and landowner, John Verney, married in 1680 his wedding breakfast was a modest one, he paid eight shillings for four fat chickens eaten by his seven guests and five shillings for a dish of cherries in London; these were town prices. A cloth worker earned twelve shillings a week, one wonders what they ate, not chicken or cherries, one surmises.

Both in town and in the country the most common of meats were chickens, ducks and geese, with pigeons and turkey more occasionally (they arrived to be reared in Norfolk in 1538 but goose remained the most popular Christmas bird), which were generally roasted on a spit in front of an open fire, though ovens were known and used, but they were notoriously unreliable, easily burning food or undercooking it. People preferred to see their food cooking in front of them. The smaller birds though were often boiled, chicken made good soup and broth, so was especially valued. But with the meats, whether roasted or boiled, there would always be a sauce. This was, of course, *de rigeur* in the medieval meal and the sauce seems to have carried on in popularity. In Sarah Loveland's household book she makes a sauce for mutton from spearmint and sugar or of broom buds, French beans, clove-gilliflowers or cucumbers. (The last, a medieval favourite, was always eaten cooked). For a change she stewed anchovies in claret mixed with the gravy from the roasted bird. She made a sauce for the goose from sorrel, sugar and scalded gooseberries, for pork she used sage, currants, melted butter and verjuice mixed with the gravy and the brains from a pig.[110] This sauce is a traditional medieval one, though they would not have had the gooseberries, making do with that gooseberry flavour that the sorrel gives. Interestingly, Sarah Loveland uses both. Boiled meat puddings were another speciality, encased in suet mixtures of meat and offal, and were wrapped in a cloth and suspended by string into a cauldron. Areas were renowned for their own speciality; there were local versions of black or hog's liver puddings. Sarah Loveland gave a recipe for her own, where she parboiled the liver, beat it with a mortar, added thick, sweet cream, eggs, breadcrumbs, beef suet, chopped dates, currants, spices, salt and sugar; wrapped in a cloth it was then allowed to stand for a while before being boiled gently over a low fire.

The winter season was always a difficult time people subsisted on from so many stores made in the summer and autumn months. Fresh meat was scarce, for there was still not enough fodder to keep a large amount of livestock throughout the winter, though there would be by the following century. So many of the carcasses in the autumn were pickled and powdered with dry salt. There were two methods, one wet, the other dry, the carcass being butchered into pieces the right size for cooking, then either plunged into brine with spices, or else rubbed and rolled in salt and hung up to dry out, where it would shrink. The pig carcass was rubbed with salt and saltpetre, pickled in strong ale, sugar and baysalt for a few weeks then brought out and hung to be smoked over a wood fire. Barrels of herrings were pickled in spiced vinegar, or sliced, boned and dried. The summer vegetables had been pickled, fruit made into conserves or bottled, flowers candied and flower wines brewed.

The powdered beef had to be soaked in water for a day or two before it could be cooked and eaten. Sir Hugh Platt informs us in *Delightes for Ladies* that it could be kept after it was 'sodden' for another two or three months if it was wrapped in a dry cloth and placed in a tightly closed cupboard. Preserving food meant a constant search – fish, Sarah Loveland claims, is first fried in oil, then steeped in white wine vinegar and a fresh salmon could be preserved a whole month 'in this perfect state and delicacy' by putting it in 'apt and close vessels in wine vinegar with a branch of rosemary therein.'[111]

In the summer many different salads were eaten, prepared from the herb and vegetable garden; here again, medieval tradition, helped by all the labour in the still room which analysed the properties of various herbs and plants, was still strong. It would take up to another two hundred years to dissipate such a tradition, in greater urbanisation and the industrialisation of landscape and peoples. But now salads could be made using borage flowers, rosemary, violets, rue, broom buds and cowslips. For leaves there would be cress, mints, chickweed, dandelion, orache, purslane, rocket, burnet and lettuce. The salads were dressed with oil, salt and something sharp like verjuice or vinegar. What small amount of grapes that were still grown in the unsettled climate were generally unripe so they were pulped, then strained and the green liquid, sharply acidic, called verjuice was used in cooking and had made a favourite sauce for the last seven hundred years.

But the staple food of the day was undoubtedly bread. As we have seen, the nobility only ate the fine wheat bread that used to be called manchet, the next bread down in quality was referred to as yeoman bread, which had a little bran left in it. The flour which had rye and wheat grain mixed together was called still, as it always had been, maslin or messeldine flour, and this was the flour that the farmers and the urban middle class used daily; puddings and loaves made from barley were eaten by country labourers, though in the north they tended to prefer a dark rye bread and further north in Scotland oats still reigned supreme. Milk puddings were made using rice, sago, oatmeal or breadcrumbs sweetened with sugar with an added dollop of jam preserve. Boiled puddings used maslin flour, as did pastry, which made a rather heavy paste which must at times have been a trial to eat – no doubt many a lady felt too refined to chew the stuff and left it on the plate. Sarah Loveland's White Pudding was made from suet, sugar, salt, cloves, pepper, currants, dates and oatmeal steeped in milk for a day, she then poured into it hot boiled cream with the yolks of eight eggs per pint of cream, it was then boiled in a cloth for five hours. Her Quaking Pudding was made from a pint of cream, ten yolks of eggs and three of their whites, rosewater, sugar and a little fine wheat flour, which was then boiled for half an hour and served with a sauce of rosewater mixed with sugar and butter.

Imbals were a kind of shortcake made from fine flour again with butter mixed with fruit purees, rolled out thin, then baked and iced with sugar and rosewater. We must still be slightly surprised to see that the food for the Christmas festivities, both the pudding and the mince pies, had meat added to it, but nearly all the medieval dishes with minced meat had mixtures of dried fruit added to them, so this was a traditional dish; still, the pudding has a surprising amount of ox tongue and chicken flesh, well ground, and mixed in with the eggs, dried fruit and candied peel, sugar and spices while the mince pies had ground beef added to the currants, raisins and candied peel. Much fruit was tended in the gardens, the idea of eating it fresh was also becoming appealing, but some of that medieval nervousness which allied fresh fruit with stomach disorders and worse still, the plague itself, still remained. So the bulk of the apricots, cherries, currants, pears, plums, peaches, apples, gooseberries, raspberries, strawberries, medlars and quinces were either bottled or made into preserves and cordials. Fresh fruit in town commanded a high price and was beyond the scope of a working man's wage. Oranges were still considered a great luxury, all of them imported, but some came from the orangeries of the nobility.

Cheese was gaining in favour as the way of finishing a meal, which was partly because the change from ewes to cows which began in the Tudor period had continued; this was due to the decline in English wool exports, as fleeces from Castile had taken over as the major European supplier. So, beef and veal was now being eaten almost as often as mutton. In lowland Britain cow's milk became the acceptable source for cheese making, sometimes cow's milk was mixed with ewe's and, on being skimmed, a sharp hard cheese was made. Town dairy shops grew up in all the large urban centres and milkmaids would walk the streets bearing pails slung from yokes across their shoulders. These young women had often walked in from the countryside bringing in the milk themselves, some even rode with the milk in barrels hooked onto the saddle. But now throughout the century the practice of keeping the cows themselves in the towns became commoner. Also farms that had been on the edge of a village were now swamped by the growing town itself and absorbed by it. These town cows lived off scraps like the pigs – empty bean pods, brewer's grains and cabbage shells – and the milk often tasted off-puttingly of these. Moreover town milk was often diluted with water and as it was carried through the streets in open pails all sorts of extraneous matter collected on the surface. Accordingly, town milk began to get a bad reputation, better by far to have the cow milked outside the door into your own pitcher which you knew was clean. Some of the cows were allowed to pasture in the green spaces in the midst of towns – cows were often seen pasturing in St James's Park and from thence their milk was sold.

Milk was heated with bread or flour to make pap for children and the infirm and with wheat to make the age-old frumenty, which was always so popular. It was also used in possets, a milk drink which was curdled with ale and chosen spices or other flavourings; the posset curds could be drained of the whey and pressed, then sliced and eaten with honey and cream. Curds could also be put into tarts in a sauce of egg yolks and cream with fruit purees and sugar as well as being made into fritters. Inherited from the Elizabethan age was the love of fools, trifles and whitepots, the first being a seasoned cream, sweetened and flavoured, then thickened with egg yolks by boiling, while the whitepot was the same but with added currants and it was baked in a pot. A trifle was a thick cream with sugar, ginger and rosewater warmed before serving. All were immensely popular in the seventeenth century; they might even be thickened with ground almonds, or thinned with sack or even flavoured with sage. The herb had a reputation for preserving mental agility, hence its ancient name, and was used in cooking extensively. Clotted cream was also popular and the clotted cream from the southwest was becoming famed, hence it was sometimes called western cream, the recipe given by the Countess of Kent was entitled 'how to scald milk after the western fashion'.

Of course in such a century big changes inevitably happened. Throughout the Interregnum you had an emphasis on plain, good comfort food. An unpleasant book which attacked the wife of the Protector, Joan Cromwell's cooking was published in 1664; this was the Restoration when traducing the Cromwells was the sport of the day. The anonymous writer's basic contention was that Joan Cromwell cooked the same simple country food she always had cooked even when she was mistress of the most important establishment in the country – Whitehall Palace – and had to entertain foreign dignitaries. She kept three cows in St James's Park and her friends praised her butter – how shocking. She called her cooking 'fitter for a barn rather than a palace'.[112]

There was, of course, a distinct difference between the cooking for Protestants and that for Catholics, though the latter never labelled themselves, except for the most devout. The courtiers that Charles II surrounded himself with were all secret Catholic sympathisers, but though the king had promised Louis XIV that he would convert publicly and was paid a large sum of money for this promise, he feared rightly to do so until his deathbed. Court food aped the French dishes that they had eaten in exile, yet one of the first changes was the diminution of the banquet. It still existed at court, for the new nobility that had accompanied Charles to France clung onto it, for they all came back with French notions about food, but when the task merely of preserving angelica took a whole day, according to the Countess of Kent, such labour intensive food could not be part of the weekly duties outside the court circle. By the beginning of the next century the word 'banquet' for the last course would not be used anymore, and the word 'dessert', the French name, would now be used instead.

The diet for the poor was as bleak as it always had been, for the urban poor possibly worse, living off scraps that they could pick up from the street. We can gather a picture of the rural poor from the Reverend Richard Baxter who wrote of their limited diet. He thought they could not afford to eat except once a month perhaps, the few that could kill an old bull did so, dried the beef in the chimney and cut a piece off it once a month to place in the stew pot. To pay the rent they had to sell their eggs, chickens, piglets, apples, pears, butter and cheese. The family made do with the poorer stuff that would not sell, the skimmed milk, cheese and whey curds, the scabbed apples and unripe pears. The reverend cleric ended his description by saying: 'and through God's mercy all this doth them no harm.'[113] No doubt they had a different view, we know that many did, leaving their rural hovels and moving into the growing urban centres where there was work and wages and the hope of something better.

Women and Food

Eighteenth century English society though hierarchical and status conscious like other European nations was certainly not a caste society where status was determined by birth except in regard of colour. It was an achieving society where honours and status could be won with hopefully the acquisition of wealth. For wealth in Britain was valued more highly than rank, unlike other European societies there were no legal barriers between different strata in society so there was complete freedom of movement between levels in geography and occupations. It was similar to how the world viewed America in the last century, a country where hard work and great ideas could gain a man a fortune. It was this freedom that allowed the beginning of the industrial revolution here and rampant consumerism to flourish. The fashions of aristocracy were copied by merchants and farmers, then taken up by servants and could even affect labourers. Of course, the *nouveau riche* were satirised in plays and novels, libelled in gossip and ridiculed behind their backs. But that did not stop them entertaining their detractors and feeling that they were securing a place in society. But it was certainly not in any way an equal society in regard of gender. Beneath the ploys of social discourse men and women were anxious about trespassing on each other's territory. And in a time where trade and empire were booming, at a time of affluence and plenty, these matters seemed even more pressing. For men when making their fortunes used their women, their wives and daughters as clothes pegs for their wealth as well as their houses to exhibit it in. Women were confined to the role of reflecting a rich man's position in society, a role which served capitalism but demeaned them.

'The want of education in women was discussed as an admitted fact, one side defending it as necessary in order to keep wives in subjection, while the other side, led by the chief literary men of the day, ascribed the frivolity and the gambling habits of ladies of fashion to an upbringing which debarred them from more serious interests.' I have argued elsewhere[114] that at birth of consumerism which began in the late seventeenth century and grew explosively throughout the next four centuries, which is also, of course, the rise of capitalism, caused a radical change in the expression of gender and with that the role and character of the food produced. Basically the male became the entrepreneur, the adventurer, the bold, grasping capitalist bent on wealth and position in society, with his houses, land and possessions, which included his wife, all being a reflection of his wealth. So why should this woman, who was dressed in silks, lace, damask and satin, who wore priceless jewels be educated? Because husbands required their wives to act as hostesses, who would have a mastery of flirtation, be a ready wit and succinct in repartee, she had to dazzle and glitter as beautifully as the jewels she wore, she had to be admired and longed for, so that the husband was envied. We must not forget how very public this urban world was, the promenade, the opera, the concerts, the constant succession of balls, both private and subscription, the tea gardens at Marylebone and Vauxhall. It was still very much a man's world, however (has it ever stopped being?) with his woman on his arm and I would argue that the food too reflected him rather than her. Where the Tudor and Stuart eras in their use of fruits and confectionery, of possets and cordials, reflected the feminine; with a redoubtable and brilliant queen upon the throne the female influence was pre-eminent. But now, as another queen, Queen Anne, died, the pendulum moved back again to the masculine.

In many ways preposterous when you consider how many recipe books were published now by women authors, or that is our impression because we remember their names: Mrs Raffald, Martha Bradley, Mrs Fisher, Hannah Glasse, Mary Holland are but a few in the eighteenth century. Moreover, many of the books written by men had anonymous women to write out the recipes. Gervase Markham's book in its later editions owns up that it was 'an Honourable Countesse'. And Markham was not the only man to pillage women's recipes and not name the source. Also, women tended to be either over modest or worried that declaring themselves openly female might harm their sales, so though they used their surnames they often only placed initials in front. So for what it is worth, in the thirty years from 1700 to 1730 twenty books were published and only three openly by women. It was not until after the 1750s that women placed their names upon their works, and it was around then when it is thought that the middle classes were almost universally literate and that books were being produced to satisfy the thirst for self-improvement. However, in examining the cookery books of both men and women there would not be any great discernible difference between those produced by either, because they all plagiarised each other.

I would suggest that the real pointer to the character of what was consumed lies in the amounts of meat sold in Leadenhall Market, the huge covered market building that was erected after the Great Fire. Here we find that there are a hundred stalls selling beef, and a hundred and forty stalls for mutton, veal, poultry, geese and rabbits. Ever since the Reformation there had been a gradual build up of cattle herds as more and more beef had been eaten, which is partly because there is a strong liking for the meat and partly because cow's milk was preferred to ewe's and more cheese had been made from the cow. Women are not usually partial to great mounds of meat served upon the plate, but this is what various writers tell us of the time. The French visitor, Henri Misson, for example, Samuel Pepys, Guy Miege, or Cesar de Saussure who in his letters home so full of gossip, detail and astute observations noted how huge the joint of beef was which came to table for them all to eat – at times he thought it must be all of twenty pounds – they all, without fail, give the impression that roast beef was the pre-eminent choice, soon followed by roast mutton admittedly, then beef puddings and meat pies of all descriptions.

Of course men have always dictated what kind of food is served and eaten, yet beneath this desire to reflect masculine desires there is always a sub text which is solely feminine, of creating the kind of food that pleases and fulfils them. They after all, were really in control of the purse strings therefore the quality and amount of produce bought, but not the way it was prepared and cooked. There is little that men can do to interrupt that process, apart from learning the skill and art of cookery itself and taking over altogether. But in the eighteenth century in the movement towards education for women there is a distinct feeling that they have silently opted out, certainly they have left the business to their sisters who have the will to write the books and cook the food. One lady whose puddings were much admired so that her guests believed she had a special, secret way to making them denied it. 'I have no recipes for puddings, nor ever had, I make them always by guess. Indeed I did teach Mrs Fountain, but it was with letting her see me mingling them. But I'll tell you everything I use to put in them and give you the best directions I can and then you must put them together to your taste.'[115] There is a delightfully wilful almost flippant attitude exhibited here, as if she is also saying, 'can't we discuss something more interesting?'

The list of ordinary self-taught but learned women is heartening, for example Mrs Elstob who spent her life studying Anglo-Saxon, produced a grammar in that language, and translated Aelfric's Homilies. Then there was Mrs Bland who studied Mrs Elstob's book and made herself so skilled in Hebrew that she taught it to her son and daughter. Elizabeth Blackwell wrote a *Curious Herbal* listing five hundred of the most useful plants. The *Spectator* was worried stating that 'Female virtues are of a domestic turn. The family is the proper province for the private woman to shine in.'

The food that is cooked still celebrates comfort, pleasure and security, even more so. But it strikes one as heavy cooking – the Rowlandson cartoons where the meat steaks hang over the plate, the huge round steamed puddings, the general problem of obesity and gout tells us of unremitting indulgence in overeating as if the hundreds of years before of near hunger and malnutrition are now being erased by food, glorious food in an obsessive and uncritical way. The elephantine fat squire with his gouty foot tucking into more roast beef is a stock character from so many novels and plays of the time. It is all suet and pastry; there is no finesse in cooking, no delicacy, and no subtlety. There seems now to be only one large meal per day, dinner which was eaten about one o'clock but it could be later; both breakfast and supper were made upon snacks, bread, cheese, a little sausage, tea or coffee, and in the evening there was generally much to drink. It is, of course, in the story of tea drinking that women reigned supreme; it is as if they abdicated all interest in the grossness of mounds of meat consumption and retreated to the tea table, to delicate china and to the rituals and precise niceties of the tea gathering among their own.

Signs of the waning influence that women now chose to have over food styles is the absence of sugar in savoury dishes, even that great standby favourite, the sweet and sour sauce now seems to be only used with venison. A favourite sauce was a thick butter one emulsified with water and lemon. Mary Kettilby in *A Collection of above Three Hundred Receipts* (1714) tells us that sweet sauces are old fashioned and that you must watch that your maid does not sugar a dish of beans; while T. Hall in *The Queen's Royal Cookery* does give a recipe for a sweet and sour sauce but adds that it may be eaten without sugar as that is the fashion now. Even that medieval love of adding dried fruit to meat sauces has become unfashionable and is not the done thing anymore. Mary Kettilby loves to use a sauce which is a combination of wine and anchovy – she uses it in hare stew and in chicken fricassee – and the sauce is also dominant later in Elizabeth Smith's *The Compleat Housewife* (1727) which, though written by a woman, reflects male tastes in food completely. There is, for example an asparagus soup, which uses twelve pounds of lean beef and a pint of brown ale to fifty asparagus spears, celery, spinach and vermicelli. These flavours are aggressive, they hardly seduce the palate, they assault it.

Where women still retained an interest was in puddings, tarts, cakes and creams, where, of course, sugar was still used extensively. What a relief it is to find recipes which are delicate, which have subtle flavours, which are not huge mounds of stodge. For example, a thin and delicate pancake recipe in Mary Kettilby's book flavoured with orange flower water and a little nutmeg. Cakes without yeast but made light by beaten egg whites, trouble and skill employed to get clear jellied preserves – amber-coloured apple or white quince. How apt Mary Kettilby is when she writes 'you must carefully watch the colour, because it turns muddy and black in a moment and the colour is as delicate as the taste…' A sign of growing urbanisation is that the directions for making a syllabub which was to milk the cow straight into the jug, have now gone. Creams, possets and syllabubs are a very English dessert, Elizabeth Smith gives 21 different recipes in her book flavoured with fruits and perfumed in one recipe by ambergris. (This is a waxy substance secreted by whales found floating in the sea which had been used in the making of perfumes since medieval times. It is mainly cholesterol but has the most amazingly beautiful aroma. There was a craze for it in the midst of the seventeenth century, but now its addition is marked as optional.) Mary Eales, confectioner to the late Queen Anne, in a reprint of her book of recipes (1718) gives a recipe for chocolate cream, where the chocolate is grated into boiling water, dissolved, then a pint of cream added and two beaten eggs, which may have then been poured into a pastry case, or placed in a mould and sliced.

The first ice houses were built in the royal parks as early as 1620 and in the grounds of private houses after the Restoration from 1680, but recipes for ice creams were slow to get printed. What seems to be the first one was given again by Mary Eales in 1714, where the cream is left unflavoured, though you have the option of flavouring it with fruit or sugar and most of the instructions are laboured ones on the freezing process, which involves ice, straw and bay salt. Recipes for ice cream do not appear until after 1750, when the ice house stopped being such a novelty.

The Desire for Display

What then was the underlying impetus in the seventeenth and eighteenth centuries towards gastronomy? Perhaps it did not even exist? The monarchy had eschewed the divine; they were Teutonic in temperament and style, a bulwark against Republicanism, puppets for a mercantile community which headed a growing empire. As to food, they were not leaders of any style or champions of any gustatory ambitions, they were trenchermen chewing their way though great mounds of meat plainly roasted or stewed, they ate like the rest of the male middle class, representative of the dullest, most bourgeois elements in it.

Male cookery writers kept the flame alive of the old style of court cookery and of display, and even if it hardly existed in the royal palaces and even if the flavours were missing, a semblance of gourmet fecundity limped on. Decorative dishes were much celebrated in Robert May's book, *The Accomplisht Cook*, in the Catholic and French tradition which was aped, as much as the economy allowed, in the Restoration court; in the following century such dishes were still being triumphed as food for feasts, great baroque pyramids of marchpane in various gaudy hues, of sugar paste flowers and fruit. John Middleton tells us how to make a miniature orchard in 1734 and though others were before him few followed him. For taste about that time swung against such profusion, it was seen as both vulgar and pretentious. A Frenchman, Confiseur, (which shows that this style was basically both French and Catholic and imported to England by the Stuart monarchs or Henrietta Maria, the wife of Charles I who clung to the Catholic faith and ate accordingly, doing much disservice to her husband's reputation) comments: 'What has become of those pyramids erected with more labour and effort than taste and elegance, which used to be seen on our tables? What has become of that confused piling-up of fruit which was more of a display of profusion then of intelligence and refinement.'[116]

For a revolution in taste had happened in France and it could not help but percolate through to other countries. The melange of spices, the sweet and sour sauces, the dense mixture of flavours were all spurned as antique interlopers, remnants of medieval cuisine, that must be banished from the modern French kitchen. There was an emphasis on natural flavours, on refinement and delicacy. It now became common for French travellers roaming across Europe and visiting England to complain, to express surprise and disdain when they encountered sweet and acidic spicy sauces, pronouncing them inedible and indigestible. The Marquis de Coulanges wrote home as early as 1657, when visiting Germany, about the weird combinations of meat with fruit and spices, such as chicken with cloves and gosling stuffed with prunes and apples. Then Jouvin de Rochefort expressed his annoyance at being served in Flanders a sugared salad, which he also encountered in Ireland. While in Spain the Countess d'Aulnoy found the meals she was offered in Madrid and Toledo either disgusting, 'meats reeking of perfume' or inedible, 'full of saffron, garlic, onion, peppers and spices'.[117] There is a frightful arrogance about these remarks which is now distinctly off putting, besides the fact that our contemporary tastes find the sound of these dishes attractive. Though eminent food historians today rate this revolution in French cuisine as highly significant I have always been unimpressed. Elsewhere[118] I have said as much for I think English cooking was also tending towards the same resolutions. The arrogance above reflects the fact that under Louis XIV France at this time (but not later in the century) was the most powerful nation in Europe; the nobility simply threw their weight about more than usual, like the English traveller would in the future, complaining that foreign food was always disgusting. For today's historians to take this as reasoned assessment of a dish is absurd.

What is also too easily forgotten is that France, implacably Catholic, was eager to replace the Protestant Hanoverian dynasty with the Catholic Stuarts and attempted to fund rebellion with that in mind. In this climate it was difficult to be sympathetic to many French ideas and one cookery writer inveighed against the French spiritedly. Hannah Glasse (1708-1770) wrote anonymously *The Art of Cookery* (published in 1747) giving the authorship as 'by a lady', not true, but like other cookery writers she learnt from observation and being a servant to the gentry – Hannah worked for the Earl of Donegall in Essex – her book was a large comprehensive collection with many of the recipes plagiarised from other writers though this was common at the time. Her distaste for French cooking and its extravagance must also come from working beneath them in large country houses, but surely too such distaste was also fuelled by the Jacobite rebellion of 1745. For she must have been finishing her work when Bonnie Prince Charlie led his army as far as south as Derby; at that point, the chance of a Stuart king being returned t the throne must have looked likely and then Catholic French food would have been the rule. The fact that Hannah Glasse exaggerated, whether knowingly or not, only encouraged the myth that French cooking was an unnecessary luxury, yet most of the innovations were pursued by the English anyway. William Verrall was an exponent of the new style learnt from the cook, Mr de St. Clouet to the Duke of Newcastle; Verrall ran The White Hart Inn at Lewes in Sussex and his collection of recipes which was first published in 1759 could be cooked today without anyone suspecting the date of their provenance.[119]

Yet display continues because the need to show off, to make a celebration dish which is well over the top, is always there and comes into play directly a festivity needs to be enjoyed, especially if wealth and position demands it. Hence, great serving dishes are used piled high with an assorted number of meats and poultry with requisite sauces, even Hannah Glasse believes such dishes must be good for company, but as she plagiarised so wilfully, even raiding Patrick Lamb's book, *Royal Cookery* (1710) who was cook to four monarchs, she is still guilty of regurgitating court cooking of fifty years before.

But there is something new in English cooking that makes its appearance in this century and it is due to women quietly getting on with what they had accomplished and did so well – country cooking at its best. Especially I would stress that gastronomy was kept alive by women in the development of the pudding and the dessert course, most of our classic puddings deriving from recipes which first appeared in the eighteenth century. These were dishes which had been in the English repertoire for centuries, they stayed there because they were much loved and now they began to be written down and in the writing they were often reinterpreted and refined. Even the French traveller Henri Misson goes into a paroxysm of delight: 'it is a manna that hits the palates of all sorts of people; a manna better than that of the wilderness, because the people are never weary of it. Ah, what an excellent thing is an English pudding.'[120]

I have mentioned above the creams, burnt cream, ginger cream, snow cheese, possets and syllabubs, which were varied, using sharp fruits like damsons, wine and eau de vie. From these stemmed trifles, custards, fools and tipsy cakes, tipsy squire and whim wham – all varieties of trifle, the specific English concoction. The traditional boiled pudding which had been a cottage staple, hanging from a thread in the cauldron over a cottage fire for many hundreds of years, came out from the twilight to be reassessed as a culinary marvel. Both the cloth and the pudding basin were used, so as to get a really light mixture with whipped eggs, for lightness meant fluidity and that meant it leaked through the cloth and into the poaching water, but not if the cloth was placed into a buttered basin. As every schoolboy who went to a boarding school knew these puddings could be heavy and tasteless, but not if made with skill; such as the notorious Spotted Dick or Dog, a suet roll studded with currants like a Dalmatian dog, a Cabinet Pudding, a treacle or jam pudding, a Sussex Plum Duff and a Sussex Pond Pudding.

Other ancient puddings were all the milk ones, baked slowly in the oven made from cereals, sugar and creamy milk, rice, tapioca, sago – I cannot make a case for these as a gastronomic experience, they are personally for me dire. But I recognise that their food value was high and it must have helped many a poor labouring family to survive especially in hard winters. They could be left all day in the embers of a fire and they would not spoil, then at night they would be warm and nourishing. Next the baked puddings and the most eminent one bread and butter pudding which can be spread with marmalade, quince jelly or any preserve of your liking, then there is baked syrup roll, jam roly poly, bakewell pudding and the Queen of puddings. And lastly, all the tarts and pies made with the fruits in season – cherry pie, blackcurrant pie, Kentish apple pie and in that section too I should add the cheesecakes, for they have pastry or biscuit bases and they were a favourite dish of the medieval diner. For I personally like the thought of a dish having a long and distinguished history. The French could jettison all their medieval heritage, or thought they had, but the English were still careful to build on it.

This is indeed homely, comfort food, smelling of farmhouse kitchens, the very quintessence of English cooking and both the cooking and the development of the recipes stemmed from women cooks. This was all done as a matter of routine, for though I believe that the eighteenth century woman was rattling the cage which men had placed her in, she was still locked into performing domestic tasks. But the situation is complicated by what was happening in France.

Here cooking was the male preserve; in France there were no female cooks, while in England there were within the middle classes only woman cooks. But French male cooks were employed in England by the nobility and the wealthy. From the beginning of the eighteenth century as a by product of the Grand Tour, your luggage on return being piled high with paintings, statuary, curios and bibelots, might also include a French chef, and this English middle class women cooks resented. They also resented what they thought were luxurious ways of cooking, unnecessary garnishes and sauces, which the French had imported and their resentment made them misunderstand those influences. There were wild stories of dozens of hams and partridges being reduced to no more than a tablespoon of sauce, which Hannah Glasse was delighted to speak intemperately about. But the French cooks that were working for the English nobility continued to bring in new ideas, the best of which were accepted, either because people genuinely liked them or because they were modish, in which case they would be followed for a time before being conveniently forgotten.

The Countrywoman

But what did French cooks and *nouvelle cuisine* matter outside the great urban centres, which now grew at an alarming rate? This century brought in new crops and machines, new thoughts on rotation and breeding livestock, as well as the terrible impact of the series of enclosures which took away the common land from the agricultural worker, leading him either to emigrate to new lands overseas or into the great maw of the industrial midlands. So much was coming into the land from overseas, tea, coffee, cotton, tobacco, sugar – even the wood to make their furniture. Not English oak but mahogany, the drawing rooms of England glowing with the dark burnished golden sheen of this wood that came from Africa or South America.

To the country born lady the outside world seemed to have everything in it that she desired. Christiana Spencer of Cannon Hall, Yorkshire, wrote to her father who was in London, asking him to send her a bottle of salad oil, soap, anchovies, capers, pickles, tea and coffee, other members of the family desired him to bring back a bookcase, a dozen mahogany chairs, dress material and a hat. The father, John Spencer, had some domestic difficulties too, his new cook expected to dine in the housekeeper's room at a second table set up there and both the cook and the housekeeper objected to sleeping in the same room as the rest of the servants, while the housekeeper objected to the cook even eating with her.

The Georgian countrywoman was very alive to all the new developments. A Mrs Clarke discussed the relative merits of broadcast sowing by hand or drilling wheat by machine, another asked the question of whether you planted the whole potato or just the eyes, a Mrs Coke found that chicory was an excellent feed for her pigs. A Mrs Boxer and Miss Hayes helped in improving Southdown sheep and others for breeding the best bulls and horses in the district, in Cardigan women farmers won prizes for such varied endeavours as reclaiming five acres from wild to arable, making a water meadow, a crop of buckwheat, rye grass seed and a wheat crop.[121]

In 1780 a cookery book was published anonymously called *The Farmer's Wife; or Complete Country Housewife* which gives a vivid picture of the life of the countrywoman. It gave instructions on the breeding and management of turkeys, fowls, geese, ducks and pigeons, fattening hogs, curing bacon and pickling pork, how to make sausages and hog's puddings, the method of making cider, Perry, mead, cherry-brandy, the best way of making butter, Gloucestershire cheese as well as Cheshire and Stilton, how to pickle fruits and vegetables, how to brew beer and ale, how to keep bees and use their honey. All this as well as recipes 'for dressing such dishes as are commonly made in the farmhouse' contained in 132 pages. The book reveals that little had changed for a thousand years, much the same activities continue producing much the same rich diet rooted in the plants and animals that abound within the countryside.

It is doubtful that the writer ever read a French recipe book, yet there are no complicated sauces with a dozen different spices in them, instead there are plenty of butter sauces and roasts served with their juices, just as the new fashion decreed. No doubt the writer would have said, but isn't it obvious that that is how you cook, simply and using the flavours of the vegetables, fruits and meats that you have. Wasn't that what farmhouse cooking had always been?

An English response to French cooking is clearly communicated in the diary of the Reverend Stotherd Abdy during a three-week visit to his patrons, the Archer family, to celebrate a family marriage. He often described the dinners as elegant though mostly the settings rather than the flavours or appearance of the food itself, yet when the French cook departs and their hostess apologies for the plainness of the cooking, there is jubilation among the guests. 'We, instead of being mortified at this account sincerely rejoiced at hearing it, as our eyes had not been blest with such a sight for above a week. When we came to table we had the pleasure of seeing seven good eatable dishes and could really tell what they were, and we enjoyed our meal thoroughly.'[122]

Even a French woman, Madame du Bocage who for two months moved among the gentry in England in 1750, decided she preferred English food... 'the simple cookery of the English, of which we have so bad an opinion; their large joints, their pudding, their fish which is cheaper than in Paris and which is served at every meal, their chickens in butter sauce, are excellent.'[123]

CHAPTER NINE

The Triumph of the Bourgeoisie

Middle–class expansion in the nineteenth century was huge in terms of numbers, wealth and influence; the population of London for example is typical, from over 900,000 in 1801 in the midst of the Napoleonic wars, it doubled to two million by 1851, the year of the Great Exhibition and then almost doubled again by the end of the century. The effect of this huge number of middle class upon British cookery was dire, though they were hardly one class, similar in income, taste and rank. The class in all its white collar complexity was driven by one powerful emotion and desire, social aspiration; and much of that was centred upon the kitchen and dining room while it also relied upon the number of servants income allowed. For the cooking was left too often to servants who were ignorant and illiterate, the kitchens were in the basement too far from the dining rooms, dishes had to be kept warm for too long, all vegetables were thoroughly overcooked, there was a love of mock flavours, like turtle soup, (made from a calf's head with chopped oysters), crab (Pollock and boiled crab shell) and lobster (monkfish and paprika). It was thought raw salads were bad for you because they harboured germs, the emphasis was on appearance of the dish and not in its flavour. The dining room became a minefield of social etiquette where one small mistake could damn you for a lifetime. That relaxed exuberance of the eighteenth century, the moral laxity and sensuality was now smothered by a hard carapace of moral rectitude, for food like sex could destroy their defence against chaos and poverty. Stories abound in popular books for children and adults of good people turning into drunken monsters through addiction and too great a fascination for food led obviously to strong drink, the two were twinned, one led to the other and both led to damnation, drugs, debt and the gutter. Best then to bless God for the gift of our daily bread and leave it at that.

French chefs were still the height of fashion; they continued to cook for the upper classes and those new industrial magnates that were earning huge fortunes out of the boom in iron, steel and coal as well as the expansion of shipping and the railways. England had never been so rich and so powerful, the Empire – as Free Trade proved its efficacy – brought in huge profits and there was for a long period, broken only by the Crimean War, a period of peace. No wonder the population steadily rose as well as prices and the gap between the very poor and the lower middle classes steadily widened. Family life was at the heart of middle-class expansion governed by a powerful *paterfamilias* that was strengthened by public opinion whose voice was uniform in its conservatism. Though middle-class values dominated society it was also an age where new ideas were in ferment at the heart of society. The fact that Darwin at last wrote and published his great work, which immediately became a best seller and has never been out of print, is as significant as the fact that he hesitated for half a lifetime. So though I detect that the overriding values tended to throw a pall over the development of good food, I also recognise that in the work of a few gastronomy was kept alive.

The First Celebrity Chef

The century started well returning to the regal values of a monarch-substitute in the Prince Regent who was greedy and self-indulgent enough to employ a chef of genius, thus the stimulus was there to create dishes of gastronomic brilliance. Carême (1784-1833) had a hard and brutal upbringing as a Paris street urchin, in 1792, while the French Revolution was at its height, he managed to find work as a pot boy at a cheap chophouse. He survived there for ten years but must have shown character and guts for at fourteen he was apprenticed to Sylvain Bailly, a noted pâtissier. Bailly recognized his talent and after some years Carême opened his own shop, the *Pâtisserie de la rue de la Paix*, which he ran until 1813, fortunately for him an enthusiastic Tallyrand would regularly visit.

By now Carême had gained fame in Paris for his baroque window displays, his elaborate constructions used as centrepieces, sometimes several feet high, made from sugar, marzipan, and pastry. These were, of course, a straight crib from the medieval *sotelty*, for he based them on temples, pyramids, cascades, windmills and fantastic castles in the best romantic tradition. He is thought to have invented many of these confections that became immensely popular, but there was nothing new that he did that the medieval cooks had not done before him.

His success opened opportunities that he would hardly have dreamt of, he worked as a cook for Tallyrand then for Napoleon himself. Carême was set a test by Talleyrand: to create a whole year's worth of menus, without repetition, and using only seasonal produce. How very contemporary this sounds. Talleyrand actively encouraged Carême to produce a new refined style of eating, using fresh herbs and vegetables and simplified sauces with fewer ingredients. Careme always spoke highly of him saying that he understood the genius of the cook and was a great judge of the most subtle of improvements while his expenditure combined wisdom with generosity. The Prince of Wales was Regent from 1811-1820 when he became George IV and Carlton House, his palace upon the Mall, was of incredible magnificence in its interiors but of an imposing simplicity outside. It stood where Carlton House Terrace stands now. Carême had two dining rooms in which to serve his feasts, the gothic dining room by John Nash looking like a rehearsal for the Royal Pavilion at Brighton, and a smaller more informal one for private dinners for the Prince. Though on the flamboyant side the Prince was a discerning patron of the arts, he read both Jane Austen and Sir Walter Scott, he bought paintings by Constable, Turner, Reynolds and Gainsborough and his choice of Henry Holland to rebuild Carlton House and Thomas Hopper and John Nash to design the spacious and opulent interiors was inspired. So Carême had the right setting both here and in Brighton for his food and especially his set pieces for dessert; there was a perfect marriage in taste, each mirrored the other exactly.

Take Carême's way with turbot, a favourite dish that the Prince liked while at Brighton. Into the turbotiere the great fish would be gently laid in a mixture of white wine, milk, salt and lemon juice, where it was gently poached. The flesh had to be as firm as chicken but more moist and when it was lifted gently from the kettle, great care had to be taken not to break the skin. Traditionally the fish was then served with a white sauce flavoured with either tarragon or fennel, but Carême made a lobster sauce, while the lobster coral was worked into a butter. Around the edge of a vast oval platter he piped creamed potato and over this medallions of lobster flesh, alternated with medallions of black truffle. The fish was placed inside the border, while tiny pastry baskets would be filled with a pale pink rose made from lobster butter, and the fish was covered with a veil of lightly fried parsley. Each person would be given a small slice of turbot, a slice of truffle, a piece of lobster and a tiny basket of lobster butter and they would help themselves to the lobster sauce. So delicate was the flavour of the lobster and the contrasting slice of truffle, so light and crisp the little baskets with the richness of the lobster butter and so stimulating the sauce that the flavour and consistency of the turbot was brought out and in no way lost. 'A perfectly balanced dish', said Carême.[124]

It is perhaps odd that I am including with enthusiasm a distinguished French chef in a book about British food, but I do so because of his years with the Prince Regent and the influence his cooking had on future generations of English cooks. I also feel that his cooking while in England was, though flamboyant, still tempered with good taste and that once he returned to France and became chef to Baron de Rothschild all sense of moderation flew out of the window. He, like so many others, was ruined by his success, he lived in the same style as his wealthy hosts; he had a number of aides attached to his staff, a box at the opera, a carriage and four. He sermonised: 'Bourgeois kitchens of limited means would be wise to follow simple methods and not try to imitate the ways of the *grandes*.' Indeed, who would attempt to imitate *jambon braisé et farci à la Rothschild*? Start with a simple braised ham then envelop it in minced pheasant breasts, at the centre contrive a large rosette constructed of overlapping pheasant breasts, alternating with strips of truffles, surround with soubise sauce and a ragout of cock's combs and cock's kidneys, scallops of *foie gras* and julienne strips of pickled tongue and mushrooms. There was another similar recipe *Ham à la Berchou* which was hidden under a blanket of minced chicken, then ornamented with crawfish tails and truffles with much the same concoction beneath.[125] Obviously, *nouvelle cuisine* in all its simplicity and natural flavours died sometime before. This, of course, is *haute cuisine* the oppressive hand of which would be laid over all cooking for another hundred and fifty years well into my own lifetime.

Carême never stayed anywhere for long, his sojourn in Russia at the behest of Tsar Alexander was brief because he hated working for one of the victors of Napoleon. But as he was impressed by the *service à la Russe*, he brought back the style to Paris where they were still stuck in that medieval mode of *service à la Française* where all the dishes that comprised the first three courses were displayed on the table at once. In Russia you were served each course separately and it began after you sat down at table, as we still do now. Carême much preferred it because such a style respected the food. In his short lifetime he improved the system of heat controls on ovens, so that he could better regulate the temperature, and he reduced a bewildering mixture of sauces to a basic triad – Espagnole, velouté and béchamel – from which he created variations which altogether amounted to one hundred sauces. He invented the modern way of making soufflés and stole from another chef my own favourite pudding –

Nesselrode Pudding named by that chef, M. Mouy for the Russian count of that name. (It is a vanilla ice cream bombe stuffed with chestnut puree with dried and glace fruits further flavoured with kirsch.) His iced bombe made from almond milk and whipped cream topped with fresh fruit purees was one of his specialities. He also brought back from Russia borscht, created fanchonettes (a small, deep tart filled with various flavours of pastry cream and topped with meringue), and roasted veal with anchovies piercing the joint rather than garlic. Almost every dish depends on the previous preparation of flavoured butters and purees, essences and sauces and almost every recipe relies on reductions, concentrations and several stages and layers. He was in pursuit all his life of blends of ideal flavours rather than a juxtaposition of contrasts.

'...he consigned the static elegance of the Versailles court to oblivion, his work reflects the freedom of thought and action that flooded France during the years that followed. He had the intellectual ability to analyse cooking old and new, to simplify methods and menus, and to define every aspect of the art that today is known as *haute cuisine*. He also had a practical brilliance which led him to become the most sought after chef of his generation with an international career in the capitals of Europe.'[126]

But Carême in the end only stayed two years with the Prince Regent and that great building, Carlton House was demolished in 1820. Carême hated the English climate, was sensitive to the jealousy of English cooks (though the leftovers from his pâtès, offered illicitly after a banquet, fetched high prices) and was highly critical of English food. 'The essentials of English cooking are the roasts of beef, mutton and lamb; the various meats cooked in salt water, in the manner of fish and vegetables...fruit preserves, puddings of all kinds, chicken and turkey with cauliflower, salt beef, country ham and several similar ragouts – that is the sum of English cooking.'[127]

He gives us a vivid and terrifying picture of the ordeal suffered in being in one of these great kitchens preparing and cooking a feast. 'See twenty chefs coming, going, moving with speed in this cauldron of heat, look at the great mass of charcoal, a cubic metre for the cooking of entrees, and another mass on the ovens for the cooking of soups, sauces, ragouts, for frying and the water baths. Add to that a heap of burning wood in front of which four spits are turning, one of which bears a sirloin weighing forty-five to fifty pounds, the other fowl or game. In this furnace everyone moves with speed; not a sound is heard, only the chef has a right to speak and at the sound of his voice, everyone obeys. Finally, the last straw, for about half an hour, all windows are closed so that the air does not cool the dishes as they are being served, and in this way we spend the best years of our lives. We must obey even when physical strength fails, but it is the burning charcoal that kills us.'[128]

The refreshing aspect of Carême was that with all his high flown ideas and baroque imagination, skill and finesse, he was a realist, due, I suspect, to the wretched struggle he had in infancy. However, no one could deny that his food was the food of luxury living and it would remain so, the high suppers of a dying breed. The question is how deeply does the food of luxury living affect the rest of us? Does it just occur in a rarefied and well-insulated hotel in the sky or is it attached to the main stream below? Was middle-class cooking at all changed by Carême's existence? He would not be in this book at all if I did not think so. Yet I wonder if he thought the same, for in an echo of the above sermonising he says it again rather more eloquently: '…it is an error for those of lesser station to try to pattern their tables after the rich, crowding them with badly prepared food, badly served because of inexperienced help. Better to serve a simple meal, well prepared; and not to try and cover the bourgeois table with an imitation of the rich.'

His cooking appeared to be effortless in its simplicity, an aspect that all great art has. But that hid a complicated process, which was not to impose flavours but to uncover them. That ambition surely is very clear in today's cooking, while Carême's techniques of reduction, sieving and straining, extracting and concentration are also very present in the technical armoury of today's chefs. There is no doubt he introduced them and I suspect they never left the luxury kitchen of the great restaurant or hotel for long in the interim between now and then. So that supreme fastidiousness reflected in pernickety techniques, nothing slapdash about Carême's kitchen, has been a constant factor ever since. But such technical prowess is labour intensive, it is not, as Carême said, for the middle-class kitchen. Let us look at one by an English contemporary who was seventeen when Carême left London and was busy starting a school, but she must have been aware that the Prince Regent had lost his chef, for it was hot news.

Eliza Acton

Born in 1799 in Battle, Sussex, Eliza Acton was the eldest of five girls but was brought up in Suffolk and didn't publish her cookery book until 1845; it was a huge success, however, and remained in print until 1914. Interestingly enough the long title: '*Modern Cookery for Private Families*, reduced to a system of easy practice in a series of carefully tested recipes, in which the principles of Baron Liebig and other eminent writers have been as much as possible applied and explained' then continues with a quotation by a Dr Gregory which would have delighted Carême. 'It is the want of a scientific basis which has given rise to so many absurd and hurtful methods of preparing food.' Furthermore, the citation of Baron Liebig would have further reassured Carême, for it was Liebig who had radically designed the new ovens which Carême then improved still further. But Eliza surely was just responding to the public's anxiety about new cookery methods and the fact that a search for scientific truth and its pertinent veracity to the commonplace was very much in the air; after all, the significance of life itself for the majority comes down to whether the supper is burnt or not. A happy home, for most of us, then and now, is a perfectly cooked and deliciously edible daily meal. Perhaps this is why, from the moment the printing presses began, cookery books of basic self-help started to appear and over the centuries never stopped being published.

Her book then begins by making sensible references and continues to make salient points; she writes well and on the first page of the preface makes it clear she is very much aware that some in the community do not even have enough food to sustain existence. She speaks of the relationship between food and health, her points on the subject are all trenchant, she pins down for example a popular myth: ' It is a popular error to imagine that what is called good cookery is adapted only to the establishments of the wealthy and that it is beyond the reach of those who are not affluent.' She continues to claim that she has been painstakingly detailed on the instructions, covering all the points, she hopes, checking others and giving for the first time directions for boning poultry and game.

Modern Cookery came out sixteen years before Mrs Beeton's great tome and the latter's book was in many ways to eclipse it. One should look at the difference. Mrs Beeton, at a very young age in her early twenties with no housekeeping experience whatsoever, reproduced the recipes that had been sent to her, for her husband, Sam, edited the *Englishwoman's Domestic Magazine* and had asked readers to send him their favourite recipes. The response was huge, recipes were sent in their thousands which Isabella religiously tested and the book faithfully records what the middle classes ate and how they cooked and entertained. It is, because of that, a valuable social document. Mrs Acton's book, begun in her late thirties and published when she was forty six, collects recipes that she has known and cooked all her life and reflects, I believe, a less urban class somewhat lower than the middle-middle class that responded to Mrs Beeton.

There is no point in making other comparisons for both document the cooking of the people in a way which Carême never set out to do, but both are well aware of his existence and other chefs who followed him. Mrs Acton begins the book with a vocabulary of terms like *Assiette Volante, Blanquette, Croustade*, which must have been necessary and a godsend to those trying to climb the slippery rungs of Victorian society. She structures her book with simple authority; Chapter One is devoted to Soups, then there are chapters each on Fish, Shell-fish, Gravies, Sauces, cold sauces, store sauces, forcemeats, boiling and roasting, Chapter Ten deals with Beef, then Veal, Mutton and Lamb, Pork, Poultry, Game, Curries, Vegetables, Pastry, Soufflés, Omelettes, Boiled Puddings, Baked Puddings, Eggs and Milk, Sweet Dishes, Preserves, Pickles, Cakes, Confectionery, Dessert Dishes, Syrups, Liqueurs, Coffee, Chocolate, Bread, Foreign and Jewish Cookery, Trussing and Carving. It is exhaustive, a mammoth production, yet any of us could use it now and only benefit from the advice and recipes.

The recipes themselves range from basic, a turnip soup, to fairly complicated like the Lord Mayor's soup which is made from a couple of pig's trotters, but on balance the choice of recipes reflects the ordinary day to day food that a family on a small income (having to watch what they spend) would eat. The recipes then have the impact of a hard won reality, one is fascinated by the difference in a 'common carrot soup' and a 'finer carrot soup', – the latter has added butter, not a lot, three ounces to 2 quarts of liquid and one and half pounds of carrot, but enough to burnish the flavour and texture.

She tells us that the most common sauce 'melted butter' is so often badly made, that foreigners call it the 'one sauce of England' for it is the basis of so many other sauces. She gives a recipe and it turns out to be what we call now white sauce, just flour, butter and milk, but she adds the butter last.

One treasures her observations. 'In Cornwall the sole is laid into thick clotted cream and stewed entirely in it, but this method gives to the sauce, which ought to be extremely delicate, a coarse fishy flavour which the previous boil prevents.' On Irish Stew, 'the potatoes should be boiled to a mash, an additional quarter of an hour may be necessary…but two hours are quite sufficient.' On roasting a fore quarter of lamb: 'The time will vary a little, of course, from the difference in the weather and in the strength of the fire, Lamb should always be well roasted.'

Elizabeth David wrote in her Introduction to a collection of Eliza Acton recipes edited by Elizabeth Ray: 'Her book was the final expression, the crystallization, of pre-Industrial England's taste in food and attitude to cookery. The dishes she describes and the ingredients which went into them would have been familiar to Jane Austen and Lord Byron, to Fanny Burnet and to Tobias Smollett. They would have been served at the tables of the great political hostesses such as Lady Melbourne and of convivial country gentlemen like Parson Woodforde.'

I recommend her book as one to dip into and have beside the bed, her cooking sums up the comfort, pleasure and security which I pinpointed in chapter eight as the qualities that the middle classes were looking for in their food and they achieved it immeasurably in the cooking of Eliza Acton. She fulfils the end of that particular need, for after her the cooking declines for many reasons which I explored fully in my book, *British Food*. When this food is dedicated to achieving those qualities above, as I believe it was throughout the eighteenth century and including the lifetime of Mrs Acton, it can be a rewarding gastronomic experience, but when there are other goals that lie behind the cooking then it withers and dies.

The Way It Looks
The semiotics of the food we select, prepare and eat is as personal to us as the clothes we put on. Both inform the rest of society about us and the life we choose to live; for the most part we do it quite unselfconsciously, unaware of how informative it is to others. If we do know, we tend to suppress it as being so acutely self-conscious it becomes an added burden. The food we cook and eat is largely a private matter between us and the family group, unless we give dinner parties where the menu is selected with enormous care and adjusted constantly so that the semiotics are the ones we want communicated (quite often, an entirely false picture is displayed, of a way of living several notches up the social ladder).

Compared to ours Victorian society was very public; on Sundays after perhaps an early morning fast the whole family attended a church service, perhaps more than one. There was a ceremonial dress for this outing that covered every detail of gloves, hat, shoes and tie and on returning there was a special meal, the most important meal of the week where a large part of a dead animal was eaten. (I am sure our great-grandparents never thought to see how exactly similar their own programme was to that of the Ancient Greeks, beginning with a fast, then a special dress, then a religious ceremony and finishing with eating a part of a roasted ox.) Because Victorian families were large and led their personal lives in front of many servants they were on show at home too. So how it looked was, if anything, the most significant aspect of their lives. (Those invisible eyes that stare from out of the shadows, the ears that hug the wall, the unnameable other, always watching your behaviour, the way you dress and speak, eavesdropping on your secret conversation, noting what you what and how you eat it.)

We have spoken of the heritage of Carême, hymning his praises as an intellectual cook and innovator, but not explored what were some disastrous influences. He made his name and fortune out of the way his food looked, but then he had the skill, money and labour to turn food into art if not architecture which it aped. His followers had neither the skill nor the artistry, they had money and the minions for labour, so what was produced tended to be second-class and often vulgar. While the middle classes themselves could not afford to do it all properly which is why so much in their life was entitled mock. One of the very worst fashions that Carême brought in was his love of aspic, of a cold platter with perhaps salmon or cold cuts laid out upon it, then covered in aspic and allowed to chill, with the aspic decorated with bits of food, thinly sliced cucumber, shaped radishes, mock truffle, strips of pimento, hard-boiled egg and parsley sprigs. How the Victorian dinner party loved this dish in all its many guises. The chef, Francatelli, who had trained under Carême, created a whole supper menu made up of aspic dishes. The desire to embellish and decorate overrode everything else; examine the illustrations of any late Victorian cookery volume. Whether savoury or sweet, what a riot of colour it was, with the kind of finicky detail and exact modelling of natural shapes that you find in a Pre-Raphaelite painting.. When so much attention was paid to the finished appearance of a dish was there enough emphasis placed upon the flavour? Did not the taste of any dish suffer when it was held up in the kitchen for all this primping and petting? But this is true of any restaurant or hotel, any kitchen almost at any time, to a certain extent. But I would say that it all took a greater length of time and labour when *haute cuisine* reigned, because how it looked was so supremely important.

In this obsession with appearance that society was enthralled by, everything else tended to get sacrificed towards it. The imperative to create gastronomy which this book attempts to trace down the years, was now diverted towards appearance and appearance only. It is the emperor's clothes in reverse, for in this version the clothes are truly magnificent, so eye catching that there are gasps of astonishment at their beauty, at the way the textures dazzle and glitter, at the radiant colours, the jewels, the furs, the silk and lace, but there is no emperor only a mechanical doll inside which struts within. The clothes are all, the emperor has vanished.

This kind of cooking is a product of highly affluent, powerful societies, there may be within those societies pockets of real gastronomy but these tend to be ignored, except by the most discriminating, because the need of such societies is to make a show of it all, to be grandly exhibitionist, to draw gasps of admiration from their audience. For the very rich, the *beau monde*, the theatrical setting for the new gastronomy was the luxury hotel which began to be an international feature, growing huge and palatial they were to dominate every capital city in Europe. Their dining rooms a mecca for the elite to show off their own finery, to be seen, talked of, their companions and peccadilloes duly noted for upper class gossip columns, even, of course, what they ate and drank would be reported. So with the eyes of the world now upon them Victorian society was acutely aware of its empire strung across the globe and its conquering elite performed masterfully for them.

That new setting, the hotel dining room, responded, pillared with marble and decorated like a Renaissance palace emblazoned in gold, laid out with crisp starched linen, silver and crystal, with chefs like Escoffier rising to star status, in partnership with Cesar Ritz (they met in 1880) who provided him with the context to shine. Escoffier's influence was as pervasive as Carême's, his maxim was '*faites simple*' but truthfully I can see little sign of it. It is said that he rediscovered the fumets and reductions of ancient French cookery that are the basis of today's lighter sauces, but if anyone did that it was Carême. Escoffier certainly reorganised the hotel kitchens in an efficient and practical manner, he created new recipes and he had an imaginative flair for reducing flavours to their essence. There's no doubt that he ruled over *haute cuisine* long after his death in 1935. His main work, *Le Guide Culinaire* was published in 1902 and collects over five thousand of his recipes, but this book naturally has little to do with domestic cooking; it is a painstaking record of his restaurant work over decades, useful for aspiring caterers and chefs, peppered with technical terms and relies on basic sauces and essences to build up other recipes from. He is also remembered for creating so many individual dishes, all of these in honour of some distinguished person which bore their name, the most famous being *Peche Melba*, but quite often they were named after members of minor royalty (which Escoffier had a great penchant for) like Sole Alice which honoured a granddaughter of Queen Victoria, Princess Alice of Athlone. The dish is fillets of poached sole with oysters flavoured with onion and thyme in a white wine sauce.

Escoffier must have produced cooking where the flavour was paramount as well as the appearance; both must have fused as one, for his reputation would have vanished if he had not. While his stated aim was to simplify flavours down to their natural essence, his celebrity guest list often had coarser tastes, for example Edward VII wanted game stuffed with smaller game and truffles served with a rich Madeira sauce, so I rather doubt that the dish named after his niece would have much pleased him. They just could not help but add unnecessary embellishments, such as in a dinner described by Colonel Newnham-Davies at Escoffier's Carlton Hotel. The colonel wrote for the *Pall Mall Gazette* which reviewed restaurants and had an eagle eye on the fashionable spots in London. The dinner was first arranged with the chef in the morning, but the consommé they started with had hard-boiled eggs and chopped truffles added to it, the filets de Sole Carlton was poached in Champagne with vermicelli, crayfish tails and Parmesan added. They went on to ortolans with raisins (a medieval touch here) then a fish soufflé 'orientale', a salad and raspberries. But it was the cooking which Escoffier inspired throughout the international world which became so dire, the aping of *haute cuisine*, all show and no taste, which destroyed utterly the idea of *haute cuisine* as acceptable gastronomy. The emperor's clothes were torn away to show the vacuum within.

Escoffier made a fortune as did Carême; a new and dominating reason had now entered the equation at the heart of what drives gastronomy. Escoffier lived to a fine old age, long enough to enjoy his wealth, you might imagine, but there was none. For at the heart of the partnership between Escoffier and Cesar Ritz there was corruption. In 1898 the Savoy sacked the two of them, it was all hushed up then and remained so for eighty years, but in the Savoy's possession locked up in a safe were two confessions from the two men that they had taken bribes and kickbacks from suppliers which amounted to over a million pounds of today's money. Escoffier was paid 5 per cent of all the goods supplied to the Savoy kitchens, in six months there was three thousand, four hundred pounds of spirits missing from the bar in 1897, and the Savoy also noticed other anomalies in the accounts because suddenly the kitchen was not making the same profits, yet they were always full. What particularly galled them was noticing that they had to pay the bills at numerous Savoy dinners and luncheons when Ritz was entertaining his investors and partners in the new Carlton Hotel that he was starting. There lies the nub of the pall of silence that surrounds this corruption, for the Savoy group knew that Escoffier and Ritz would be taking their most illustrious client with them to the new hotel – the Prince of Wales, who was a constant visitor to the Savoy with his mistress, Lily Langtry. If the scandal broke, then their relationship would be exposed and the old Queen would be assailed again with another scandal around her eldest son and heir to the throne. The Prince must have placed pressure upon the Savoy, some of the money was paid back and the pair left to go to their new hotel that was upon the site that New Zealand House now stands on.

Certainly he had cooked for kings, emperors and queens, but the reigning Queen did not care much for gourmet food, she liked her meals to be plain and simple; her son, however, the Prince of Wales like his Regent forbear was avidly greedy and ate voraciously. He began the day with a breakfast that comprised haddock, poached eggs, bacon, chicken and woodcock followed by a twelve course luncheon and a fourteen course dinner. Faced with the Prince, a chef with any sensitivity towards his craft would have felt he was feeding an eating machine. Besides, two hundred years earlier the Hanoverians had expunged any last remnant of the divine in their sacerdotal relationship with their position, so that element had long gone. No, the royals that flocked to Escoffier, trailed by all the remnants of their family and the titled houses, the opera singers and actresses were all there to eat well and to be seen to be there. It was another show. And it has remained so. What drove both Escoffier and Ritz was Mammon, as their scandal exposes, which is not to underestimate the skill and artistry of their cooking, nor to suggest that Mammon does not bequeath the same dynamic energy as the religious impulse does; it is impossible to judge.

Escoffier's influence was to simplify, but much of what he did hardly touched the style of *haute cuisine* that still trumpeted wealth, power, and empire. If we glance at an eight-volume compendium of cooking published at the end of the century one of the details that Escoffier was said to have banished is prominently displayed in all its gaudy detail. Atelettes are silver skewers with ornamental tops called the 'diamonds of cooking which ought to be shown only on solemn occasions, to be too prodigal with them is to diminish their value and their charm.' Pierced by these skewers are sculptured crayfish, truffles, mushrooms, cockscombs, prawns, 'star of aspic jelly with centre of barberries surrounded by rings of carrots with green peas in the rings.'[129] One simply knows that the carrots and peas are there for their colour and shape not for their flavour.

Escoffier also failed to rid restaurants of sugar work. In 1889, a C. Norwak was awarded a gold medal for his table ornament in caramel and sugar work of The Crucifixion. The detail of these pieces is astonishing, sometimes referred to as 'artistic emblematic *grosses pièces*'. One, called 'Sporting', is described as 'the stand and figure is moulded in fat and can be used for other purposes. The body is a galantine of game, ornamented with shapes cut out of fat, livers, truffles, tongue and aspic jelly. The wreaths are of chopped jelly aspic croutons and a ring of soufflés of game standing in chopped jelly with each one being ornamented with a truffle at its base.' Another is called 'Dancing' with the stand emblematic of Terpsichore, 'a temple surmounted with a design in musical instruments and palm leaves. The lower part forms a tray for fresh fruits and the upper part upon which two figures in sugar are dancing in an arrangement of candied fruit over cake'.

It is so vividly reminiscent of the middle ages or the Renaissance celebrating their own power, prestige and wealth. Escoffier's art and influence is impotent against the power of the Empire and the monarchies of Europe which insists on celebrating their riches on the tables of the elite. But what does such a book tell us of the food that the middle classes might be consuming. It lists the favourite cheeses which might well serve for today, there are as many from Europe as there are from England. Of the former that perennial, Parmesan, heads the list followed closely by Gruyère, Camembert, Roquefort and Gorgonzola, of the English cheeses, Stilton, Cheddar, Single Gloucester and Blue Dorset are front runners, followed by something called Devonshire toasting cheese. As one would expect the most favourite food is beef, there are 240 recipes from Irish stew to vol-au-vent of beef tendons, while potatoes get 106 recipes, including a short entry on varieties. The book also shows particular tastes which no longer exist, there are 44 recipes for eels, in aspic, galantines, fricassees, pies and tarts and 10 more recipes for conger eels. There are 46 recipes for macaroni dishes, including a soup, rissoles, salad, pudding, pie and omelette, 18 recipes for liver dishes and 78 recipes for lobster, which include soufflés, as one might expect, but also rissoles, fritters, patties, pilau, pie, brochettes, and lobster is devilled, creamed and curried.

A few 'artistic luncheon dishes' are mentioned, 'stewed, scalloped or roasted oysters, snails, fried frogs or served in a thick cream sauce, stuffed fried mussels or fried with champignons.' Ketchup can be made from anchovies, barberries, cockles, cucumbers, elderberries, mussels, oysters, pepper, walnuts, tomatoes and wine. Kedgeree is referred to as 'one of those fanciful Indian preparations' and there are six different recipes, only the last of which has spices in it. The book also tells me that truffles are found chiefly in Hampshire, Wiltshire and Kent, then gives 36 recipes which include a pudding, a sauce, a tart and what is this – an ice. It shows us yet again there's very little which is original, the best ideas return again and again.

The Death of *Haute Cuisine*
The last century had similarities to the fourteenth century, both brought unimaginable devastation into a world that had seemed secure and stable, in so doing it revolutionised the life of the working people who had survived the

disasters. The Great War and the flu epidemic were like the Black Death, each killed millions of the very young, but they brought into our awareness an intimate knowledge of great suffering which has scarred our perception. The Victorian and Edwardian world of the *beau monde* juddered to a halt in 1914 and with it the type of food they felt were its celebration. It should never have been seen again, yet it crept back, a poor, withered ghost, for people who had the funds still wanted the sense of play and grandeur to reassure them the world was much the same.

In the real world the men who became soldiers were often so malnourished that they found army rations gave them the best food they had ever had in their lives. Not much gastronomy there and though many of them had never eaten or drunk French food or wine the tastes they had while fighting in the trenches were hardly a revelation. For the world they had left was one where they grabbed a bit of food to keep body and soul together and hardly noticed the taste, while the rest of society was divided neatly into two. There were the nobs who only ate Frenchified food, unlike the workers who passed the menus outside the hotels and never understood a word written there; then there were the comfortably off, who ate English food which smelt good, meat and gravy, pies and puddings – you could even eat a bit of their food if you worked for them as a gardener, odd job man, that kind of thing.

Looking back on that pre-1914 world it seems to me quite incredible that the whole of the upper class only ate French food (I qualify this below), they only employed French chefs, they only listed the dishes in French, for the most part they only drank French wine and used French words for the table settings and everything else to do with the dining room. For a country which had fought wars with their nearest neighbour for over a thousand years to adopt such a fashionable stance over the most basic of acts – eating – when still fighting the Napoleonic wars strikes me as profoundly astonishing. But was the food they ate completely French? Well no, they still ate traditional English food, game, meat, fish, much of it in thoroughly eighteenth century English recipes but they now gave such food French titles.

It was, of course, because it marked them out as a class apart. The semiotics of this demarcation was a crude one, if you did not pronounce the menu in impeccable French you were not part of the set. It is for this reason that it took so long for *haute cuisine* to die, snobbery kept it alive; the need for the upper classes to recognise and know their own. If they did not have *haute cuisine* what other signals existed to show the others who they were? (There was in those interwar years a delicate new style which did appear, still enormously attractive to us today, but it died with the Second World War. Besides it never reached those upper echelons of the old aristocracy who clung, in this new changing world, to the food and dishes they had eaten before the war.[130]) There was also a territorial aspect to their French appropriation, as it was only six hundred years earlier that they had possessed two thirds of France, and it was only three hundred years before that, when the Normans conquered England itself and the ruling clique spoke in French. France, its food and language was in their blood, why, if it was invaded did they not send armies to defend its soil? Also, France was worshipped as the fount of all culture, after all the Russian aristocracy also spoke in French; it was the language of civilisation.

The other side to this adoration was that English cooking tended to suffer because it was disparaged, scorned and thought a fit subject for comedy and jokes. So all the more value was placed upon *haute cuisine* as the only gastronomy worthy of notice. Yet, what in all this time had the bourgeoisie to say about the food which the elite still ate, which luxury hotels still provided in an unstoppable flow? Alas, they loved it too. The middle classes thought this food, which their masters and betters ate with such enjoyment, must also be the food of the gods. The *hors d'oeuvre* trolley with its little compartments filled with the mundane and the stale, the chopped beetroot in malt vinegar, the sliced unripe tomatoes, the tinned anchovies, the hard-boiled egg covered in bottled salad cream which had formed a skin upon it, the Russian salad out of a tin, then the main courses, the piped potato in swirly shapes, the tinned grey petit pois and pulpy asparagus, the radish roses, the macedoine of vegetables in aspic, the flabby fillets of sole, the overall reliance on shaped vegetables and fruits to redeem a dish like a Vandyked orange, tomato or lemon or cutting a lemon into a basket shape or carving a mushroom cap - all of it was lauded. Indeed, without the willing compliance of the middle classes *haute cuisine* would have died long before it did. Of course, it vanished in the Second World War and through the years of rationing in the early fifties it was shorn of most of its finery – those sculptured vegetables for example were too valuable to eat as food to be wasted as decoration – but the bare bones of the cuisine lingered on. That ubiquitous trolley was astonishingly popular in the 1950s and 60s, especially with children, it spelt out treat time, though the food within it always tasted too vinegary to be really pleasant. Children also liked piped food as it made pretty shapes, they did not mind much if it made the food cold, but then in the fifties any food which was even vaguely different, in form, colour or flavour, was welcome.

But the revolt also came from the middle classes, a few small, independent restaurants in the mid-fifties opened, started by idealists who had read the recently published books by Elizabeth David. They also recalled with great pleasure the food of Italy, France and Spain and began cooking using garlic, fresh herbs, lemons and olive oil. They did not know then that these were the flavours we had once loved in the past but certainly these places as they became known were like an oasis in the desert. Many did not last, but the genii had been let out of the bottle, we knew others were out there and the network began to strengthen. While writers like Dorothy Hartley and Florence White reminded us of a culinary past which had infinite riches, the fifties too was when Constance Spry published her comprehensive book, heavily influenced by the notion that French food was by far the best; nevertheless she also celebrated the best of English food, enough to remind us that it existed and it was nothing to do with *haute cuisine*. The luxury hotels were the last to change, they clung onto the artefacts of the *grande cuisine*, using it for functions, because people seemed to expect it; these were the clichés, the setting, the food, the routine of the dinner menu, familiar and now on the shabby side, the food of the Masonic Ladies Night which they ate convinced they were having a good time and convinced too that this is what good food tasted like.

The old dragon not breathing fire anymore, senile and spent was finally speared to the heart by a small group of knights in the early seventies: Paul Bocuse, Michel Guérard, Jean and Pierre Troisgros, Roger Verge and Raymond Oliver.

Nouvelle Cuisine

The group were named by Henri Gault and Christian Millau (who ran a restaurant guide) with a title which was hardly original, first used in the 1740s to describe the cooking of La Chapelle and then in the 1880s to describe Escoffier but it might easily have been used in the 1820s to describe Carême, for the ideal goals this new group espoused were so similar to the earlier ones. They revoked all unnecessary complications in cookery. They reduced cooking times for seafood, game birds and green vegetables. Ingredients must be bought daily being the freshest possible. Short menus to avoid any prefabricated dishes. No strong marinades for meat or game, the latter should be cooked fresh, not left to hang and go high. Thick flou-based sauces were out, in the words of Henri Gault: ' Banishment of terrible brown sauces and white sauces, these espagnoles, périgueux, financières, grand-veneur, béchamel, mornay that have assassinated so many livers and covered up so many insipid pieces of meat.'[131] Better by far to use lemon juice, meat jus, vinegar, fresh herbs and good butter or olive oil; they looked at the newest technology with interest and used it whenever they could; Bocuse experimented with the microwave oven. They bore in mind dietetics and the nutritional balance of a meal. Most of this new group owned and ran their own restaurants which were often outside Paris. In England their style of cooking was taken up by Anton Mosimann at the Dorchester and the Roux brothers at Le Gavroche and the Waterside Inn and Raymond Blanc at Le Manoir aux Quat'Saisons.

In one stroke these new chefs turned themselves into stars, for it was a simple act, in the kitchen they arranged the food upon the plate themselves, and then the waiter took it out to the dining room and the clientele. They banished forever what was called silver service where the maitre d', that is the hotel manager, the one that commanded the restaurant, served from a large silver platter using a fork and spoon, placing the food upon the plate in no particular design. You waited to be served, acutely aware that some plates were getting cool, but manners forbade tucking in. All that was changed, the chef knew what he wanted, knew what the plate must look like and arranged it all, and stepping out to become the celebrity he has remained.

Some of their dishes struck people at first as being so esoteric that that must have been the sole reason for creating them. Michel Guérard's aubergine cooked in saffron steam, Alain Senderen's calf's sweetbread in sea-urchin cream, Jacques Manière's eggs Celine with caviar and a little vodka, sounded to gourmets of the time that they were just hard up for ideas, as if they had searched their imagination and latched onto the first weird combination. But it is always the task of chefs to strike out and find new departures for their talents and new combinations of flavours and this group flung their net wide.

What is so interesting is that in each of the so-called revolutions in culinary history they have all been done in pursuit of simplicity, as well as searching for the natural flavours of the freshest ingredients, jettisoning all the complications. It is surely that each age reinterprets what simplicity means, what natural flavours are, then, as each succeeding age slowly clutters up the original concept the need to return again to basics arises, or in trying to reinstate the basic ideal it only ends up by complicating it further, hence the need every now and again for *tabula rasa*. Though *tabula rasa* does not exist, it is a myth, we never have this so-called clean slate, because as historians know only too well, we build on the past, even if the accretions are scraped away it still leaves the basic structure and also the remains, the skeletal ghost, of what was scraped away.

A great influence upon *nouvelle cuisine* (which was not always welcomed) was the magazine which had coloured pictures of food for its cookery columns. Coloured photography of food dishes began in the fifties with Paul Hamlyn's book productions, which induced magazines to follow the same path, suddenly realising that black and white pictures were a dismal invitation to cook and gave an unrealistic picture of the dish. Photography also became technically far more refined and ambitious in its scope. Moreover, the chefs themselves saw that the arrangement upon the plate of the food, the sauce, the garnish was of pre-eminent importance. Suddenly we were thrown back a century to 'the way it looks' which again now had to be as important as the flavour. But there are many cooked dishes, which though delicious to eat, photograph badly like stew, a casserole, a ragout, unless you take a close up of a small chunk of meat, arrange a whiff of steam, scatter a little parsley flakes, catch the edge of a tiny sliver of carrot or pimento, manage to make the cube of beef glisten and add a drop of wine sauce. But all of that the photographer learnt to do later. Such photographs were not suitable for *nouvelle cuisine*.

The chefs look at the plate as Mondrian might have looked at his canvas. I believe contemporary painting[132] was as much an influence on this style of cooking as the coloured photograph, certainly the diners would stare down at their plates as they were served and express sounds of genuine astonishment at their aesthetic beauty. So their cooking by the nature of its notoriety had to omit from its repertoire certain dishes that could never photograph well, or reinterpret the dish with the photograph in mind, or only photograph a selection from it.

Gault in 1995, looking back on the two decades, commented: 'This *nouvelle cuisine*, wishing to be without roots and open to every influence, was the band wagon on to which jumped along with the authentic cooks, a crowd of mountebanks, antiquarians, society women, fantasists and tricksters who did not give the developing movement a good reputation. Furthermore fashions, mannerisms and trickery attached themselves to this new culinary philosophy: miniscule portions; systematic under-cooking; abuses of techniques in themselves interesting (mousses, turned vegetables, coulis); inopportune marriages of sugar, salt and exotic spices; excessive homage paid to the decoration of dishes and "painting on the plate" and ridiculous or dishonest names of dishes.'

In Britain it spawned a new consciousness of what food might be, a new re-evaluation of how to cook to achieve the best flavours and fusions, but at the same time we had our version of *cuisine bourgeoisie* and the growing intrusion into our domestic lives of television, which was not slow to see the potential interest the subject held for its audience. Delia Smith was (and still is) the goddess of the kitchen who sits astride the bourgeois world as completely as Mrs Beeton did in her century. Aware of all the traditional dishes in the British repertoire she has brought them up to date for the contemporary world, nor does she ignore the styles of *nouvelle cuisine* or any other contemporary cuisine that holds fashionable sway, but takes from it what she feels she can use.

In the years since *nouvelle cuisine* came to prominence cooking has moved on. Enterprising and imaginative restaurants are not always in large urban centres or capital cities, as in France if a restaurant is superlative it gets known and has a following. One of the first was The Walnut Tree Inn near Abergavenny, where Franco Taruschio cooked Italian food of the Marche region; hardy British then in any way but expressive of the new and growing interest we have always had for the superlative food of other countries. From around then, country house restaurants became a fashion almost in themselves – there was John Tovey of Miller Howe, a hotel in Windermere, Cumbria, who produced a modified *haute cuisine*, camp, exquisite and seductive. There was a period when they all went in for a rather tiresome ritual of serving the plates of food beneath domes, the ritual required a waiter per diner, and the waiters stood behind the diner and lifted the dome in unison, where the beautifully arranged main course lay. I recall then worrying a little that the arrangement of the food meant a lot of manual handling in the kitchen of pieces of hot food (and wondered about licked fingers) and hoped for thorough cleanliness. I still do not like this whole business of fussy serving and presentation.

Young chefs like Marco Pierre White would suddenly get a reputation, their restaurant booked out for weeks in advance, their personality dissected in the media, their personal life as newsworthy as a film star, while their cooking was still endlessly praised. Pockets of gastronomy would appear as in Ludlow, led by the brilliance of Shaun Hill, a scholar cook, who learnt to cook in Robert Carrier's kitchens in Islington in the sixties, and who now approached the subject with a strong historical sense; there was Alastair Little with a restaurant in Soho, London, Rowley Leigh, who studied with him at Cambridge, Gary Rhodes from Bristol. Chefs of talent, imagination and exuberance now on the British scene were numerous, there was no doubt that a new renaissance of British cooking had begun, was growing and flourishing, but what was behind all of this new obsession that the public had for good food and the media had for milking every story from it?

Affluence

One of the necessary attributes of a burgeoning middle class, which has power to influence fashion and social trends, is a continuing and growing affluence. I am writing this at the end of 2010, at a time when the affluence has halted. So perhaps the last 25 years can be seen more clearly as economic boom time, certainly in that time restaurants of quality have sprung up, often where customers have to book weeks in advance, restaurants where they might have such a thing as 'tasting menus' where the chef can show his ingenuity and imaginative flair in twenty or so tiny tasting dishes; such menus are priced individually and can easily cost a hundred and fifty pounds. The fact that these restaurants are still flourishing as I write shows that the economic boom has not finished for some people. I would also have no hesitation in recognising that there is a new wave of gastronomy that has swept the nation.

In this new obsession with food that has gripped society, which television feeds avidly, what is the nature of the new energy that drives these restaurants and chefs? One cannot dismiss the obvious, of course: riches, fame and celebrity are reached through the culinary avenue. So Mammon rears its glorious head beckoning to the unknown teenager that this could be the path to glory, television trumpets this almost every night of the year in one way or the other. But the existence of Mammon behind the drive does not explain society's obsession and real enjoyment of the subject of food itself, but not necessarily the reality. As we know, watching food programmes or buying cookery books does not necessarily lead to cooking and enjoying the result. Part of the obsession can be explained by people's curiosity as to how the social strata above them live and enjoy themselves, as pointed out earlier this has been a consuming passion ever since the advent of printing cooking books, and the books themselves catered for the need. They still do. Yet the books and the television are only fantasy pictures of this social strata, an idealised romantic picture so what is still being sold is a Hollywood version of gourmet food. Here then, is an affluent middle class chasing the treasure at the end of the rainbow, a necessary, elusive but useful symbol to energise the consumer society into continual spending.

Another darker aspect of the obsession for food, whether it is fantasy food, healthy food, or plain grub taken as fuel, is the fear that it may vanish altogether. The future is uncertain. There are elements of desperation and recklessness in our consumption of food, the sheer indulgence, and the problems of obesity, diabetes and coronary-related afflictions are like a glimpse of ancient Rome in sybaritic feasting hearing but ignoring the barbarians at the gate.

Food security is a newish term and as it is spoken by food gurus and scientists it suggests an uncertain future caused by climate warming, where if we continue to eat as we do, food scarcity and malnutrition will grow rapidly, famine and devastation in Africa is bound to ravage that continent and it will even effect the affluent western industrial world as well as the rising new world powers, China and India. We will all have to change our ways. Then, gastronomy itself will become an austere and Spartan art. One of the preparations towards such a radical change has been and will continue to be highly technical experiments with the growing matter of food itself, the cellular structures of the edible material.

Science

From the moment meat was touched by fire, the moment the raw flesh began to shrink, change colour, sizzle and exude moisture and aroma, science began to be central to the act of eating; and science has helped the development of our consumption ever since from methods of harvesting grain to channelling water, to shaping cooking irons and cauldron pots, turning spits and shaping flues, to the first pressure cooker of 1679 which cooked a meal for the Royal Society and Charles II, to Baron Liebig redesigning ovens. Science is the handmaiden of the art of eating.

Heston Blumenthal[133] is one of the most original chefs working today, following the example of the brilliant Spanish chef Ferran Adrià; he has examined the nature of foods, and cooking techniques afresh. What he calls his philosophy is in fact an interesting essay on the analysis of taste and its complicated, multi-sensory nature, but what he pursues is anything which can possibly contribute to cooking, he revels in culinary avant-garde, in the use of enzymes, liquid nitrogen, sous-vide, dehydration, modern thickeners and sugar substitutes. He utterly rejects the term 'molecular gastronomy' which was a term coined in 1992 by a workshop with chefs and academics. Yet his understanding of its existence, his knowledge of what is happening when food undergoes chemical change,s is at the heart of his cooking.

The fact that Heston Blumenthal has reached the eminence he has in such a short time, and also had a television series which exhibited the quests that drove his culinary experiments, underlines our own anxiety and fascination for the subject of food itself. What all affluent societies choose to forget, what they hide from themselves, is the necessity of food, how without it we very quickly grow ill and die, so we eat too much, we create festivals of foods and feasts to celebrate all sorts of triumphs, create awards and medals, so that the true nature of its life-giving chemistry may be obscured.

Chris Horridge is another chef who is pursuing a goal where his ultimate dish fuses gastronomy with health. He is doing astonishing work which, I feel, is showing the way forward to this highly uncertain problematic future. His food is dairy, gluten and sugar free and each ingredient he uses boosts the nutritional value, what is more he looks at the nutritional benefits or lack of them when various ingredients fuse together; for he is aware that some ingredients which contain minerals and vitamins may nullify another set of nutritional factors from another ingredient. His armoury of ingredients is extensive, he mentions bee pollen, echinacea and ginseng, and is aware of the 'nutritional and potential medicinal elements of herbs'. He is aware of the traditions of his culinary past, which is highly impressive, and turning the chef into a chemist like Blumenthal, yet Horridge is not sacrificing flavour to nutrition, nor presentation, he calls it a three dimensional cuisine, 'presentation, flavour and nutrition'.

Now, we need all the science we can muster upon the subject to answer the great questions of the immediate future. On one side there are multinational companies like Monsanto who state that genetically modified (GM) foods will solve all the problems. We understand why they should say this, locked into the capitalist system as we all are, that with their control of seeds and agriculture, (75 per cent of the world's seed companies is owned by just 5 companies) they have Mammon to serve, but a closer examination of what they have so far produced to answer the ever urgent problem of famine in the developing world does not reassure us. The 'golden rice' for example, which has added vitamin A in its genetic make-up to halt blindness in those societies which have to almost solely live off it, requires each person to eat several kilos of rice per day to achieve the right amounts of the vitamin. Or there is the soya bean which has been spliced with omega 3, the crop will only thrive in the temperate zone and these areas under climate warming are dwindling, so I feel the crop has been designed for health-conscious westerners (not the starving populations in hot climates) to spread on their morning toast to stop coronaries.

If Monsanto wants to win over the GM critics, they should begin by creating food crops that can withstand drought, will fix soil with nitrogen, produce food which is easily prepared for human digestion, are disease and saline resistant and which will absorb carbon dioxide from the air. This little miracle package would go a long way in answering the most besetting problems. However, it still leaves another worry which is that it confounds completely the rules of natural selection. A genetic mutation made in the laboratory sometimes between two different species (a fish and a vegetable for example) which is impossible through natural selection, strikes me as a dangerous precedent. The Darwinian discovery is a process whereby living things react to outside stimuli and respond to combating it by their own behaviour that gradually leads to genetic changes. The scientist in the laboratory cannot comprehend those stimuli in all their myriad complications, therefore cannot arm the plant with the means to combat them, so inherently they must fail or else respond in an eccentric way that could be destructive to the environment. There is also the potent problem of the engineered gene dispersal by wind, insect or tyres of farm vehicles through buffer zones which are risibly narrow, so once sown there is no guarantee that engineered plants can be controlled. Pandora's Box has been opened; we are now vulnerable to the results.

Jettisoning the rules of natural selection in livestock does not concern research scientists either, so that much work has been done in crossing species and not just breeds. Transgenic pigs that carry human growth genes have been created, so that the possibility of eating meat which is partly and possibly human in origin could happen in the future. Could one produce a pig that gave a milk which could be marketed? As if we haven't now got enough cow's milk! Pig milk chemically is far nearer our own and so we should in pre-history have taken to it, but the choice was made then because litters were large and piglets were considered of more use than the milk they consumed. Calf genes could be spliced with chicken to give chickens with greater flesh and thighs, but that so far has proved a failure. Sheep spliced with mouse genes can produce more wool. Turkeys can be induced to produce more eggs. But so far transgenic animals have been an area of failure, the creatures themselves are often frail and deformed, develop diseases and suffer from stress. While the public are revolted by the whole idea, the process is kept as secret as possible, this is one aspect of the food industry that does not want the exposure of publicity.

Technology

What does kitchen technology do to our cooking? Or more precisely, what do we think it does? We believe it improves the quality of our dishes. We believe it saves time. The first belief is debatable and could only be proved via experiments with an army of tasters testing blind. As to time saved, if machines are simple to take apart and clean then mixers and beaters obviously save time and something of the chore in cooking labours. But there are people who love making mayonnaise in a bowl with a wooden spoon and I doubt whether any time would be saved using an electric beater. Much of the belief that clings around 'labour saving devices' is little more than myth. Many of us merely use kitchen technology because it is there.

The great cooking time-saver was of course the invention of the gas and electric oven; no longer did we have to start the day by clearing the ashes away and making a fire before we could heat water to boil an egg. A cleaner method of producing heat that could be controlled and modulated was the first great step towards kitchen equality. Earlier the lowest paid servant was told to do the filthiest jobs, but with the coal and ashes removed, the need for kitchen labour gradually declined. Yet oven temperatures were still not thermostatically controlled until with gas ovens in 1923 and ten years later with electric ovens, at last a soufflé could be cooked with more security and less anxiety.

We all know the phrase that 'necessity is the mother of invention' and we may be able to cite endless examples of it, but take the internal combustion engine which superseded the ox cart or horse drawn vehicle and introduced speed into travel. It was hardly necessary to go quicker, by land, sea or air. Or take the watch, which superseded the sundial, is it necessary to know the time to the second? Or the vacuum cleaner, was that necessary when a broom, dustpan and brush are perfectly efficient? Certainly many technical inventions make our life greatly more pleasant, take glass windows which let in light and air into the home, or the gramophone which allows us to hear great music. The invention can be slight, take the handkerchief, which the Romans knew, but which disappeared for over a thousand years until the Renaissance, but how necessary it is to have something which mops up snot, phlegm and sweat! While on a larger scale, a sewage system connected to domestic water closets was undoubtedly a necessity to preserve health, fight disease and improve the quality of life. What is odd is that though such sewage systems existed in the ancient cities of the Indus and Mesopotamia and of course Rome, further civilisations were not as vigilant in the details of human waste disposal, so it was not until the nineteenth century (between 1775 and 1866 nearly 300 patents were taken out relating to water closets, earth closets and urinals) that our cities had a workable system.

Technology related to our food supply and its preparation and cooking is similar in that many inventions are superfluous to necessity, yet others, like the domestic refrigerator few of us would consider doing without. Yet a cool larder with plenty of ventilation works perfectly well, but that needs space which in newly built houses is never planned. One can cook with no utensils at all over an open fire by burying food protected by damp leaves buried in the embers, or pierced by a stout, long stick and grilled. However, the first terracotta pot made stews possible, an improvement on boiling in skins. And as the tools grew in practical design certain dishes, soups and stews within the utensils undoubtedly became tastier and slightly more complex because of all the added flavourings and slow cooking. It then could not help but be noticed that long, slow cooking of meat, vegetables and herbs in embers or suspended over a modest fire was pleasanter because of the herbs than without. Herbs, which may well have been noticed, had already become known as antidotes to aches, fevers and illnesses, so because they tasted good greater notice was taken of them and they were studied; many hundreds of generations later we are the inheritors of such knowledge, even if some of it has been lost in time.

One of the most irrelevant inventions in recent kitchen technology must be the microwave oven, irrelevant, that is, in the quest for good food. This machine which uses radiation, heating the food, thus cooking it, but never browning or baking it, so that the great pleasures of cooked food, like crispness, difference in texture, range of flavours edging towards caramelisation, can never be achieved. A huge number of new kitchens are installed with these objects, yet often they are seldom used or only used for one or at the most two functions, making porridge or thawing frozen food. They seem popular with people that live alone; they are practical for small portions of prepared meals, so they have like so much technology the social effect of isolating the individual away from the group. How very different from the microlith, in its many shapes, forms and sharpness, where all the women would have been in a circle chatting as they worked preparing vegetables for a communal pot.

What greater domestic technology does, and this effect was noticeable after the Black Death when individual baking ovens were built into modest cottages, is to separate the individual from the group. It is isolating, cuts people off from a neighbourly clan, which on a personal level for some may well have advantages, but for others the distancing is unhelpful. But this isolating factor which is an outcome of ever greater cooking technology has an unfortunate effect in society itself. Social democracy works if it is built up pyramid style from closely bonded groups; by constantly isolating individuals, who are often not part of any group at all (not even the local pub), the social machinery then gets taken over by the professionals. It is only in a national crisis that groups appear again, that is how vital they are. Social isolation, of course, now starts at an early age, because of the computer and the internet (nothing to do with cooking here) and some might argue that it is a means of social communication through Facebook, blogs and Twitter.

Contemporary cooking from our most talented chefs relies heavily on new cooking techniques, but this is to be expected, as kitchen technology becomes both more daring and more subtle. Though I think all chefs might well agree with me, that what one relies on is a sharp knife and a smooth wooden surface. Sophisticated technology is not necessary for great gastronomy.

Summing Up

At this moment in history it strikes me that we stand trying with great difficulty to balance upon a peak, that great incline of technology, of great scientific progress, which has brought about huge population growth. We balance there not knowing how long we can contrive to do it, too aware of the crowds below us, so that it is inevitable we will fall, but when, oh yes, but when? Soon, is my own inadequate answer.

The over production of food has been our undoing, the cutting down of rain forest for beef production, the size of the herds of livestock and their production of methane gas, the pollution into our water supplies from factory farming, the dissipation of aquifers for mono-agriculture, the almost total reliance on staple foods, cereals and rice, the complete lack of proper government legislation over private companies who have been allowed to control and manipulate the food industry, not for the good of the community, but for their own private profit, the belief in the free market, the demands from a rising population for heat, light and entertainment in the home. All this has led to pollution of the earth and the atmosphere, a situation where the nutritional quality in the food that is still grown is rapidly declining. If we could return to the first chapter in this book, to a virgin land which had just emerged from ice, we would eat a range of foods of astonishing quality in flavour and nutrition, but such a natural larder only feeds small groups of people. There are now far too many of us.

Mother Gaia has her own immutable laws, if it is possible we should listen, though I think we have forgotten how to.

Notes

1   See report in *The Guardian* August 11th 2010

2   See *Fairweather Eden*, Michael Pitts & Mark Roberts, Arrow (1998)

3   See *Britain BC*, Francis Pryor, Harper Collins (2003)

4   *Ecological Energetics*, Phillipson (1966)

5   See Stringer, Chris. *Homo Britannicus*, Penguin (2006)

6   See Stringer

7   *Feeding Strategies in Prehistoric Times* – Catherine Perles. Ed: A culinary History from Antiquity to the Present, ed. Albert Sonnenfeld, Columbia University Press. (1999)

8   See *Facing the Ocean*, Barry Cunliffe OUP (2001)

9   See Cunliffe (Ora Maritima 101-6)

10   The agriculture is about a thousand years earlier than in Britain because it is on the continent.

11   Report in *The Guardian*, November 8th 2008

12   See:*The Archaic use of Hallucinogens in Europe: an archaeology of altered states:* Richard Rudgeley. Addiction, 1995. P.163-164

13   Miles, David

14   See Pryor, Francis

15   Ale had to be drunk fresh soon after it was brewed, for it quickly became vinegar. Hops preserves the ale and turns it into beer, but this discovery was not made and used until the time of Charlemagne (AD 742-814), while other historians believe it did not reach England until 1530.

16   See *The Tribes of Britain*, David Miles Weidenfeld & Nicholson (2005)

17   *The Roman Banquet – Images of Conviviality*, Katherine M.D. Dunbabin, C.U.P (2003)

18   Agricola, xxi. Tacitus

19   Mattingly, David. What did the Romans do for Us? *History Today*. Vol 57. June 2007.

20   See page 150 *The Tribes of Britain*, David Miles, Weidenfeld & Nicolson (2005)

21   See page 605 *Iron Age Communities in Britain*, Barry Cunliffe. Routledge (2005)

22   See John Wilkins in *Culinary Biographies*, ed. Alice Arndt, Yes Press (2006)

23   See *Vegetarianism*, Colin Spencer, Grub Street (2000)

24   *Art, Culture & Cuisine, Ancient & Medieval Gastronomy*, Phyllis Pray Bober, University of Chicago Press (1999)

25   Odin, the supreme god in Valhalla loves wine, so it remained a special drink in Norse feasting, but at this time the international system of trade and commerce in vintage wines had broken down. The large estates were split into many smallholdings, wine making was no longer a speciality trade.

26   I am not denying that they did not exist in the Roman Empire, of course they did, but they were not integral to the history of British food.

27   Roman Britain had a population of around 5 million, in the fourth, fifth and sixth centuries it fell by 50% , perhaps even more.

28   See Dyer, Christopher. *Making a Living in the Middle Ages, The People of Britain 850-1520.*

29   See Dyer

30   It is a brassica with numerous names, false flax, wild flax, German sesame, Siberian oilseed, native to northern Europe and has been grown for three thousand years. The oil has up to 45% omega 3 fatty acids is 50% polyunsaturated, is highly stable, resistant to oxidation and rancidity.

31   *Harleian Manuscript*, No 603, British Museum

32   'ubi ab ostio aulae tota fere villa et late patens ager arabilis oculis subjacet intuentis.'

33   Now to be viewed in the Birmingham Art Gallery

34   Aulus Corneluis Celsus had written 'because it contained more nutritional matter than any other food.' see *Food, a culinary history from antiquity to the present*, edited Albert Sonnenfeld, Chapter 15, Massimo Montanari.

35   Anthimus. *On the Observance of Foods*. Translated and edited by Mark Grant, Prospect Books (1996)

36   Pollington, Stephen. *The Mead Hall. The feasting tradition in Anglo-Saxon England*, Anglo-Saxon Books (2003)

37   The Romans had eaten the tendrils of hops as a wild delicacy but it the northern peoples who tended the vine, that is those in what we now call Finland, Latvia and Estonia. See Phyllis Pray Bober

38   Oxford (Bodleian Ms Hatton 115, fol. 60v-1)

39   Though the term 'Viking' was unknown then, it was invented by Sir Walter Scott and from then on caught the public imagination with another invention, their winged and horned helmets and long hair. They shaved their heads except for a tuft in front and the word 'viking' is Icelandic for pirate.

40   See Pray Bober

41   See Beech, George. The Naming of England, article in *History Today* Vol. 57 Oct. 2007

42   Binski, Paul. The Cult of St. Edward the Confessor. *History Today* (Vol.55.Nov.05)

43   *The Normans in the South*, John Julius Norwich, Solitaire Books (1981)

44   See Chapter 3 *British Food An extraordinary thousand years of history*, Grub Street (2002)

45   *Chronicles of the Kings of England:* translated by Rev. John Sharpe, 1815. J.A. Giles editor, London, George Bell & Sons (1904)

46   See *The Rohan Master*, introduction by M.Meiss and M.Thomas (New York, Braziller,1973)

47   De Naturis Rerum. Quoted in Wright, Thomas.

48   See Wright, Thomas.

49   Dyer, Christopher.

50   See page 33 Scully, Terence. *The Art of Cookery in the Middle Ages*, The Boydell Press (1995)

51   The couvre-feu was a pottery cover with ventilation holes that could be placed over the fire to restrain it, keep it safe until the morning. The special bell, the couvre-feu bell was rung at eight or nine in the evening to remind householders to cover their fires – hence curfew.

52   See Henisch, Bridget Ann. *Fast and Feast. Food in Medieval Society*, The Pennsylvania State University Press (1976)

53   Russell. *Book of Nurture.*

54   Quoted in Wright, Thomas

55   *The Goodman of Paris*, trans. E. Power, New York: Harcourt, Brace, (1928)

56   Spufford, Peter. *Power and Profit, The Merchant in Medieval Europe*, Thames and Hudson (2002)

57   In the counties of Lincolnshire, Norfolk, Suffolk, Essex, Cambridgeshire and Huntingdonshire alone in 1086 there were 1,306 mills.

58   It is in his prologue to his life of Thomas a Becket.

59   Quoted in Wright, Thomas.

60   A resin which exudes from the bark of *Pistacia Lentiscus*.

61   See *Arab Cuisine and its contribution to European culture* – Bernard Rosenberger. from *Food, a culinary history from antiquity to the present*. Ed.Albert Sonnenfeld, Columbia Univ. Press (1999)

62   See Dyer

63   Benedictow, Ole J. *The Black Death, 1346–1353, The Complete History*, Boydell & Brewer (2004)

64   See Spencer for details of the *Forme of Cury*.

65   See Dyer

66   James, Lawrence. *The Middle Class. A History*, Abacus (2006)

67   *The Boke of Keruynge.Book of Carving*. Wynkyn de Worde. With an Introduction by Peter Brears, Southover Press (2003)

68   See Thirsk, Joan, *Alterative Agriculture, a history. From the Black Death to the Present Day*, O.U.P. (1997)

69   Henisch, Bridget Ann.

70   *An Ordinance of Pottage*, an edition of the fifteenth century culinary recipes in Yale University's MS Beinecke 163. Constance B. Hieatt

71   For more on colour in food see Spencer, BF (page 51)

72   See Barber, Richard. *Cooking & Recipes from Rome to the Renaissance*, Allen Lane (1973)

73   *An Ordinance of Pottage*, Constance B. Hieatt, Prospect Books (1988)

74   A collection of Ordinances and Regulations for the Government of the Royal Household made in divers reigns from King Edward III to King William and Queen Mary also receipts in ancient cookery. Printed for the Society of Antiquaries by John Nichols (1810).

75   Barclay, Alexander. *Eclogues*.

76   *The Earl of Northumberland's Household Book* (London, 1770)

77   Hale, John. *The Civilization of Europe in the Renaissance*, Fontana Press (1993)

78   One of only four surviving cycles of the mystery play from hundreds that once were performed every year on Corpus Christi day.

79   Wright, Thomas, *Homes of Other Days*, Trubner & Co (1871)

80   ibid

81   Dawson, Thomas. *The Good Housewives Jewel*, Southover Press (1996)

82   *A Proper Newe Booke of Cokerye*, edited by Anne Ahmed (Corpus Christi College, Cambridge,2002)

83   Peterson, T. Sarah. *Acquired Taste, the French Origins of Modern Cooking*, Cornell University Press (1994)

84   Wilson C. Anne. '*Banquetting Stuffe*', Edinburgh Universty Press (1986)

85   ibid

86   Dawson, Mark. *Plenti and Grase*, Prospect Books (2009)

87   See Thirsk, Joan. *Alternative Agriculture, a history*, OUP (1997)

88   See Uglow, Jenny. *A Little History of British Gardening*, Chatto & Windus (2004)

89   Elizabethan spice chests with their many deep drawers behind doors that could be securely locked still exist and are striking in their beauty.

90   Thirsk, Joan. *Food in Early Modern England*, Continuum Books (2007)

91   Harrison, William *The Description of Elizabethan England*, Harvard Classics (1995)

92   ibid

93   Landsberg, Sylvia. *The Medieval Garden*, (British Museum Press, 1995)

94   ibid

95   Brears, Peter. *Banquetting Stuffe* edited by C. Anne Wilson, Edinburgh University Press (1991)

96   Ferguson, Niall. *Empire, How Britain Made the Modern World*, Penguin Books (2004)

97   Nichols, John. *The Progresses and Public Processions of Queen Elizabeth*, vol.1, London (1823).

98   Nichols, John. Also referred to in Sass, Lorna. *The Queen's Taste* John Murray (1976)

99   Sitwell, Edith. *The Queens and the Hive*, Penguin (1966)

100   ibid

101   Hentzner, Paul. *Travels in England during the reign of Queen Elizabeth*, Cassell & Son (1899) Several writers depicted this scene, also Thomas Platter and Baron Waldstein.

102   Strong, Roy. *Feast, a history of grand eating*, Jonathan Cape (2002)

103   Golby J.M. & Purdue A.W. *The Civilisation of the Crowd. Popular Culture in England in 1750-1900*, Sutton Publishing (1999)

104   Hill, Christopher. *The World Turned Upside Down*, Pelican Books (1972)

105   Thirsk, Joan. *Food in Early Modern England*, Hambledon Continuum (2007)

106   See *British Food* for how potatoes got from Spain to Ireland.

107   Fussell G.E.& K.R. *The English Countrywoman*, Orbis Publishing (1953)

108   For a fuller picture of John Evelyn and his classic work *Acetaria*, see *British Food*.

109   Webb, William. The Vale Royal of England, 1656. Quoted in *The English Housewife in the Seventeenth Century*. Christina Hole, Chatto & Windus (1953)

110   ibid (Quoted in Christina Hole who owns the ms)

111   ibid

112   See Thirsk, Joan, for a fuller and amusing account.

113   The Poor Husbandman's Advocate quoted in Fussell.

114   *British Food*

115   Quoted in Fussell

116   Quoted in Lehmann, Gilly. *The British Housewife*, Prospect Books (2003)

117   Pinkard, Susan. *A Revolution in Taste*, C.U.P. (2009)

118   See *British Food* on *La Varenne*.

119   William Verrall's *Cookery Book*, Southover Press (1988)

120   The whole lemon that is cooked in the centre of this pudding and was considered an authentic part, was only added sometime in the 1960s, but by whom is a mystery.

121   Fussell

122   Quoted in Lehmann

123   ibid

124   Quoted in Ayrton, Elizabeth. *English Provincial Cooking*, Mitchell Beazley (1980)

125   Aresty, Esther B. *The Exquisite Table*, The Bobbs-Merrill Company, Inc. New York (1980)

126   Willan, Anne. *Great Cooks and their Recipes. From Taillevent to Escoffier*, McGraw Hill (1977)

127   ibid

128   ibid

129   *The Encyclopaedia of Practical Cookery*, ed. Theodore Francis Garrett, 1898.

130   See Boxer, Arabella. *Book of English Food* Hodder & Stoughton (1991)

131   Davidson, Alan. *The Oxford Companion to Food* OUP (1999)

132   No one wanted their plate of food to look like a Jackson Pollock, but Miro, Kandinsky, Klee, some Matisse, there were here shapes and colours which were influential.

133   At The Fat Duck, Bray, Berkshire. It has been named the best restaurant in the world, and was awarded 3 Michelin stars in 2004.

Bibliography

Arndt, Alice, ed, *Culinary Biographies*, (Yes Press 2006)

Anthimus, *On the Observance of Foods*, translated and edited by Mark Grant (Prospect Books 1996)

Benedictow, Ole J., *The Black Death, 1346-1353, The Complete History* (Boydell & Brewer 2004)

Birley, Anthony, *Garrison Life at Vindolanda: A Band of Brothers* (Tempus 2002)

Bradley, Richard, *The Social Foundations of Prehistoric Britain: Themes and Variations in the Archeology of Power* (Longman, London 1984)

Bober, Phyllis, *Pray, Art, Culture & Cuisine, Ancient & Medieval Gastronomy* (University of Chicago Press 1999)

Burnett, John, *Plenty and Want: A Social History of Diet in England from 1815 to the Present Day* (Routledge 1987)

Clark, Grahame, *The Stone Age Hunters* (Thames and Hudson, London 1967)

Cunliffe, Barry, *Facing the Ocean: The Atlantic and Its Peoples, 8000 BC to AD 1500* (OUP 2001)

Cunliffe, Barry, *Iron Age Communities in Britain* (Routledge 2005)

Dunbabin, Katherine M.D., *The Roman Banquet – Images of Conviviality* (C.U.P. 2003)

Dyer, Christopher, *Making a Living in the Middle Ages: The People of Britain 850-1520* (Yale University Press 2002)

Fox, Cyril, *The Personality of Britain: Its Influence on Inhabitant and Invader in Prehistoric and Early Historic Times* (National Museum of Wales, Cardiff 1932)

Hieatt, Constance B., *An Ordinance of Pottage, An Edition of the Fifteenth Century Culinary Recipes* (Yale University's MS Beinecke 163)

Lawrence, James, *The Middle Class: a History* (Abacus 2006)

Lehmann, Gilly, *The British Housewife* (Prospect Books 2003)

Meiss, M., and Thomas, M., *The Rohan Master: A Book of Hours* (Geo Braziller, New York 1973)

Miles, David, *The Tribes of Britain* (Weidenfeld & Nicolson 2005)

Norwich, John Julius, *The Normans in the South, 1016-1130* (Solitaire Books 1981)

Oxford, Arnold, Whitaker, *English Cookery Books to 1850* (OUP 1913)

Pitts, Michael and Roberts, Mark, *Fairweather Eden: Life in Britain Half a Million Years Ago as Revealed by the Excavations at Boxgrove* (Century 1997)

Pollington, Stephen, *The Mead Hall : The Feasting Tradition in Anglo-Saxon England* (Anglo-Saxon Books 2003)

Power, Eileen, trans, *The Goodman of Paris* (Harcourt Brace, New York 1928)

Pryor, Francis, *Britain BC: Life in Britain and Ireland before the Romans* (Harper Collins 2003)

Roach, F.A., *Cultivated Fruits of Britain, Their Origin and History* (Basil Blackwell 1985)

Rudgley, Richard, *The Archaic Use of Hallucinogens in Europe: an archaeology of altered states* (Addiction, Volume 90, Issue 2, pages 163-164, February 1995)

Sahlins, Marshall, *Stone Age Economics* (Tavistock Publications, London 1972)

Scully, Terence, *The Art of Cookery in the Middle Ages* (Boydell Press 1995)

Sonnenfeld, Albert, ed., *A Culinary History from Antiquity to the Present* (Columbia University Press 1999)

Spufford, Peter, *Power and Profit: The Merchant in Medieval Europe* (Thames and Hudson 2002)

Stringer, Chris, *Homo Britannicus: The Incredible Story of Human Life in Britain* (Penguin 2007)

Sutcliffe, A.J., *On the Track of Ice Age Mammals* (Harvard University Press London 1985)

Smith, Christopher, *Late Stone Age Hunters of the British Isles* (Routledge, London 1992)

Thirsk, Joan, *Alternative Agriculture: A History: From the Black Death to the Present Day* (OUP 1999)

Willan, Anne, *Great Cooks and Their Recipes: From Taillevent to Escoffier* (McGraw Hill 1977)

Index